A History of
THE CIRCUS

By the same author:

The History of the English Toy Theatre

The History of the English Puppet Theatre

Punch and Judy: a History

Edited by:

Professional and Literary Memoirs of Charles Dibdin
the Younger

Bawdy Songs of the Early Music Hall

A History of
THE CIRCUS
by George Speaight

London: The Tantivy Press
San Diego and New York: A. S. Barnes and Company

In Memory of Miranda
who tried to stop me writing it

© 1980 by George Speaight

The Tantivy Press
Magdalen House
136-148 Tooley Street,
London SE1 2TT

A. S. Barnes & Co., Inc.
11175 Flintkote Ave.
San Diego, CA 92121

Library of Congress Catalogue Card Number:
ISBN: 0-498-02470-9

Typeset by Unwin Brothers Ltd, The Gresham Press (England)
and printed in the United States of America

Contents

Acknowledgments

IT IS A PLEASURE for me to acknowledge my thanks and indebtedness to the many people and institutions who have assisted me during the collection of material for this book.

For my quotations from manuscript sources I acknowledge the gracious permission of Her Majesty the Queen for the republication of material from the Royal Archives – Queen Victoria's Journal – which is subject to copyright; of the Master and Fellows of Trinity College, Cambridge, for extracts from the diaries of A. J. Munby; and of the Gemeentelijke Archiefdienst van Amsterdam for the extract from Jacob Bicker's account, which they kindly transcribed for me.

For permission to make use of unpublished theses I am indebted to John F. Polacsek and Bowling Green University, and to Saffana Al-Khayer and the University of Exeter.

For personal assistance when researching in their collections I am indebted to Mr Joe Ging of the National Museum of the Music Hall, Sunderland; to Mr Robert L. Parkinson of the Circus World Museum, Baraboo; to Miss Judith St John of the Osborne Collection, Toronto Public Library; to Dr Jeanne Newlin of the Harvard Theatre Collection; to Dr Günter Böhmer and Frau Columba Wilhelm of the Puppentheatersammlung, Stadtmuseum, Munich; and to the ever-helpful staffs at the British Library,

the Bodleian Library, the Theatre Museum, the Bibliothèque de l'Opéra in Paris, and the Toneel Museum in Amsterdam.

For answering my enquiries and conducting research on my behalf I am grateful to Mrs M. J. Johnson of Chiswick District Library; to Mr V. J. Kite of the County of Avon Library; to Mr A. P. Lake of the King's Lynn Library; and to Mr J. Smith of the Liverpool Record Office.

For editing circus journals, whose articles have so greatly contributed towards our knowledge of the subject, I owe much particularly to David Jamieson of *King Pole*, Fred D. Pfening of *Bandwagon*, Don Stacey of *The World's Fair*, and L.-R. Dauven of *Le Cirque dans l'Univers*.

And for giving me the benefit of their knowledge in many hours of pleasurable discussion there are too many names to record, but I recall in particular Dr A. H. Saxon, Mr Stuart Thayer, Miss Marian Hannah Winter, Miss Kathleen Barker, Mr Sandy Davidson, Mr John Vinden, and Mr Paul Schickle.

Finally, I express my acknowledgments and thanks to the owners and copyright owners of the illustrations reproduced in this book, as separately listed, and to The Circus Fans Association of Great Britain for lending photographs from its archives.

G.V.S.

6

Introduction

THE CIRCUS is an international art. That is a sentence that will be repeated several times in the course of this book. This means that to tell its story properly one must write of its history in many countries; and that implies either a book of adequate detail but of enormous length, or a merely cursory review within a moderate compass. It is perhaps because a historian of the Circus is confronted by these two equally unsatisfactory alternatives that no comprehensive general history of the Circus has ever been written in English, and no history even of the Circus in England has appeared for over a hundred years.

But the fact that the Circus *is* so international an art means that its development in one country has followed closely upon its development in other countries. Performers have moved freely between London and Paris, St Petersburg and Berlin, Madrid and Rome, New York and Sydney, Buenos Aires and Cape Town, Tokyo and Delhi. A new act in one country has been quickly imitated elsewhere. Thus it is, that – in one sense – the history of the Circus in one country is the history of the Circus everywhere.

So, I have attempted to solve the historian's dilemma by concentrating upon certain countries and certain periods. The Circus, as we know it today, originated in England; so it has seemed logical, after reviewing the origins of Circus in Europe, to concentrate upon telling the history of the development of this art in England, and in greater detail than has hitherto been attempted.

The Circus in England first inspired, and was then much influenced by, the Circus in America. Yet, the Circus in America has developed in a manner somewhat differing from that of the Circus elsewhere in the world. So I have next told the story of the Circus in the United States. These two sections provide, as it were, the pillars that hold up the structure of the book.

No history of the Circus can, however, omit Europe. Rather than attempt a similar treatment for every country in turn, however, I have concentrated upon the peak of art and appreciation that the European Circus achieved in France in the last quarter of the nineteenth century. That is a chapter that cannot be paralleled elsewhere.

This book is primarily a study of the *development* of the Circus as an art and entertainment form, rather than a chronicle of performers and proprietors. So I have concentrated upon trying to establish just when each of the types of circus act recognized today first appeared in the ring. Here I must offer a word of caution. The archives of Circus are so sparse and scattered, those bills and advertisements that survive are so packed with exaggeration and lies, that an authoritative history of the early Circus is an impossibility. When I write that somebody did something for the first time, it must always be assumed that I imply the rider, "as far as I have been able to discover". Some of my instances may be spurious. In other cases earlier examples may be found. I hope that the chief result of my research will be to establish a *terminus ab quo* for the various forms of circus acts, and that other students of this subject will be inspired to record examples "earlier than Speaight".

When someone comes to write the history of the Circus in the twentieth century and later, it would be an enormous assistance if some recognized body existed to authenticate and record new achievements in circus feats. I commend this idea to the various national organizations of circus enthusiasts: the Circus Fans Association, both of Britain and America, the Circus Club International, the Club du Cirque, the Gesellschaft der Circusfreunde, the Club van Circusvrienden, the Amigos del Circo, the Circus Fans of Australasia, and others. Perhaps an international recording body could be set up by these societies to undertake this task.

The Circus had developed into what seems its definitive form by the end of the nineteenth century. Acts and presentation have, in many respects, improved since then, but the formula has not been fundamentally altered. Many of us hope it never will be. Hence, the detail in my story becomes thinner as we enter the twentieth century. This is not because I am not interested in the Circus today, as I hope the final chapter of the book will demonstrate; but because there is less fundamental development to chronicle, and anyhow the story of the Circus in this century has been well told in many books of reminiscence already.

As well as drawing fine limits in space and time to this history, I have also limited myself in subject matter. Once the Circus was historically established, I have not dealt with – or, at best, only mentioned incidentally – circus-type acts performed in pleasure gardens, or music halls, or over Niagara Falls, or wherever; nor have I dealt at any length with hippodromes, or Wild West Shows, or menageries; nor with plays performed in circuses; nor with circuses presented in theatres, or on ice. Interesting though all these are, they belong rather to the periphery of the subject. I have limited myself to telling the story of that entertainment of human bodily skills and trained animals that is presented in a ring of approximately 13 metres in diameter, with an audience grouped all round it. That, to my mind, is the essence of Circus.

G.V.S.

Opposite: Circus-type acts in the bull-baiting "ring" of the Nuremberg Fechthaus in 1689.

8

I
THE ORIGINS OF THE CIRCUS

1
Histriones and Minstrels

IN THE YEAR 421 B.C. a dinner party was given in Athens by a wealthy dilettante called Callias; among the guests was Socrates. The philosophical discussion round the table was interrupted at one point by the entry of a troupe of entertainers. A jester cracked jokes; a girl and boy played music and performed a mime; and a girl juggled with hoops, placed a ring of sharp swords on the ground and threw somersaults among them.[1]

Five hundred years later, during a pause between the courses of the epic banquet given in Rome by Trimalchio, a troupe of rope dancers and acrobats was introduced to entertain the diners. For one of the turns a boy climbed up a ladder held by the master of the show, balanced himself on the top rung while dancing and singing, and then, clenching a filled goblet between his teeth, leaped or perhaps somersaulted through an iron hoop, round which blazing torches were fixed, without apparently spilling the liquid.[2]

The performances at these banquets were typical of the feats presented by the acrobats, tumblers and jugglers who entertained the Greek and Roman worlds for many centuries. A few years after Trimalchio's banquet a rope dancer exhibited his skill at the Games so effectively that it was reported that "in his buskins he seemed to be walking on the winds";[3] some accounts speak of the use of a *petaurum* or springboard; a girl acrobat stood on her hands while shooting an arrow from a bow with her feet; some performers swallowed swords or ate fire; some juggled with balls and others with daggers; some walked on stilts.[4] By the first century A.D. trained animals were making an appearance: we read of a dog playing the chief role at the theatre of Marcellus, of bears which acted a farce, and of elephants walking upon ropes.[5]

Some of these performances may have taken place in the great arenas that were called "circuses" by the Romans, but it is a mistake to equate these places, or the entertainments presented there, with the modern Circus. They were of enormous size (the Circus Maximus could accommodate perhaps as many as 385,000 spectators); their shape was elliptical, with a "spine" running down the middle; and they were used principally for athletic games and chariot races. The amphitheatres were closer to a circular shape and nearer our modern conception of a circus arena, but these also were too large for any intimate displays of skill – Flavian's Amphitheatre, the Colosseum, in Rome has an arena 282 by 177 ft and could seat up to 50,000 people; their entertainments were principally gladiatorial shows; animals appeared in them, but to be slaughtered, not to display their skills. The origins of the Circus must be sought elsewhere.

A Roman statuette of a Negro juggler, believed to come from Thebes.

In the performances of the acrobats that we have already considered, three aspects should be especially noted. One is that women and men performed equally in their shows. Another is that a comic character, a *stupidus* or a *sannio*, appeared frequently in association with the acrobats. And the third is that there was little distinction between acrobats, dancers, mimes and actors. They were all *histriones*.

Minstrels

A thousand years later the situation was not very different. Early in the thirteenth century a great feast was given at Bourbon, in the Auvergne, in honour of the king and queen of France. After mass the whole company sat down to a banquet in the great hall of the castle, and when the meal was finished the entertainers – two hundred jongleurs – came in. Some recited stories, some sang ballads, some played music, and some performed feats of skill:

> Here one that made the puppets play,
> Or gave a juggling knife display,
> One somersaulted on the ground,
> Another capered in a round,
> One tied his body in a loop,
> Another dived straight through a hoop.[6]

The medieval minstrel was a performer of many parts:

singer and musician certainly, often a jester as well, and also, as likely as not, acrobat, juggler, conjurer, puppet showman and animal trainer. He might balance a sword by its point on his chin, or a cart wheel on his shoulder; he might spin a basin on the end of a stick and toss it up to catch it on another one; he might juggle with balls and knives simultaneously; he might walk on his hands, or on stilts, or on a rope; he might jump through a hoop; he might contort his body while hanging from a pole. He might train animals: dogs and goats danced on their hind legs to the beat of a drum; monkeys turned somersaults; cocks walked on stilts; hares beat the tabor with their feet; horses reared on their hind legs, or – a remarkable feat this – beat a roll on a drum with either their fore or hind hoofs; bears lifted their ponderous bulk on to two legs to dance or allow a man to wrestle with them.[7]

Little bands of such entertainers, led usually by a *trouvère* or poet, wandered across Europe throughout the Middle Ages, playing sometimes in the castle or the palace but more often gathering a crowd at the street corner or village green with a drum and trumpet.

And in other continents the same, and sometimes greater, skills were being practised. There is a long tradition of acrobatic performances in Egypt, and in the thirteenth century A.D. there is a good description of the entertainers in an Egyptian market-place at that period. They included a boy acrobat who could

A plate spinner and a performing goat, from the 14th-century manuscript, "The Romance of Alexander".

stand on the points of swords and pick up rings with his eyelids, men swallowing swords, stones and sand, tight rope walkers, and men who could carry live coals in their hands; trained animals included snakes, a lion led on a collar and chain, an elephant kneeling on command, a goat who pointed out the best boy in the crowd, bears who went to sleep when told to, dancing dogs, and a cat who played with mice without harming them.[8] There may well have been some limited traffic between the entertainers of Asia Minor and North Africa and Europe.

2
Feats of Activity

B Y THE SIXTEENTH CENTURY we begin to find records that enable us to learn a little more about the performers of what were often described as "feats of activity". The accounts of civic expenditure in English towns sometimes record a fee paid to a performer or troupe of players who passed through the town and gave a performance for the mayor and other officials. In an analysis of these payments we find that the most common, and presumably the most popular, form of circus-type entertainment was rope dancing, of which I have noted twenty-two references between 1570 and 1663; then comes tumbling with thirteen references, vaulting with seven, and juggling with five.[1]

Most of these performers were, to judge by their names, English, but there was some international exchange for we find specific mention of Italian and French tumblers, a Dutch vaulter, and Turkish and French rope dancers. At least one English troupe of rope dancers, the Peadles, toured the continent, and were in Germany in 1614–15. Some of these performers were also actors, and when a famous Italian Arlecchino, Drusiano Martinelli, brought his company of Commedia dell' Arte players to London in 1578 his requirements included a mattress and hoops, indicating that acrobatics were part of the performance. Other of these tumblers and rope dancers combined their feats with conjuring, puppet shows, or selling medicines. At least one of the rope dancers in England during this period was a woman, and the Italian players who visited London in 1574 were attacked for "the unchaste, shameless, and unnatural tumbling of the Italian women". This was, of course, at a time when no woman could appear as an actress upon the public stage.[2]

Few details were recorded about the nature of these performances, but occasionally some kind of description has been preserved. In 1546, when Edward VI was passing through the city of London before his coronation, a Spanish rope dancer stretched a rope

An English 17th-century rope dancer. An engraving by Jn. Bellange.

13

from the steeple of St Paul's cathedral to the ground and slid down it, lying on his breast with his head forward and arms spread out, "as if it had been an arrow out of a bow". This dramatic and dangerous feat, which was repeated several times during the next two centuries, was achieved by fastening a grooved board to the flyer's chest and providing several mattresses at the bottom to break his fall. In 1553, when Mary I was passing through London before her coronation, a Dutchman balanced on the weathercock of the steeple of St Paul's, kneeling, standing on one foot, and waving a streamer five yards long. The sensational effect of the Italian tumblers was described by an observer who saw one perform before Elizabeth I at Kenilworth in 1575, amazing him with the ease and lightness of his "goings, turnings, tumblings, castings, hops, jumps, leaps, skips, springs, gambols, somersaults, carpettings, and flights, forward, backward, sideways, downwards, upward, and with sundry windings, gyrings, and circumflections".[3]

There are also references to animals being toured round the countryside for exhibition: a lion and porcupine in 1585, an elephant in 1623, a camel in 1638, a beaver in 1623, an opossum in 1678, apes or baboons in 1572 and 1616, a dancing horse in 1628, a serpent in 1568, a monster in 1639, and even "a strange beast" shown by a poor man who was rewarded with six shillings at Nottingham in 1671.

Many of these animals were exhibited merely for their rarity, but some of them were trained to perform tricks. We hear of a baboon "that can do strange feats" and of "Jack-an-apes to ride on horseback", that is a monkey riding on a horse's back, a turn that is still popular and entertaining in circuses today. A popular act was an ape trained to jump over a chain for the king of England but to sit obstinately still when asked to do so for the Pope.

A performing animal that acquired considerable fame was a horse called Morocco that was trained by a showman called Banks and is referred to by many Elizabethan and Jacobean writers. A pamphlet of 1595 reports that "this horse would restore a glove to the due owner, after the master had whispered the man's name in his ear; he would tell the just number of pence in any piece of silver coin newly showed him by his master"; other accounts tell how it "would fetch out the biggest knave in the company with his mouth" and go to a person in the crowd and bow to him "making curtsy with his foot", and would discern maids from maulkins (sluts). The horse was, of course, obeying inconspicuous signs from its master, and would count by pawing with its fore leg as many times as was indicated. A well-trained horse or pony will, in fact, recognize tiny indications from its trainer, such

Vaulting on a wooden horse in a 17th-century Dutch theatrical entertainment.

as the clicking of finger nails, a sniff, a shift in the position of the hand, or in the inclination of the body.[4]

These are feats that caused great amazement at the time but they have been repeated by many horses in circus rings since. In 1668 Pepys saw "a mare that tells money" at Bartholomew Fair, which "come to me, when she was bid go to him of the company that most loved a pretty wench in a corner. And this did cost me 12d. to the horse, which I had flung him before, and did give me occasion to baiser a mighty belle fille that was in the house that was exceeding plain, but fort belle."

Feats of horseriding were uncommon, but are occasionally recorded. As early as the fourteenth century a man amused Edward II by comic falls from the horse he was riding, and in about 1530 Peter Tremesin gave a display of riding on two horses at once at the court of Henry VIII. A tumbler is recorded at Bristol in 1575 as "showing certain feats of vaulting upon a horse". This horse, however, was almost certainly a dummy wooden horse, as is used to this day in gymnasiums, though they have now lost their imitation heads and tails. There is pictorial evidence that this piece of equipment was already in use by the seventeenth century.[5]

The performances that we have been considering

seem, for the most part, to have been presented as separate and individual items, but an opportunity was now presenting itself for them to be brought together into one entertainment. This was the institution of permanent theatre buildings.

The Elizabethan theatre developed from the bear gardens and bull baiting rings, which were circular arenas surrounded by three tiers of galleries. The entertainment or sport here consisted usually of bears or bulls being attacked by dogs. There is some truth in Macaulay's dictum that "the Puritan hated bear-baiting, not because it gave pain to the bear, but because it gave pleasure to the spectators", but, though no one will try to defend this sport today, it is as well to realize that what attracted the Elizabethan spectators was not the bloody corpse of a dog or the bleeding flanks of the bear but the sheer inexplicable courage and stark bravery of the mastiff dogs who charged again and again in an assault upon their heavier adversary. There is no parallel with circus entertainment, but spectators who were thrilled by the bravery of animals would also be likely to admire the skill of trained animals and the bravery of human acrobats performing daring and dangerous feats.

And so it was. Apes sometimes rode on horseback in the bear rings; some kind of wrestling show with dwarfs or puppets, followed by fireworks, was seen by Lupold von Wedel at Paris Garden in 1584; William Vincent exhibited feats of activity, vaulting and rope dancing at the Fortune between 1622 and 1642; a clown, a John Pudding, was arrested at the same theatre for dancing on the ropes during the Commonwealth in 1648; vaulters, fencers and rope dancers performed at the Globe during off-seasons;[6] and according to the latest scholar of this theatrical period, "jugglers, tumblers, acrobats, dancers on ropes, puppeteers, human freaks and exotic foreign beasts had from time immemorial been the standard offerings of the minstrel troupes: it is entertainers such as these that kept the Hope in business on playing days after the actors had quit."[7] Precise details of these performances have not survived, but there is sufficient evidence that they took place.

The bear baiting rings, and the theatres developed from them, provided, indeed, a perfect setting for a circus-type entertainment. They were circular, or sometimes square, in shape; intimate in atmosphere, with an arena of about 55 feet across (the width of the "pit" of the Fortune); and the galleries provided an excellent view of anything taking place in the central ring. In addition to the bull and bear baiting rings, ten theatres had been built in London between 1576 and 1614, all with similar architectural plans. The mixture of entertainers was available. All the ingredients were present. The idea was in the air. In 1620, and again in 1634, an elephant exhibitor named John Williams, with John Cotton and Thomas Dixon, put forward plans, that eventually came to nothing, for building a huge Amphitheatre that would have housed, among other things, exhibitions of riding and managing horses, running, jumping, vaulting, tumbling, dancing on the ropes, and pageants. Why didn't the Circus start here?

Or did it? Can we not see every element of Circus in those barely reported entertainments at the Hope and the Globe and the Fortune on Bankside? Given a few more years, surely a tradition would have been established and that is where circus historians would be making their pilgrimages today. But this gradually evolving form of performing art was snuffed out in 1642 by the Civil War and the establishment of the Commonwealth. Theatres of all kinds were closed, performances of all kinds were prohibited, and arenas with their association with the filthy sport of bear baiting were especially detested by the Puritans; no kind of entertainment that was in any way associated with the bear gardens could hope to survive. By the Restoration in 1660 the old arena theatres had all been demolished or fallen into ruins. And so we had to wait a hundred and thirty years for the simple concept of a variety of human and animal performers playing in a circular arena to be discovered afresh.

This use of round or square open-air theatres for circus-type entertainments can be paralleled on the continent. The Fechthaus in Nuremberg, erected in 1628, was strikingly similar to the Fortune and its design may well have been due to the influence of English acting companies touring Germany; woodcuts illustrate this theatre in use either for bull and bear baiting, or for rope dancing, tumbling and a performing ape.[8] Other arena theatres in Europe, like the Hetz Amphitheater in Vienna erected in 1755, were circular or oval, and similar entertainments would have fitted naturally into them. The countries of Europe escaped the experience of England's Puritan Commonwealth, but the destruction and chaos of the Thirty Years' War must have inflicted comparable damage upon the emergence of a new form of performing art.

3
At the Fairs

DURING THE EIGHTEENTH CENTURY these feats of skill and animal training found a welcome home in the great fairs that were developing all over Europe. In London there were Bartholomew, Southwark and May fairs, as well as the little theatre at Sadler's Wells on the hills of Islington, a short walk from the city. In Paris there were the great fairs of St Germain, St Laurent and St Ovide, and from the 1760s a permanent row of theatre booths and fairground entertainments that sprang up along the boulevard du Temple, the famous "boulevard du crime". An analysis of the entertainments at the fairs of Paris from 1678 to 1787, for instance, shows some seventy troupes or individual rope dancers, thirty-one leapers, five vaulters, ten balancers, three strong men, four strong women, and one fire eater.[1]

Some details can be gleaned of the feats of the human performers. The springboard now came into use to assist the leapers. This originally consisted of planks sloping down from the level of the back row of benches in a booth auditorium to a spot just in front of the orchestra pit, where they joined a short springy plank inclined upwards. There was great competition to record the greatest leaps: in 1697 a Frenchman leaped across the orchestra with a flaming torch in each hand; in 1727 an Englishman threw a somersault over fourteen people; in 1741 Nicolini Grimaldi, said to be the grandfather of the famous English clown,[2] leaped from the stage to the chandelier over the forestage, knocking down some of the glass lustres on to the head of the Turkish ambassador who was sitting in the front row; in 1742 a Frenchman leaped over twenty-four men with drawn swords; in the 1780s le beau Dupuis leaped over a horse and rider and somersaulted over seven men each with a lighted candle on his head.

The equilibrists or balancers achieved some remarkable feats. A fifteen-year-old Pole balanced a pyramid of thirty glasses and thirty lamps on the point of a nail while playing a drum in 1774; the next year a Saxon called Joseph Brunn held a fork horizontally in his mouth, while balancing another vertically on its end, with a third horizontally from its tip, on the handle of which a sword was balanced on its point. The mind boggles at the care and patience involved in these feats, but Brunn was an expert juggler, too; he could take three forks, one in each hand and one in his mouth, and throw three apples in the air to catch each of them on the point of a fork.

A strong man, known inevitably as Hercule, supported a table with twenty men on it on his shoulders in 1782, but a strong woman in 1774 had drunk boiling oil, lifted an anvil with her hair, and carried eight men on her stomach. A stone eater provided an alternative to fire eating in 1789. A ladder dance was sometimes featured, often by a woman, which consisted in climbing an unsupported ladder and performing a kind of stilt dance at the top. Women spun round with swords apparently sticking into their eyes, or danced with glasses of liquor balanced on the back of their hands. Posture masters, who might be contortionists or tumblers or balancers, were popular in the English fairs. And in every entertainment the clowns played a part, whether they were called Merry Andrew, Jack Pudding, Punchinello, Scaramouche, or Gilles.

It was the rope dancers, however, who were the stars of the booths. Their acts were something more than merely balancing on a tight rope, they were *dancers* and their reputation rested on the skill and style with which they could combine acrobatic balancing with artistic dancing steps. In 1784 Mlle Malaga was described as "a young person of sweet and dreamlike appearance, a rope dancer of the abstract school, full of poetry and expression, who danced on

Mahomed Caratha, or the Turkish equilibrist, 1749.

the rope with the wings of a sylph and the modest graces sung by Horace". But there were, of course, acrobatic feats also: at the beginning of the century Mr Barnes danced on the rope in boots and spurs with two children hanging from his feet; Antony, called de Sceaux, was famous for his drunkard's dance; Laurent danced with chains round his ankles and baskets on his feet; Mlle Violante danced on a board eight inches wide that was balanced on the rope; in 1754 Gagneur threw a backward somersault from the rope seven feet above the stage; in 1783 Mlle Charini, like many others, danced with her feet in chains while playing the mandoline.

Famous rope dancers in England were Jacob Hall, with whom Pepys spoke, and Mrs Finley, known as Lady Mary, about whom Steele wrote. Later in the century came Paulo Rédigé (actually a Dutchman, Pol Roediger), known as le petit Diable, and his comrade, known as Placide. They were dancing in the Paris fairs in the 1770s and visited England, where

they met with great success, about 1780. They later made their way to America. The Little Devil introduced a trick of dancing on the rope with wooden shoes, leaping in the air, breaking the shoes by clapping his heels smartly together, and alighting on the rope in his stockinged feet. Most rope dancers used a balancing pole, but one of Rédigé's company, la belle Espagniola, danced a hornpipe and a Spanish fandango, clicking castanets, without a pole.[3]

Early in the century there are distinctions drawn between dancing on the low rope, vaulting on the high rope, on the slack rope, and walking on the sloping rope. The tight rope on which dancing was usually performed does not seem to have been normally more than four or five feet above the ground. In 1747 a Turkish performer, Mahommed Caratha, boasted that he would dance on the slack rope, which was clearly a more difficult exercise than dancing on a tight rope, but two years later an Englishman at May Fair repeated the same feat.

The famous Dutch Woman
la fameuse Hollandoise
Famosa donna Thelesca

The famous Dutch Woman on the rope, from a drawing by Laroon, c. 1690.

The Celebrated Miſs Wilkinſon, The Female Wire Dancer.

Another view by Laroon of the Dutch Woman on the rope, altered to show a later performer on the wire.

An important development in the art of rope dancing was the introduction of a wire, which was destined eventually to replace the rope altogether. The earliest reference to this that I have noted is in 1750, when Mahommed Caratha, who had returned to England the year before with a company of rope dancers from Turkey, offered "new equilibres on a small wire"; two years later a noted English performer, Mr Maddox, was balancing at Sadler's Wells "on a small wire scarce perceivable", and Duncan Macdonald, a Scottish Jacobite gentleman who was reduced to earning his living as an equilibrist during his exile in France, was said to perform wonderful feats on the wire. Within the next few years a number of other wire performers were advertising themselves, but the quality of the wire was not very reliable – stranded wire ropes were not developed until the 1830s – and in 1753 a wire broke at Bartholomew Fair and the performer was thrown to the ground and seriously injured. Ropes seem to have continued in use for

perhaps another hundred years, but it is uncertain whether the phrase "rope dancers" always signifies dancers on *ropes* – we still use the term "tightrope" quite incorrectly today.

The wire seems at first to have been used as a slack wire for a swinging and balancing kind of act: Mahommed Caratha played with ten balls on the wire and Maddox claimed to toss twelve balls, but neither of these claims, if they mean keeping this number of balls in the air simultaneously, is really credible; Maddox also sounded a trumpet, played the violin, and wheeled a wheelbarrow "in full swing". Writing in the late 1760s, Tobias Smollett described a visit to Sadler's Wells by a Welsh lady's maid who recounted seeing the "rolling of wheelbarrows upon a wire (God bless us) no thicker than a sewing-thread".[4] The feat with the wheelbarrow was a popular one: Brunn, the Saxon equilibrist, wheeled a wheelbarrow with a child in it along the wire, but this had been performed by several artistes previously on the rope; in the reign of

Queen Anne an Italian Scaramouche at Bartholomew Fair had danced on the rope "with a wheelbarrow before him with two children and a dog in it, and with a duck on his head", and had sung a song while doing so.

A spectator's view of rope dancing is provided by a racy description of Bartholomew Fair, written by Ned Ward in 1699.[5] He was not greatly impressed by most of the performers; the tumbling pleased him mightily, but two of the rope dancers who discarded their petticoats after a few dances to reveal breeches beneath were mere "plump-buttocked-lasses"; an Irish woman had "buttocks as big as two bushel-loaves, which shaked as she danced like two quaking puddings" and "she waddled along the rope like a goose over a barn threshold". A Negress, however, gave a good display on the slack rope, swinging on it "as if the Devil were in her, hanging sometimes by a hand, sometimes by a leg and sometimes by her toes". And Ward was deeply moved, too, by a German girl who danced on the rope, "playing with her feet as if assisted with the wings of Mercury"; the proportions of her limbs and vivacity of her movements inspired him to think "that if she be but as nimble between the sheets as she is upon a rope, she must needs be one of the best bed-fellows in England". This may be the performer usually known as "the famous Dutch Woman" – the corruption of *deutsch* to Dutch was not uncommon. Ned Ward, franker than most reporters, provides a pretty plain explanation for the enormous popularity of rope dancing, especially by female rope dancers, at this time.

We can recapture something of the atmosphere of the fairs from a description of the costume worn by Dupuis, the leaper, that helps us to visualize the swaggering, gawdy appearance of these performers. He wore trousers of flesh-coloured silk, decorated with pipings of silver; the jacket of the same material was without sleeves and fastened by a little chain attached to silver-gilt buttons; the half-beaver hat, turned up in the style known as "à la Suisse" (like Polichinelle's hat), was decorated with silver braid and had two silver tassels hanging from each corner at the back. Something, too, of the swashbuckling character of these booth performers may be glimpsed from the comment of a contemporary on Paulo Rédigé and Placide: "If one didn't know these chaps to be Nicolet's rope dancers", he wrote, "you would imagine you were encountering murderers in a forest if you met them on the boulevards. Their attire is a long gown, a great cloak, a turned-down hat, hair rolled in plaits, and a big gnarled stick in the hand; their behaviour is to insult every one, harm whoever they can, drink in every wine shop, and mix with scoundrels." We

are told that the dancing girls in their troupe had to take turns to sleep with them, and that they claimed by right the pretty girls in any town they visited.

Trained animals, too, played a part in the entertainments of the fairs. An analysis of the shows in Paris reveals a little horse in 1749 who danced to the violin, performed the cup and balls conjuring trick, and carried a ladder in its teeth with a man hanging under it; a Turkish horse in 1772 could distinguish the colours of materials, count the number of buttons on a man's coat, add, subtract, multiply and divide numbers, fire a pistol (no doubt by pulling a cord with its teeth), and jump through a hoop. An ape in 1748 was dressed like a soldier and rode on a dog's back; others could play the violin and dance a minuet dressed as a woman, or play the hurdy-gurdy; a monkey called Turco, taught by a clever trainer named Spinacuta, imitated a well-known actor. A learned dog in 1750 could count the number of persons present up to thirty, write their names, tell the time, and answer questions on the Metamorphosis of Ovid, geography, and Roman history by indicating appropriate cards to spell out its answers. A deer and a ram could count. A canary in 1774 could tell the time, perform the four rules of arithmetic, and answer questions by indicating letters of the alphabet; a pigeon had performed similar tricks in 1717. All this was, of course, achieved with the aid of inconspicuous directions from the trainer, as with Banks's Morocco.

Among other animals we read of two lion cubs and a tiger, shown together at St Germain in 1750, who were said to be as obedient to the commands of their master as the gentlest dogs; however young the animals were, and however elementary the commands that they obeyed, this must, I think, be the earliest big cat act in modern European history. Similarly, what may be the earliest performing elephant was recorded by Robert Hooke in London in 1679, exercising the musket and flourishing the colours. A hare beat a drum roll on a hollow box with its feet. Rats danced on a rope, carrying little balancing poles like human rope dancers, and performed a saraband to the music of a violin. A gifted trainer called Bisset taught cats to play the dulcimer and squall to the notes, turkeys to execute a country dance, a tortoise to write names on the floor with its blackened feet, and a learned pig to answer questions. In 1778 an unusual act presented serpents dancing on silken ropes to the sound of music; and during all this period dancing bears were commonly exhibited in the streets.

Any study of the fairs reveals how closely the pattern of entertainment and entertainers in their booths repeats the characteristics that have already shown themselves throughout history. The performers come from many countries: as well as French and English, the fairs of London and Paris contained Scots, Irish, Italians, Prussians, Saxons, Dutch, Danes, Hungarians, Poles, Portuguese, Spaniards, Negroes, Turks and Indians. Women performed almost as frequently as men, and sometimes – usually the widow of a booth proprietor – directed a performing troupe. And the rope dancers and tumblers were closely linked with the actors and puppet players. The pieces with which

the fairground theatres challenged the state monopoly of drama, both in England and France, were a mixture of acrobatics, conjuring, dancing, scenery and histrionics. We are very close now to the evolution of the Circus as a distinct form of art and entertainment, but we must never forget that its roots lie deep in this often desperate and brawling world of fairground booths and theatres.

A performing bear and monkey in the streets of London, 1785.

4
The Riding Masters

BY THE MIDDLE of the eighteenth century there had emerged in England a school of riding masters who had achieved such mastery of their horses that they could combine riding with the feats that vaulters had hitherto only performed on wooden horses. These horsemen would hire a field or open space adjoining an inn or tea garden, rope an area off, and announce an exhibition of their feats. In London the most popular areas were on the edge of the town: in the south, in the Lambeth fields where one of the bridges across the Thames gave access to the south bank; and in the north, on the Islington hills, where visits to pleasure gardens or spas with chalybeate springs were becoming a popular excursion from the city.

The first of these men to exhibit his skill in London was an Irishman, Thomas Johnson, who performed in a field adjoining the Three Hats inn in Islington in 1758. He rode standing on the saddle of one horse, then with feet astride on two, then with feet further astride on three horses.[1] He continued these exhibitions, sometimes with companions, for the next eight years; in 1763, when he was riding somewhere in Chelsea, probably in Cromwell's Gardens, his audience included James Boswell who wrote in his journal: "I was highly diverted. It was a true English entertainment. The horses moved about to the tune of Shilinagarie [an Irish Jacobite song]; for music, such as it is, makes always a part of John Bull's public amusements." Evidently the displays of horse riding were already acquiring some of the features of a rounded entertainment. Among the audience Boswell was delighted to meet a prostitute, the first in a long line of women with whom he had slept, who now claimed to be respectably married to an army officer, though Boswell thought she must be joking. Other references speak of the popularity of these riding

displays with the nobility, so they were clearly drawing a genuinely mixed audience of all classes.

In 1767 Johnson's place at the Three Hats was taken by Sampson, an ex-cavalryman who had previously been performing outside an inn at Mile End, on the eastern edge of the city. He was partnered by his wife, who was said to achieve feats of riding that "proved the fair sex are by no means inferior to the male, either in carriage or agility"; contemporary prints, however, indicate that the ladies wore long riding skirts for their feats, so their agility must have been somewhat hampered. In 1769 Mr Sampson displayed his skill at Garrick's Shakespeare Jubilee celebrations at Stratford on Avon, and he was certainly appearing here and there about the country.

In 1772 Sampson is said to have been involved in some marital troubles involving the loss of his horses, and he was reduced to appearing as a member of Coningham's troupe at the Three Hats, but the programme was far more ambitious than before.[2] Coningham played a flute while riding, without reins, standing astride two horses, whereas Johnson had held long reins in his earlier exhibition; Coningham also leaped repeatedly over a galloping horse and claimed the sensational feat of diving through a flaming hogshead, or barrel, carried on two horses' backs.

Meanwhile a rival equestrian had appeared upon the scene. Thomas Price, a member of a family that was to make its mark in the Circus later, had been giving riding displays up and down England. In 1763 he was at Bristol, where he inspired a local poet to pen some lines in his praise:

Upright he stands, and swift as rapid tides
With ease at once upon three horses rides.[3]

In 1767 he began exhibiting his riding at Dobney's

JOHNSON, Standing on One, Two & Three Horses in full Speed.

Mr Johnson in three of his feats of horse riding.

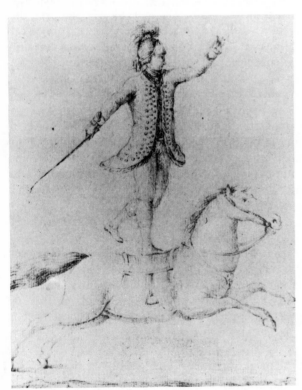

An anonymous drawing of an 18th-century trick horse rider.

Bowling Green in Islington, not far from the Three Hats. He jumped over a bar while standing on two horses, picked up a whip from the ground at full gallop, and so on. In 1772 Daniel Wildman, who was to appear two years later in Paris, demonstrated his trained bees while riding on horseback there. We are told that the space occupied by the bowling green was surrounded by refreshment boxes which provided good accommodation for the spectators; "a circle was formed on it, and there was an Amphitheatre immediately without further trouble or expense".[4] The elements of a circus arena were beginning to take shape.

At this time a discharged cavalry sergeant major, Philip Astley, who had achieved some excellence in the control of horses during the wars, took note of the popularity of these displays and got himself a job as a groom at Sampson's Riding School in Islington. Here, as well as parading the neighbouring streets blowing a cracked trumpet to advertise the show, he took every opportunity to study the tricks of the Islington riding masters and, in the words of his close friend, Jacob Decastro, "studiously endeavoured to glean from them all their superior methods of teaching and breaking" horses. Thus prepared he set up his own Riding School in 1768 in a field called Halfpenny Hatch on the south side of the Thames beside a footpath linking Westminster and Blackfriars Bridges, where he and his wife exhibited "activity on horseback". In the same year Mr Wolton was performing horsemanship on one, two and three horses at St George's Spaw, by the Dog and Duck in St George's Fields, Southwark.

There were now a number of these English or Irish riding masters touring the provinces with their displays, and some of them were travelling abroad. A rider of whom we shall hear later, called Charles Hughes, claimed that he had appeared in Africa and America in 1770;[5] Potts was in Vienna in 1770;[6] two English equestrians, John Sharp and Mr Faulks, certainly performed in America in 1771;[7] and Wolton was in Spain in that year.[8] Hyam, known as the English Hero, caused a sensation in Paris in 1774 and 1775; his partner, Miss Masson, rode standing on one foot with the other in her hand, and Hyam put on a superb display of leaping on and off his horses, over them, riding standing with a child on his head, hanging from the stirrups, in every kind of attitude, firing pistols at the culmination of every trick.[9] In 1777 he paid his first visit to Vienna, where he later founded his own riding school and became a favourite of the Viennese ladies.

The most famous of the English equestrians to travel abroad was Jacob Bates, who hailed from Newmarket.[10] It is interesting that both he and Johnson are depicted in contemporary prints as wearing jockeys' caps; clearly there were horse racing as well as

cavalry influences upon the developing art of display horsemanship. As early as 1763 Bates had made his way to St Petersburg;[11] in 1766 he was the subject of a print published in Germany; and in November of that year he appeared in Amsterdam on the drill ground near the Ox Market, where a large circle had been marked out. We are fortunate to have a detailed description of his act at this time.[12] He rode with reins, standing, on up to four horses at a time; he rode standing in the inside stirrup of two horses galloping side by side; he picked up a pistol from the ground at full gallop and fired it, like a hussar, under the belly of the horse; he leaped a foot high while standing on the horse, and then stood on one foot, all at the gallop; he leaped on and off the horse, at full gallop, several times, and then several times "right and left over the horse, only touching it with his hands"; he knelt beside his horse, which then lay down as if it were dead; he jumped a pole three feet above the ground, standing on two horses, "all at full gallop and in a round circle". These tricks were soon to be surpassed, but they were regarded as "incredible things" at the time, and attracted "an inconceivable concourse of all sorts of people . . . gentlemen of the government with their ladies as also other leading members of society with their ladies and family . . . and of the common people both men and women". Bates was performing in Paris in 1767, in 1772 in Philadelphia, in 1773 in New York, in 1774 back in Paris in a circular amphitheatre type of building, and again in 1778.

Trick horse riding by Mr Wilkinson, c. 1790.

23

5
The Circus is Born

WE ARE NOW very near the moment in time when the Circus began to assume the form that we know today, and it may be of some interest to trace in detail the developments during the crucial half dozen years between 1768 and 1773. The scene is London.[1]

On Easter Monday 1768, Mr Wolton commenced his exhibitions of horsemanship at St George's Spaw. This was, at that time, quite an elegant pleasure garden on the south side of the river, with a spring producing water that was supposed to have curative qualities, a long room for breakfasting, a bowling green and a swimming bath. In May he was joined by a young lady, but the hazards of his occupation were demonstrated on May 27 when he was injured and the performances were suspended for a week or so. On August 18 the young lady became Mrs Wolton – husband and wife teams in equestrian acts were to become quite common. On September 9, in a benefit performance for a Southwark resident whose house had been burnt down, there was added between the performances rope dancing and tumbling "by one of the best in England". This is the earliest instance of trick horse riding being combined with traditional feats of acrobatics, a pointer to things to come and a milestone in the history of the Circus. On September 24 the performances closed down and the horses were auctioned.

During the early Spring of that year Mr Sampson, with his sixteen-year-old son, had been performing at the Globe in Whitechapel, and from Whit Monday he transferred to the Three Hats in Islington.

Mr and Mrs Astley began performing at Halfpenny Hatch in June. Astley's act at first consisted only of trick riding and of a horse that lay down as if dead and got up again on the word of command. In July Astley added a comic act of pretended bad riding called The Taylor riding to Brentford. The story of this turn is a curious one, and has not, I think, been told before. In 1768 John Wilkes, the radical politician and scourge of the government, had been prosecuted for publishing seditious and obscene libels and had been expelled from the House of Commons; he determined to challenge the government by standing as a candidate for parliament for the county of Middlesex. The election was held at Brentford, then a village on the Thames a few miles to the west of London, on March 28 and attracted enormous public interest. Wilkes was the hero of the mob, and coaches and even barges were provided from many places in London to convey his supporters to the poll. In the event Wilkes was returned with an enormous majority and the issue was kept alive by further triumphant elections in 1769 (three times), 1774, 1780 and 1784.

The story of a tailor who rode inexpertly to Brentford to vote for Wilkes was evidently a popular piece of folklore, as it was the subject of more than one print, the earliest perhaps published by Sayer on June 10.[2] Inspired by this, Astley created an act in which Billy Button, the tailor, first cannot mount his horse; when he eventually succeeds it won't move; then it gallops so fast that he is thrown off; and finally it chases him round the ring. It was the first clowning entrée in the history of the Circus, and was to enjoy a long life in many lands.

Astley's season closed on September 3, but he resumed for a week at Christmas, adding the act of a monkey riding on horseback, and tumbling by a young gentleman from High Germany. A good warm room was provided from which to watch the performance.

In 1769 Astley opened his season in May at a new

24

The original tailor riding to vote for John Wilkes at the Brentford election.

site by the south end of Westminster Bridge. The programme consisted of horsemanship and the Taylor; in July he added a little learned horse, "three feet high, from the deserts of Arabia", which performed conjuring tricks, and a horse which sat up like a dog. In August Astley performed conjuring tricks with cards on horseback as he galloped round the circle. Conjuring was at that time developing into a very popular entertainment with several eminent performers, and this is reflected many times in these equestrian performances.

In August a broadsword match was fought, with the contestants using blackened sticks and wearing white jackets so as to show the marks; the object of this was to enable the match to be decided by a system of marks rather than by the traditional method of fighting to a bloody finish. In October a sack race was introduced, with the competitors having sacks over their heads as well as round their legs, and with obstacles to be surmounted. Both these quasi-sporting events proved very popular and were repeated on many occasions subsequently. For the Christmas week there was also lofty tumbling, "after the manner of Sadler's Wells".

During this year, 1769, Mr and Mrs Sampson had been at the Three Hats until July, and then at the Dog and Duck, where they were joined by "the surprising German Youth (with undaunted courage)".

In 1770 Astley's was the only equestrian display to be seen in London. The husband and wife team was joined by Master Griffiths, who was fourteen years old, and the only addition to the programme was a Palatine's tricks with lofty tumbling. A "commodious gallery", 120 ft long, a kind of covered stand, was built, from which patrons could watch the show from dry seats; it was often stressed that a light shower would not prevent a performance, but some must have been lost through heavy rain. At the end of July the exhibition ended early, as the company left for Paris. (At least, so Astley claimed, though evidence of his performances in France has not come to light before 1774.) They were back again for a week at Christmas.

In 1771 Astley again had the field to himself. The season opened at the end of March with the usual turns of horsemanship and the Taylor, and some military exercises in the style of England, Ireland and Scotland. Astley was always proud of advertising his military background. In May he was carrying a young lady on his head while riding two horses at a gallop, and picking up a shilling from the ground, blindfolded and at full speed on horseback. For a week in June Astley let a horseman called Charles Hughes take over the programme, and from then on the Astleys, Master Griffiths and Hughes made up the equestrian troupe. Astley still rode as the tailor and Hughes added a similar comic act of a drunken sailor riding from Portsmouth. On the last night of the season Astley rode standing on two pint pots, and the company left for Paris again in the middle of August. They were back, without Hughes, for a week at Christmas.

In 1772 Astley showed his little learned horse at Exeter Change, an exhibition room in the Strand, during the early months, and opened his Riding School on Easter Monday. Astley's five-year-old son made occasional appearances on horseback, and Hughes was replaced by a mysterious gentleman described as Cosmethopila who may have been identical with "a native of France" who also figured on the programme. This pseudonym, whose object was presumably to attract speculation and publicity, may have been inspired by, or even identified with, a person calling himself Cosmopolita, from Paris, who had been performing Mathematical Amusements and Sleight of Hand at a room in Bow Street earlier that year.

In July Mr Hawtin displayed "heavy and light Balances" – presumably a weight lifting and equilibrist act – and at the end of the month the company prepared to leave for Paris. There must have been a hitch in their plans, however, and after a lot of ballyhoo

Some of Charles Hughes's equestrian feats at his Blackfriars Riding School.

about their approaching departure Astley, amusingly, advertised the show in French for a few days after the announced final performance. They continued playing till mid-September, adding Mr Wildman's act with bees to the programme; after a fortnight Mrs Astley learned to take part in this with him, and later she presented it on her own. The secret was apparently to coat wherever the bees were commanded to settle with sugared water; Wildman was a conjuror who normally performed deceptions as well as the bee act in various rooms about London – doing it on horseback was only a gimmick. In August that year a piece of automata called the Chronoscope was displayed while the spectators were assembling before performances; it depicted an Eastern Nabob on his elephant.

During this year, 1772, there was serious competition for Astley, as Hughes set up his own Riding School not far away, near Blackfriars Bridge. He opened on Easter Monday with his wife, his sister, romantically named Sobieska Clementina, and an eight-year-old girl, and they presented a very full and accomplished programme of trick horse riding, including most of Astley's turns like card tricks on horseback, the Taylor and the Sailor. A quite fresh act was described as "a puppet-shew master, title ascending etc. etc., riding a single horse, holding by a strap made fast to the saddle". The details of this are far from clear, but presumably it consisted of a marionette operator standing on the saddle of a horse as it cantered round the ring and performing with a puppet as it went. In May "the famous Miss Huntly, from Sadler's Wells", and a young pupil, Mr Jones, joined the company, which now consisted of two men and three women. In July Hughes brought out his own learned horse, described as the only one in the kingdom that will fetch and carry, and Mr Breslaw, a noted conjuror, came to present his Dexterity and Deceptions in the circle. In August Mr Huntly joined the company with a display of tumbling, including the fairly modest feat of somersaulting over two horses; he was presumably the equestrienne's father, and perhaps getting on in years. The season ended in mid-September.

There was a good deal of bad blood between Astley and Hughes at this time, which was not helped when Hughes announced a benefit performance for Astley's father, who had quarrelled with his son and was in reduced circumstances. In May Mr Sampson had brought the two equestrians together and it was said that the affair was amicably decided, as a token of which Sampson rode one evening at each Riding School; but the keen rivalry continued.

In advertisements at this time Hughes declared that "horsemanship has been his chief study for many years ... his activity far surpasses anything of the

Mr and Mrs Hughes, 1772.

kind yet attempted by any other performer ... that he had the honour of performing before their Majesties ... also in America and Africa." The next year he enlarged on this claim: "In the year 1770 Hughes exhibited before many Indian Nations, in Africa and America, and in 1772 had the honour of performing before their Britannic Majesties in Richmond Gardens." No record of his appearances has, as yet, been found in American sources, but if his claim is accepted Hughes was the first equestrian to perform on the American continent – an honour not previously accorded him in histories of the Circus.

For the season of 1773 Astley opened on Easter Monday with a more varied programme than hitherto. In addition to the usual acts of horsemanship, Horsemanship Burlesqued, and the little Military Horse there was a Sagacious Dog answering questions like "Does Beauty or Virtue in the Fair Sex more attract our Affections?", and a family from Verona performing La Force de Hercule, in which they built themselves into a pyramid on each other's shoulders. In July Mr Astley's sister joined the company, which then comprised half a dozen horsemen and horsewomen; a Polander performed balancing tricks on ladders and chairs, and a Spaniard put on a terrific display of acrobatics, vaulting over a garter (what we

Dexterity on horseback, as displayed by Charles Hughes and his sister, Sobieska Clementina.

would call a ribbon today) 8 ft above the ground, somersaulting off a board 16 ft high and firing a brace of pistols before he reached the ground, jumping over fourteen grenadiers, with a boy on one of their shoulders, and jumping through a flaming hogshead suspended 8 ft from the ground.

A summons from the Surrey magistrates in July brought this promising season to an early close, though Astley survived this threat in due course.

Meanwhile Hughes, with his wife and sister, after a tour of Hungary and France, were joined by Breslaw's Italian Company in a programme of horsemanship, conjuring, an Italian violinist who played the instrument in five different attitudes, tricks with eight small birds of various species, and a droll piece of activity called the Potius of Italy, "the particulars of which are inexpressible".

To complete the equestrian entertainments of 1773, Hyam, "the English Hero", was presenting "amazing feats of horsemanship", in company with Mademoiselle Zara, at a pleasure garden called Cromwell's Gardens in Brompton for half the week and at Price's Riding School (late Dobney's Bowling Green) for the other half. In between the acts of horsemanship there were capers on the tight rope by Signior and Madame Paliasette and their family; postures by Mons. Julian and his family; a grand piece of machinery (probably automata); Signior Paliasette leaping over five horses, a boy sitting on the middle horse with a lighted torch on his head; and Madame Margaretta performing a grand equilibre on the slack wire, which included her balancing thirteen glasses, full of liquor, on the end of a tobacco pipe, while standing on one leg on the wire without a balancing pole. The exhibition concluded with the drunken Taylor riding to Brentford. Visitors entering London from Heathrow Airport

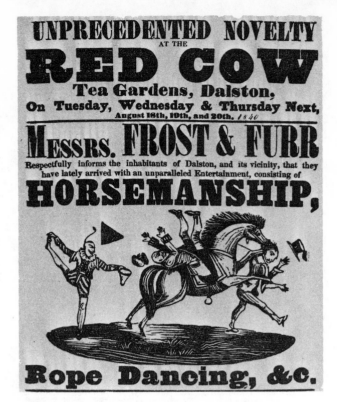

The Taylor to Brentford long continued in circus programmes. A bill of 1840.

today will pass the site of this splendid entertainment as their cars carry them down the Cromwell Road.

The progression from the simple displays of horsemanship in 1768 to these three packed and varied programmes that were being presented simultaneously in London in 1773 is unmistakable. The step had been taken to bring together into one performance these newly acquired feats of horsemanship with the skills that had been displayed for centuries by generations of animal trainers, vaulters, tumblers and jugglers. The Circus was born.

Opposite: Mr Makeen, a noted performer in the early years of the Circus, was eventually killed in falling from his horse.

II
THE EARLY YEARS

Mr MAKEEN
the Equestrian Hero

6

"The Father of the Circus"

PHILIP ASTLEY has been hailed by generations of circus writers as "the father of the Circus". It is no part of the purpose of this book to rob him of that proud title, but it must be recognized that he actually originated very little himself. He was not the first man to present displays of horsemanship - Johnson, Sampson and Price preceded him and he had to learn his tricks from them; he was not the first man to present such displays in a ring - all the riding masters must have ridden round in a circle and Dobney's was provided with a proper ring surrounded by seated spectators; he was not the first man to mix riding displays with other forms of entertainment - Mr and Mrs Wolton beat him to this by three and a half months, and Hughes and Hyam were developing mixed shows of this kind at the same time as Astley; he was not the first man to combine a number of feats of skill into one show - this had been a common feature of the fairground Medleys of the eighteenth century; he was not the first man to take his displays to foreign lands - Bates toured abroad before him.

Did he originate anything? Yes, he does seem to have been the first man to combine comedy with horsemanship. His Taylor was riding to Brentford as early as 1768, and I have not discovered any earlier appearance of this act. Under various names it was copied by innumerable equestrians in many countries for many decades to come. This is some claim to fame, for horses and clowns are two indispensable ingredients of Circus. But Astley's reputation rests not so much on what he originated as on how he developed the elements of entertainment that he had inherited. He was essentially a showman by instinct. Under his forceful direction the programmes in the Riding School grew more and more elaborate, and the Riding School itself grew more and more like a theatre. He estab-

lished an institution, and that is why he is remembered - and rightly remembered - as "the father of the Circus".

The stages of this development can be traced from his advertisements. In 1776 he added to his programme "a variety of amusements from the Boulevards of Paris" and "the roasted pig on the slack rope", in which apparently a performer lay on a twisted rope and was spun round as if on a spit; in 1777 he added automata figures and a curious clock; in 1778 rope vaulting, artificial fireworks and waterworks; in 1780 Ombres Chinoises (a shadow puppet show), tumbling with a trampolin (a springboard), and a zebra walking round the Riding School; in 1784 General Jackoo, a performing monkey, dancing dogs, a learned pig, and female rope dancers from Paris; in 1785 a musical child, a fox hunt, and the English Rossignol who imitated the songs of various birds; in 1786 a musical piece and a pantomime; in 1787 dancing horses, a ballet, and a "war entertainment"; in 1788 the Gibraltar Charger, a horse that stood still while fireworks exploded all round it; in 1789 "Paris in an Uproar", the destruction of the Bastille; in 1790 "The Siege of Quebec"; in 1793 the Disembarkation of the Light Horse for service on the Continent; in 1796 a military pantomime; in 1797 a Cabinet of Monkies; in 1799 a ballet of action, a nautical divertissement, and a ventriloquist; and so on. These acts were always interspersed with equestrian exercises and with sundry appearances of the learned horse, tumblers, vaulters and strong men.

The place of entertainment was developed over the years to match the increasing variety of the programme.[1] Up to 1779 the Riding School consisted of an open-air circular arena, 95 ft in diameter, enclosing a 60 ft ring in which the entertainments were given;[2]

Philip Astley in middle age on the driving seat of his carriage.

The furprizing Learned PIG will perform this Evening at *Aftley's*, Weftminfter-Bridge.

A learned pig answers questions in Astley's first covered Amphitheatre.

this was surrounded by two or three rows of covered seats for spectators; the main building, 51 ft high, was surmounted by a carving of an equestrian standing on horseback above the entrance from the street and was decorated with painted cloths depicted the feats to be witnessed within; the back of this building, facing the riding circle, served as a grandstand housing three rows of three boxes; on each side of it lower buildings provided stabling for the horses, with boxes for spectators above; a jump was placed in the centre of the circle, and a stage could be set up in front of the main stand for feats of activity on foot; in what was described as "the small circle", somewhere to the side of the main complex, there was apparatus "for breaking and training vicious horses".

Performances here could, of course, only be given in the daytime and during the summer, but in 1778 Astley began presenting an evening entertainment of Ombres Chinoises, a learned dog and horse, and imitations of birds' cries in a room in Piccadilly. Meanwhile he was constructing a covered building on the site of the Riding School. This was opened in 1779 as Astley's Amphitheatre Riding House, and it was now possible to play in all weathers and at all times of the day. Programmes of "Winter Evenings' Amusements" were presented. It is not certain how extensive was the area enclosed within the Amphitheatre Riding House at this time, and open-air displays may have continued in the large circle during the summer, but within a few years a major development had taken place with the construction of a completely covered ring and stage.

In 1784 a pantomime or musical piece was presented "by principal performers from the theatres in Paris" and the building was briefly known as Astley's Amphitheatre and Ambigu-Comic. In 1786 the interior was painted to resemble a grove of trees – an outdoor effect was evidently still thought desirable – and it acquired the title of Royal Grove, Astley's Amphitheatre. The theatre at this time contained a ring surrounded by seats in two tiers, with a small stage introduced at one point into the circle of seats. From this time on, the stage came to play an increasingly larger part in the entertainments. In 1792 the theatre was said to have been rebuilt "on a plan totally different from any other place of public entertainment in this kingdom"; this probably involved constructing a larger stage, perhaps with access from the stage to the ring; the building was now known as the Royal Saloon, Astley's Amphitheatre. This theatre was burnt down in 1794 and was rebuilt as the Amphitheatre of Arts in 1795; in 1801, now styled the Royal Amphitheatre, the interior was entirely rebuilt; but it was burnt down again in 1803. Undaunted, Astley erected an even larger theatre to be opened in 1804; this contained a ring, 44 ft in diameter, almost surrounded by pit benches and three massive tiers of boxes or galleries; introduced into the ring of seating, and transforming the shape of the auditorium from a circle to an ellipse, was a huge and well-equipped stage.

These dry particulars can do no more than hint at the consuming energy of the man who drove the enterprise forward. He was largely self-educated and scornful of experts, who told jokes about his mispronounciations and boorishness behind his back; in appearance, until he grew fat in middle age, he was imposing, over six feet high (at a time when English-men were much shorter than they are now), very strong, and with a stentorian voice; he possessed the gift of understanding the public taste; he knew, as he used to say, "what would catch John Bull";[3] and in the process, if he did not exactly invent the Circus, he created a type of popular entertainment that was to develop within a few years into the Circus as we know it today.

Astley's open-air Riding School, as in 1777, with its 60-ft ring, from the drawing by William Capon.

7

The Circus finds its Name

ASTLEY never called his entertainment a circus. It is possible that he did not know anything of the classical associations of the name when he adopted the title of Amphitheatre for his new building in 1779, but he was certainly familiar with the use of the term in connection with boxing; Stoke's Amphitheatre in the Islington Road and Figg's and Broughton's Amphitheatres in Oxford Road has established a reputation for cudgel fights and pugilism from the 1730s and 1740s.[1] It is to be noted that the term Amphitheatre had been adopted for the ambitious

building proposed but never built in the 1620s. In the eighteenth century the term implied a building similar in purpose, and probably in general design, to the Bankside rings for bull and bear baiting; and these sports were, in fact, still being presented in the boxing amphitheatres up to, at least, the middle of the century.

Astley's use of the term Amphitheatre, so far from being a conscious harking back to Roman spectacles, was probably inspired by entertainment places nearer home and not far removed from the Bankside bull rings in which, it may be, something like the first

*MR DIBDEN in the Character of MUNGO
in the Celebrated Opera of the Padlock.*

London Printed for R. Sayer at Nᵒ 53 Fleet Street & J. Smith at Nᵒ 35 Cheapside.

*Charles Dibdin, the first manager of the Royal Circus,
and the author of its name.*

circuses had actually been performed. However that may be, Astley was no doubt above all attracted by the grandiloquent sound of the word. Like many other self-educated men he enjoyed rolling a polysyllabic title round his tongue.

We must now, however, return to the figure of Charles Hughes, whom we last saw displaying exhibitions of horsemanship at a Riding School near Blackfriars Bridge in 1773. Hughes continued these exhibitions in the intervals of touring in France, Italy, Spain and Portugal until, in 1782, he made the acquaintance of Charles Dibdin. Dibdin was a restless, gifted, quarrelsome, clever composer and man of the theatre, famous in later years for his sea songs; he had just lost his position as house dramatist and composer at Covent Garden and was looking round for some fresh opportunity to use his energy and talents and for some source of income with which to pay off his debts. He noted the growing interest in displays of horsemanship but observed that this form of entertainment was associated with what he called "blackguardism", by which he meant, I suppose, that its performers were rough, uncouth fellows and the audiences not much better.

At the very beginning of 1782 Dibdin conceived a form of entertainment that would present horsemanship in a more "classical and elegant" manner. He proposed to combine it with drama by writing plays on themes of chivalry, introducing tournaments and other medieval equestrian exercises as part of the plot, thus uniting, as he put it, "the business of the stage and the ring". He invited the cooperation of Hughes, and then engaged the financial interest of four backers. The partnership was then joined by a fifth gentleman, Colonel West, who possessed some rights to a plot of land on the Surrey side of the river, not far from Hughes's Riding School. An agreement was drawn up: Dibdin was to act as manager and provide the plays, Hughes the horses, West the land, and the backers the money. Mr Grimaldi – the father of Joey – was engaged as ballet master to instruct a troupe of some twenty children. And a building was erected. But what was it to be called?[2]

"A theatre was to be erected", wrote Dibdin, "which I proposed to call The Royal Circus." If Astley fathered the Circus, Dibdin christened it. But what made him choose the name?

Dibdin was a man of some education and was almost certainly familiar with the use of the terms amphitheatre and circus in Roman times. Astley had adopted the title of Amphitheatre for his covered equestrian theatre two years previously, and Dibdin may have simply wanted to match it with a title of similar classical respectability. But what did the term "circus" imply to an eighteenth-century Englishman? In the first place it seems to have implied merely a circular open space. Twenty-eight years earlier in 1754, when John Wood built a ring of houses round a circular space in Bath he called it The Circus. The same use of the term is found in Oxford Circus and Piccadilly Circus in London. But there was a more immediate source of inspiration.

In the centre of Hyde Park, lying between the Serpentine and what is now called Bayswater Road, there had existed since the time of Charles I a roughly circular ride for horsemen, with a diameter of some two to three hundred paces. This ride, which provided a fashionable place for gentlemen to exercise their horses, was known as the Ring or the Circus.[3]

The use of this identical name has encouraged many writers to try to find a link between the circuses of ancient Rome and the circuses of nineteenth-century Europe. But there is no link, and even the derivation of the name is probably not directly from Rome at all but from associations with eighteenth-century gentlemen riding their horses for exercise and pleasure in the London parks.

Astley's theatre retained the title of Amphitheatre

until it was closed in 1893. A number of other buildings or temporary shows, presenting similar entertainment, adopted the term: there were Amphitheatres at Birmingham, Edinburgh and Leicester up to 1840. But the alternative term, Circus, gradually gained currency: Jones opened a Circus, so named, in Marlborough Street, London, in 1785; the New Manchester Circus opened in 1793; in 1798 there was an Olympic Circus at Liverpool; there were Circuses in 1799 at Bristol, in 1803 at Nottingham, in 1822 at Glasgow and Newcastle, in 1823 at Salford, in 1828 at Stepney, in 1833 at Birmingham. Ryan had an Amphitheatre in Birmingham in 1831 but his building in Brighton was called a Circus in 1836; Edinburgh had both an Amphitheatre and a Circus in 1840, but only a Circus from then on.

Dibdin's Royal Circus did not last many years, but the name he coined has gone round the world. Wherever this form of entertainment was presented, the name went with it: *cirque, circo, Zirkus, cyrk, tsirk* . . .

8

The Circus Theatres

The Royal Circus

THE ROYAL CIRCUS opened in 1782. Its external appearance was not unlike Astley's, even to the winged Pegasus surmounting the roof in place of Astley's standing equestrian. Inside, it was an elegant little theatre with benches surrounding a ring and a circle of boxes above. Draped curtains, slender balustrades and Corinthian columns in a colour scheme of silver upon a straw-coloured ground imparted a note of simple grandeur; a small stage was flanked by stage doors in the current theatrical tradition.

Its history, however, was a stormy one. After only nine nights it was closed by the magistrates as it did not have a licence; by the time a licence for burlettas and pantomimes was finally obtained, Dibdin was being pursued by his creditors, was forced into the semi-sanctuary provided by the Rules of the King's Bench, and in consequence of his inability to discharge his duties – and perhaps for general inefficiency – was dismissed as manager. He was succeeded by Grimaldi, but the enterprise languished and Hughes then proposed to Dibdin, who had secured his liberty, that the pair of them should seize the premises and conduct the theatre in defiance of the proprietors. Dibdin agreed to this, and an accommodation was reached with the proprietors, but after a season he quarrelled with Hughes and left the Circus for good.

Hughes was now engaged in a state of perpetual conflict with the proprietors and maintained a precarious hold upon the premises despite a court order for ejection. When a compromise was reached some ambitious productions were mounted with Delpini, a brilliant clown, combining this role with that of manager, but the principal actors were arrested for speaking dialogue; at this period, of course, the Licensing Act prevented the Minor Theatres from presenting straight drama and every piece had to be disguised with music and song to rank as a burletta. That, for the time, put a stop to any attempt to marry drama with equestrianism, the theatre declined to irregular performances, and Hughes went abroad.

When he returned he succeeded in persuading James and George Jones, who had been running an Equestrian Amphitheatre in Union Street, Whitechapel, to take a lease of the theatre in 1794. The interior was completely renovated and a short period of prosperity followed, with a series of successful pieces written by James Jones's son-in-law, J. C. Cross. But the theatre was burnt down in 1805; it was rebuilt, very handsomely and much larger, the next year, but it still failed to prosper; in 1809 it changed hands and the ring was filled with benches for a pit. As the Surrey it went on to enjoy a long and successful life.[1]

The programmes at the Royal Circus did not quite

The Royal Circus, with a pony race from the stage, round the ring, and back to the stage, c. 1800.

achieve the integration of drama and equestrianism that Dibdin had intended. The displays of horsemanship were interspersed in between burlettas, dances, farragos, spectacles and fireworks – the roof above the stage could be opened to allow the smoke and fumes from these to disperse. Dibdin's contributions were lightweight intermezzos or serenatas with titles like *The Barrier of Parnassus* or *The Land of Simplicity* and pantomimes like *The Lancashire Witches, or The Distresses of Harlequin*; Cross specialized in ballets and spectacles with a historical flavour, with titles like *Gonsalvo de Cordova, or the Conquest of Granada* and *Louisa of Lombardy, or the Secret Nuptials*.

A particularly ambitious production in 1789 during Delpini's management celebrated the fall of the Bastille by a piece called *The Triumph of Liberty* with settings by the eminent scene painter, William Capon, which employed more than a hundred men on stage and was greatly superior to the comparable piece at Astley's.[2] Another effective piece in 1791 was a comic pantomime, *The Four Quarters of the World*, for which a platform was laid from the stage over the orchestra, round the circle, and up again on to the stage; in the last scene a procession of carts representing Europe, Asia, Africa and America was drawn by horses, leopards and tigers round the ring, which had,

Decastro tells us, "a very grand, sublime and imposing effect". As there is no mention of a cage being erected it must have had a very dangerous effect, too! If these carts really were drawn by tigers and leopards this is the first instance of wild animals appearing outside their cages in a ring, but the feat of training would have been so remarkable for its period – or for any period – that one must express doubt – the animals were probably men in skins. Horses, however, were introduced actually on the stage in 1800 in Cross's pantomime, *The Magic Flute, or Harlequin Champion*, set in the time of Charlemagne, which featured not only a tournament but a sagacious horse who tore down a victory banner that had been unfairly awarded to his master's opponent.

During the interregnum between the two "house dramatists" the programmes here tended to include more acts of pure circus type. In 1785 a fox hunt was introduced, which proved a very popular spectacle; later there was a stag hunt; in 1786 there were tight rope, slack rope and wire acts, and an artiste who threw a back somersault from a trampolin to a height of 22 ft and did flip flaps with his legs tied together; in 1787 the Prussian Tumblers appeared and the complete bill comprised horsemanship, including a hornpipe on horseback, a ballet, a minuet, rope dancing, a song, horse vaulting, tumbling, slack rope vaulting, wire dancing, the Taylor's Journey to Brentford, and a pantomime. In 1793 "the force of Hercules" came in, which was a troupe of acrobats standing on each other's shoulders. During the Jones management pony races were staged.

Charles Hughes has often been dismissed by circus writers as some kind of deserter from Astley's troupe who set up in unsuccessful opposition to him. This is quite unfair. There are indications that he was a better equestrian than Astley, certainly he was his match. He was already a rider of repute before he joined Astley's troupe, and he served in it for less than a year. He toured abroad more extensively than Astley, he was perhaps the first English rider to perform in America, and, as we shall see later, he founded the Circus in Russia. He is described as a handsome man and of great strength. He and Astley were bitter rivals, and anything the one did the other immediately tried

to do better; the advertisements in which they "knocked" each other make entertaining reading. Astley was, of course, by far the more successful; he was a born showman with an eye for every kind of popular entertainment, he was lucky (and astute) in his speculations, and he was always his own master. Hughes was a horseman, not an impresario, a more genuine circus personality than Astley, and he found himself out of his depth in dealing with his theatrical partners; he was unlucky to have become involved in a personality clash with a difficult character like Dibdin, and then to find himself entangled in a complex financial partnership. There may have been faults on both sides: Dibdin, who was paranoic about his ex-partners, described him as a "horse-rider with the dark mind and dastardly heart of a Portuguese-bravo"; Decastro says he "was a man of rather irritable temper . . . possessing a spirit of opposition as often as he was thwarted in his measures". He lost his

ARENA *OF* ASTLEY'S AMPHITHEATRE, *SURREY ROAD.*

Astley's third Amphitheatre, with its 44-ft ring and well-equipped stage, as in 1815.

37

licence for the theatre from some offence given to the magistrates and died, disappointed, in 1797, aged fifty. Hughes has been overshadowed by Astley, but he is entitled to an honourable place in the roll of the founding fathers of the Circus.

Astley's Amphitheatre

With the building of the third Amphitheatre in 1804 Astley's really entered upon its long career as a dual-purpose theatre. We can read of the magnificent spectacles staged there in the writings of Dickens and Thackeray and half a dozen other Victorian authors; we can see the splendid auditorium in the familiar Pugin-Rowlandson aquatint, with its three circles of open seating and the ringside spectators crowding round the Circle in which a graceful equestrian stands upon the middle one of three prancing horses while a clown directs them with a whip. Beyond the curtain lies the stage, and it was here that the union of stage and ring, conceived by Dibdin, reached its fulfilment. After the Royal Circus had abolished its ring in 1810, Astley's had the monopoly of this form of entertainment and there evolved here that curious dramatic hybrid, the hippodrama, though the Scenes in the Circle of genuine circus acts continued to play a subordinate part in the programmes.

The first really successful example of hippodrama was *The Brave Cossack* in 1807, which concluded with a set piece cavalry battle with horses galloping, rearing, plunging and dying all over the place. Although the ring was used in the course of the action, it must be noted that the main cavalry engagement took place on the stage, which was provided with strong ramps, disguised by scenic ground rows, for the horses to ascend. The stage at Astley's was, in fact, the largest in any English theatre at the time.

After this, hippodramas followed each other year by year. In 1819 one of the most popular of all subjects was introduced in *Richard Turpin*, and highwaymen holding up coaches and jumping five-barred gates remained a staple feature in the repertory. In 1824 an even more popular subject appeared with *The Battle of Waterloo*, and this was not only played on innumerable occasions but was followed by other battles from the Napoleonic saga and later by battles from every war in which British troops might be distinguishing themselves, whether in Burma, Afghanistan, the Crimea or the Sudan. Even Shakespeare provided material for hippodrama, and *Richard III* was played here with great success in 1856. Perhaps the most

"Turpin's Ride to York" was for long a circus favourite. A performance at Rampling's Circus, Margate, in 1850.

famous of all hippodramas was *Mazeppa*, based on Byron's poem, with a naked youth bound to a wild horse of Tartary that is set free to gallop across the steppes of the Ukraine; this was first performed here in 1831 but the most sensational production was in 1864 with a woman, the famous Adah Isaacs Menken, in the role of the naked youth. At the end of its long history, from the 1870s to 1893, Astley's was chiefly noted for the vast zoological pantomimes, in which an excuse was found to introduce almost every animal from Noah's Ark into almost every nursery panto-mimical theme.

I shall not try to trace the story of hippodrama any further in this book. For one thing, its history has already been admirably told elsewhere.[3] For another thing, it is not strictly Circus. The stage at Astley's was always more important than the ring, and when Menken appeared the ring had even disappeared and the whole piece was played on the stage. One of the best contemporary circus writers has enunciated the principle that while Theatre is essentially the display of what is unreal and pretended, Circus is essentially the display of what is actual and without pretence.[4] Some theatre workers today may not be inclined to accept his limitation on the Theatre, but for the purposes of this book I accept his definition of Circus. Hippodrama is great fun in itself, comparable in many ways with Western movies, but it is not really quite Theatre and it is not really quite Circus. We must confine ourselves here to acts of skill performed by men and women or by trained animals, presented in a ring, with the audience grouped around. That is the essence of Circus.

Opposite: Haute Ecole in the Golden Age of the Circus.

III
THE CIRCUS IN BRITAIN IN THE NINETEENTH CENTURY

9
Circuses

THE CIRCUS had barely established itself in London before it began to spring up all over the country. At first the entertainments were often given in existing Riding Schools, which clearly lent themselves to small-scale equestrian displays: Astley made the first of what were to become yearly visits to Dublin as early as 1773, when he played in the Riding School on the Inns Quay; by 1788 the Riding House in Tip Street, Manchester, and Ryles's Ride in Monmouth Street, Bath, had been similarly used; in 1789 the Riding School in Christian Street, Liverpool, and in 1790 the Riding School, Northampton, housed itinerant circus entertainments.[1]

Just as in London, it soon became desirable to erect more suitable buildings, capable of housing larger audiences, and before long a chain of more or less permanent wooden circus buildings had been erected across the country. Astley is said to have built no less than nineteen circuses during his career; of these we know of the Amphitheatre and the Olympic Pavilion in London, and of a circus in Paris, but where were the others? He certainly built circus amphitheatres in Dublin, Liverpool and Manchester but the complete list seems impossible to determine.

These early circuses do not seem to have incorporated stages, but they included some kind of platform from which songs could be delivered: in the Liverpool circus of 1799 there was a structure like a huge Punch and Judy booth in which the singers appeared, and at Bristol the same year there was something not unlike the rack over a manger projecting over the horse ride for the singers to stand on.[2] As more permanent buildings were erected, a stage was usually incorporated in the same way as in the London theatres. Ryan's Amphitheatre in Birmingham in 1828 had a stage 127 ft deep.

If we look briefly at three or four towns in Britain we can see how quickly the Circus established itself as a popular form of entertainment. In Birmingham Swann's Amphitheatre in Livery Street was in use by 1787; in Manchester the New Circus opened in Chatham Street in 1793; in Bristol a Riding School was adapted for circus performances in Limekiln Lane in 1792; in Liverpool the New Olympic Circus had opened at the bottom of Shaw's-Brow by 1798; in Edinburgh a circus had been sited in Broughton Street before 1788.

These were merely the first. At a rough count some eight circus buildings were erected in Manchester during the nineteenth century, ten in Bristol, and fifteen in Liverpool. No doubt other cities could tell a similar story, if only local historians would study these matters.[3]

These buildings were often crude structures, with thin wooden walls and tin or canvas roofs; their exteriors were modest, but they were not without atmosphere. A Birmingham circus of the mid-century is described as follows. "The building was large, built partly of wood and partly of brick, with a double tarpaulin roof. It was vast and dim, and the sunlight endeavoured almost in vain to peep through. Everything had a dull and tarnished appearance. The gilded parts were covered with cloth and any portion of the paint and gilt-work that was visible to the naked eye was coarse and dauby-like. The place smelt dreadfully of sawdust, decayed orange peel, and stable manure, which, coupled with a large escape of gas, formed anything but an odoriferous compound." But at night there was a transformation. "Now the scene was brilliant and striking ... Innumerable jets of gas lighted up the place till it was in a perfect glory of brightness. The coarse appearance of the paint was

Hengler's Circus in Dale Street, Liverpool. A watercolour by W. Hedman.

softened down, and all was gay and radiant. The boxes were crowded with ladies, and the house generally was full to the ceiling."[4]

Some of these circuses were of considerable size and were splendidly decorated. The Amphitheatre in Woodhouse Lane, Leeds, could hold 3,000 people. Ryan's Amphitheatre in Birmingham in 1838 could accommodate 2,000 persons and the interior was surrounded by thirty-nine Doric columns. The Amphitheatre in Leicester, erected in 1840, was described as "equal in size and beauty to any in Europe". Hengler's Grand Cirque in Liverpool, built in 1857, was a splendid building after the style of the Cirque Napoléon in Paris, with a ceiling covered with folds of chintz and the pillars supporting the roof neatly papered and ornamented with flags and shields. Newsome's Circus in Birmingham, built at the same time, was draped with many thousand yards of scarlet cloth, with black velvet ornaments and a bullion fringe a yard deep, the whole festooned and supported by flying Cupids. The surrounding columns each supported a colossal piece of classic sculpture.

When a purpose-built circus building was not available, circuses often performed in regular theatres. It is not entirely clear to what extent the theatres were adapted for the circus performances. Sometimes the performance was simply given on the stage; with the raked stages common in nineteenth-century theatres,

this must have presented considerable problems to the horses and the acrobats. Sometimes, however, as with the Rampling Cirque Continental at Margate in 1858, a proper ring was set up in the pit.

It is not sufficiently realized that for a large part of its history Circus took place in circus buildings rather than in tents. A suitable building is still the ideal place in which to watch a circus performance; the Tower Circus at Blackpool and the Cirque d'Hiver in Paris demonstrate the atmosphere and intimacy that such a building can create in the gay opulence of a nineteenth-century setting. It is a tragedy that so few such buildings survive. The Circus Krone Bau in Munich, with its great laminated wooden beams spanning the arena, demonstrates how effectively such an atmosphere and intimacy can be recreated in a twentieth-century building. It is even more of a tragedy that this is the only building of its kind outside eastern Europe.

These early circus buildings were not only hurriedly run-up and pulled down when they had served their purpose; they were sometimes transported round the country as portable arenas. In Norwich in 1833, when Ducrow's National Arena and Equestrian Studio was erected on the Castle Meadow, the local paper commented that this was the first of the temporary buildings periodically erected in the locality for entertainments of the kind; in 1840 at the same place a journalist drew attention to "the huge amphitheatre which is now in rapid progress towards completion on the Castle Meadow" and Batty's Circus claimed that it was housed in "the most elegant, spacious, and substantial building ever erected in Norwich".[5]

It is not surprising that these structures were not always soundly constructed. The gallery of the circus at Bristol fell down in 1799, injuring many people, one of whom died; in 1836 a large wooden building erected for a circus in the Ranelagh Gardens, Norwich, was blown down in a gale; in 1848 six hundred people were in a gallery that collapsed in a temporary wooden circus at Leeds.[6] The frequency of such accidents inspired some circus owners to insert in their handbills assurances about the safety of their structures; the Olympic Circus at Newcastle in 1822, for instance, stated that "the Circus is erected by Messrs Brown and Sons, Builders, who pledge themselves to warrant the above erection commodious and firm in every part".

The idea of portable wooden buildings for circuses may now seem strange, but portable theatres, both for human and puppet performances, regularly toured fairs and villages up to the early years of the twentieth century. They were formed by shutters bolted together within a more substantial framework of vertical and horizontal beams, secured to the wagons on which the show was transported; no doubt the portable circuses used the same technique. Cirques Medrano and Amar were touring in France with portable buildings of wood and metal as late as the 1930s. But when we think of touring circuses we inevitably think of tents.

As early as 1773 Astley had performed in Liverpool in a large field near a bowling green at Mount Pleasant, but this was almost certainly in the open air with no more than a walling of canvas to prevent spectators who hadn't paid for admission from seeing the performance. This was a common arrangement. In 1794 two men fell from an elm tree and were injured while trying to watch Astley's show at Oxford; in the 1820s boys caused so much damage to the trees by the Forth at Newcastle when they tried to watch Powell's Circus that the mayor, with a fine feeling for the preservation of the environment, ordered the circus to move. The ring for these open-air circuses was formed by turning the earth, or mould, over so as to make it soft for the horses' feet, and touring with such a show was known as "moulding" in the profession.[7]

The earliest recorded use of a circus tent is in 1788 at Liverpool, when Astley performed in what he called the Royal Tent in Vernon Street, off Dale Street. The venture seems not to have been successful, as he auctioned off the materials of the Royal Tent at the end of the season and performed for several subsequent years in the Theatre Royal there. It is curious that in

an age of sailing ships, when sailmakers were manufacturing vast spreads of canvas for the Navy, no further use of tents for circuses is recorded in Britain for over fifty years. Fairground shows usually had canvas tilts or roofs, and sometimes canvas side walls, but I have never seen any indication of a circular canvas tent in a fair, and the rectangular plots in which sites were laid out would have made this shape uneconomic.

The evidence for permanent circus buildings, and the lack of evidence for the use of tents during this period, is overwhelming. But all the same a sense of doubt nags at the back of the mind. When the English equestrian, John Ricketts, built a circus in Philadelphia in 1793 he constructed a circular wooden building with a conical roof – very like a tent in shape; when Philip Astley built a second theatre in London, on the fashionable side of the river, in 1806, he constructed a wooden building from the materials of a broken-up ship, with a tin roof, "in the form of a tent", and called it the Olympic Pavilion. Why "pavilion"? Why did these early circus builders make their buildings look like tents, if tents were not yet being used for circuses? Or were they?

The first substantial use of a tent for circuses in England came from America, where it had been introduced in the mid-1820s. In 1842 Richard Sands landed in Liverpool with "a splendid and novel Pavilion, made after an entirely new style, with the most costly interior Decorations and appointments forming at once a magnificent spacious Roman Amphitheatre and Arena of the Arts, the whole of which is erected in a few hours; and capable of holding several thousand persons". Sands' American Circus toured England for three or four years and the example of his tent was soon copied. In 1843 the Norwich paper recorded that the first touring circus in Norfolk at which performances were given under canvas was that belonging to Batty, who had a tent 65 ft in height and 300 ft in circumference, which could accommodate 1,400 persons, and Cooke's Royal Circus was touring in 1845 with "a magnificent new pavilion on an improved construction". But American circuses still made the running: in 1850 Macarte and Bell's Grand American Circus was touring the Midlands with "a magnificent Marquee"; in 1853 Hernandez and Stone's Great American Circus was in the Manchester area with "a portable equestrian palace . . . to hold 3,000 persons", and in 1857 Howes and Cushing's United States Circus boasted of its Great American Marquee and that "Tents now take precedent of Marble Halls".

By this time Brown's Royal Cirque Unique was touring with a "monster tent" and the English circuses had almost all adopted the idea. The usual size for an

English circus tent in the 1860s was about 120 ft in diameter (compared with about 96 ft for Batty's in 1843); in the 1880s Sanger's one-pole tent measured 185 ft in diameter, but it could be extended with 42 ft wide sections per pole up to as many as five poles if necessary. A tent at a country fair might hold 1,000 people, but Powell and Clarke's tent in the 1880s could seat 7,000.

Whether in tents, portable arenas, or permanent amphitheatres, the seating for the audience in these circuses conformed to the standard theatrical pattern of boxes, pit and gallery. There are no references in the nineteenth century to ringside seats. The normal arrangement would seem to have been that the pit was the benches surrounding the ring, the boxes were separate compartments behind the pit and on a slightly higher level, and the gallery was either the back rows of the pit or, if the building permitted, above the boxes. In rectangular fairground booths the pit might be the benches on one side of the ring, the boxes the same kind of benches but carpeted on the opposite side, and the gallery the benches by the entrance facing a simple stage beyond the ring.[8] By the 1860s circuses were talking about their best seats as stalls.

The whole seating arrangement was flexible and portable, for Wallett tells how he dismantled the gallery and pit in the circus at Leeds in one night, packed them in wagons, and transported them to the circus at Huddersfield. Unfortunately the elevation here was not the same, so that after they had been re-erected and the circus was full of spectators, the supporting beams shifted and the whole arrangement inclined forward, trapping entire rows of audience with their knees jammed against the back of the seats in front.

It may be observed that the ringside seats in circuses today are usually partitioned off into the semblance of boxes, and now that boxes have almost disappeared from modern theatres it is only in circuses that these sociable adjuncts to the watching of entertainment – so well suited to the seating of a family party – can be enjoyed.

Prices throughout the century were commonly three shillings boxes, two shillings pit, one shilling gallery, and sixpence standing. These conformed closely enough to current theatre prices, but fairground shows might charge only sixpence or threepence.

Whatever the arrangement of seating, the central element in the circus, the feature that must be essential to anything that calls itself a circus, is the ride, the circle, or the ring. We have seen that this had a diameter of 44 ft in Astley's rebuilt Amphitheatre of 1804, and this size was never to be substantially altered. At the Olympic Pavilion in 1806 the ring on the stage measured only 40 ft diameter, and at the Holborn Amphitheatre in 1875 the ring was enlarged to 47 ft diameter; within these limits we find diameters of 42, 44 and 45 ft at various places. In an art as international as the Circus it became essential to standardize the dimensions of the performing area so that the horses could find the same conditions everywhere they went. Minor variations still occur, but a circus ring, now internationally expressed as 13 metres in diameter, is the same from Los Angeles to Moscow. Attempts have been made to work with larger rings, but they have never succeeded.

This does, of course, limit the number of spectators who can be seated fairly near the ring, and in 1860 George Sanger experimented with placing three rings side by side, with two stages or platforms between them, and a race track running round the outside.[9] This was in the open air, not in a tent, but he repeated the arrangement at the Agricultural Hall in 1870. Subsequently he abandoned the idea; neither performers nor spectators liked it; but it was, however, adopted by all the big American shows as we shall see later.

There are two theories as to how the size of the circus ring was originally arrived at. According to one school of circus historians, a circle with a diameter of 42 ft provides exactly the right balance for a rider standing on the back of a cantering horse between the centrifugal forces tending to throw him out of the ring, and the centripetal forces formed when he leans inwards. I have never been able to follow this argument. If the ring were larger he could surely perform his act equally effectively by not leaning inwards quite so much. Astley's earliest arena, in fact, had a ring of 60 ft diameter. In an argument *ad absurdam*, if there were no ring and the horse cantered in a straight line, every act of horsemanship could be performed without the necessity of leaning at all. What is true, I think, is that a horse could not move easily in a much tighter circle, and a rider in such a circle would be obliged to lean so far towards the centre in order to keep his balance that he would have difficulty in keeping a firm footing on the horse's back. The 42 ft ring is not so much the ideal size as the smallest practical size for good horsemanship.

The other theory is that the size of the ring was controlled by the length of the lunge used for training the horse. This seems likely enough, and it assumes a lunge of about 20 ft. But Philip Astley's lunge was about 30 ft. In his advice for breaking a horse, published in 1775, he wrote: "Let him be led to some convenient piece of ground, with a small rope, of about ten yards long, tied to the near side of the snaffle next his mouth [and] let a boy lead him round the Circle."[10] A horse trained in this way would become accustomed

The Holborn Amphitheatre was a fine circus in London between 1867 and 1875.

to being ridden round in a circle of 60 ft diameter, which exactly accords with the actual size of the ring used by Astley in his first performances, and incidentally with the diameter of the "pit" in the Elizabethan bull rings and theatres. But a ring of this size was somewhat large to fit into a building of moderate size and, moreover, represents an uneconomic use of space.

Although Astley was not the first man to present his riding act in a circular arena, I believe he can be credited with establishing the approximate size of the circus ring. When he built his first indoor Amphitheatre he reduced the size of the ring by a third, to the smallest practical diameter for good horse riding. It was a compromise between experience and economics; a compromise that has, indeed, stood the test of time.

The ground within the ring was covered with pulverized sawdust in Astley's Amphitheatre, and this – mixed with earth – has always remained the standard material for travelling circuses. In the permanent circuses of the middle of the century, however, coconut matting was introduced; we find this in the circuses built by Wallett at Kidderminster and by Newsome at Birmingham, where the centre of the matting was covered by "an elegant circular carpet of chaste design". Coconut matting is used in some permanent circuses today, but it is somewhat slippery for the horses' feet and limits the speed at which they can work.

In addition to the ring, some portable and tenting circuses incorporated stages, like the permanent amphitheatres. This was the case with Ginnett's Circus as late as the 1860s,[11] and it is still a feature of some European circuses though lovers of "pure circus" (of whom I am one) deplore this mixture of two very different art forms.

A feature that every circus had to provide was a space for the orchestra. In Thomas Cooke's Circus in the 1840s this was placed over one of the entrances to the ring, and this has proved the most satisfactory position.

And, of course, the show had to be lit. In the early years of the Circus, as of the Theatre, the only illumination could have been from candles or oil lamps. Astley's Royal Grove had a triple circlet of candles suspended over the centre of the ring. Wicks needed snuffing, glass chimneys needed cleaning, and oil needed to be of good quality, if efficient results were to be obtained. One wonders if they often were. Gaslight was installed at Astley's in 1818, and other permanent circuses must have soon followed suit. Clarke's Circus at Bartholomew Fair was lit by gas in 1825,[12] and Cooke's Circus at Brighton was advertising "a profusion of gas light" in 1827 to show off the "costly dresses and trappings of the performers and their horses to all possible advantage". Tenting circuses made use of naphtha flare lamps, produced by dripping oil on to a heated burner, which produced a brilliant but dangerous hissing flame. The earliest use of electric light that I have noted was in 1867, when it was switched on for Maccomo's performance with the lions, tigers and elephants in Manders' Menagerie. In 1878 Ginnett's permanent circus at Brighton, the Hippodrome, was early in the field with electric illumination, but the arc lamps of 4,000 candlepower frightened the horses and had to be removed; in 1885 Powell and Clarke's tenting circus was lit by the electric illumination for circuses "as recently discovered by the Americans". The first American circuses to be lit by electricity were, in fact, Cooper and Bailey, and W. W. Cole, in 1879.[13] Before mains supply became available circuses had to take steam-driven generators with them.

For their names, most circuses simply adopted the name of their proprietor, but for a time the title of Olympic Circus was very popular. I don't know who originated it, but I suppose it was thought to be a classical variant of nomenclature in keeping with the amphitheatres and circuses. There was one at Liverpool as early in 1798, and as this was called the New Olympic this was presumably not the first. Astley adopted the name for the theatre he built in Wych Street in 1806 which he ran as a second circus establishment until 1812. Olympic circuses are found all over the place, in Europe and America too, until the 1850s. Ducrow was fond of calling his circuses Temples or Arenas of Art; and after the middle of the century the title Hippodrome became popular – another variant in classical styling – originally to denote a track for chariot racing, but it soon lost its association with the Circus and became a synonym for a music hall or Palace of Varieties.

The Rotunda in Vauxhall Gardens served as a charming small circus between 1839 and 1859.

10
Proprietors

WHO WERE THE MEN who made this burst of circus activity possible?

Some were riders from Astley's or Hughes's troupes; some came from the fairground booths, some came from we know not where; but by the early decades of the nineteenth century there were a couple of dozen or more proprietors of small troupes of equestrians and acrobats, leading their little bands across the country. The humblest of these would do no more than gather a crowd with a rider or acrobat in order to sell a stock of mountebank's wares; other would rely on selling tickets in a lottery for prizes that might be quite substantial at the opening performance, but as the news got round and spectators flocked to buy tickets the value of the prizes decreased. Some would set up in fairs, in the courtyard of an inn, or in any open spaces where they could gather an audience; some troupes combined and split up again; the larger companies played in the permanent circus buildings whose growth we have already considered, or – as best they could – on the stages of orthodox theatres.

When the full history of the Circus in Britain is written the names of all these pioneers will be suitably honoured, but here I can do no more than mention a few of the more important.

By the end of the eighteenth century John Astley, Philip's son, was taking a leading part in the running of the Amphitheatre, as his father was much occupied with establishing a circus in Paris. John was a graceful equestrian who had been christened "the English rose" by Marie Antoinette when he rode at Versailles; he lacked his father's formidable characteristics, but artistes in the company found his gentlemanly behaviour a pleasant relief from the "bear-like manner" of the old man. John seems to have been largely responsible for managing the touring companies. They travelled to most of the towns in the United Kingdom, the men riding the performing horses and the women in the baggage wagons, though the better-class actresses preferred to travel at their own expense by mail coach.[1]

Rivalling Astley was a partnership of five men, all expert performers in their own right, which had been formed by 1799 and which hired or erected circus buildings all over the United Kingdom for their performances. Parker had been an equestrian in the 1790s at Edinburgh and Bath; his wife was an actress, the best Columbine in England. Benjamin Handy was a vaulter and clown in Birmingham in 1787, where he married Signora Riccardini who had distinguished herself by standing on her head on the top of a spear surrounded by fireworks. George Smith had been a star equestrian as a boy at Birmingham and Bath in 1787-8, leaping from the trampolin and swinging on the slack rope. Mr Crossman had been another boy wonder, challenging all the horsemen of Europe to match his feats at the Royal Circus from 1788. Smith and Crossman were described as "the two greatest equestrian performers of their time". William Davis had been a pupil of Charles Dibdin the Elder at the opening of the Royal Circus, and became a horseman of repute.

When Astley's Amphitheatre was rebuilt in 1804 these five took a half share in the theatre, with John Astley holding the other half. The speculation was a successful one, and they all retired in due course to live the lives of country gentlemen. Handy became a magistrate in Bath – not bad for a former circus clown! One doubts if Mrs Handy ever stood on her head in the Pump Room.

Davis was the last of the partnership to remain working in the Circus. After John Astley's death in 1821 he took over the Amphitheatre for three years,

Some early circuses merely acted as a pitch for a mountebank salesman.

renaming it Davis's Amphitheatre and quarrelling with Astley's widow in the process.

A few more names from this early period may be noted. Thomas Ord was well known in Scotland and the north of England; he had begun performing in about 1804 with only one donkey, but he built up a good show and established several circus buildings, including one on the Mound in Edinburgh. He suffered the disasters that were inseparable from these early circus years; on one occasion almost all his horses died from drinking poisoned water in Wales, on another occasion he was bringing his show back from Ireland in two boats when one, on which his wife was sailing, was lost at sea. When he appeared in his flesh tights we are told that he seemed "a very good incarnation of a supple, sinewy, powerful and graceful athlete of the great days of ancient Greece". His daughter married John Edward Pinder, and they established a circus that remained popular in Scotland for many years.[2]

Bannister and West, separately and in partnership, toured Scotland and the north of England from about 1810. West later went to America, where he appeared with some success.[3] Price and Powell similarly formed a loose kind of partnership; Powell's equestrian booth at Newcastle in 1815 consisted of only three horses, four riders, a musician and a clown, but he went on (if it was the same man) to build up quite a decent company; there are so many Prices in the circus world that it is difficult to keep tracks of them all. Both these families continued to lend lustre to the Circus throughout the century.

An interesting character was Abraham Saunders who had been a rope dancer at Covent Garden as early as 1760 and was an attraction at Sadler's Wells in the 1780s. In 1796 he was running a Portable Riding School at Bartholomew Fair and Edmund Kean, as a young boy, is said to have joined his troupe in about 1800; he took the Royalty Theatre in 1804 and the Theatre in Tottenham Street in 1807; he toured his company to Scotland and Ireland, but lost his horses at sea. As late as 1837 he was still running a booth at Bartholomew Fair, and he died in harness two years later, aged 92.

His son, Master Saunders, was a boy wonder. In 1796, only seven years of age, he had been billed as "the Wonderful Child of Promise". He went on to appear as a tight rope dancer and an equestrian for many seasons at the Royal Circus, Astley's, and in the provinces, particularly at Birmingham where his sister joined him in a slack rope act and a small circus acquired the name of Saunders's Amphitheatre in 1806–7. The next year, while at the Royal Circus, he was seen by William Beckford, the wealthy recluse of Fonthill Abbey, who developed a passionate admiration for him and tried to persuade him to leave the family home in Duke Street and travel abroad with him as his companion and lover. It is not certain how far the relationship developed but it is perhaps indicative that in 1810, when the Bow Street runners raided a public house in Vere Street that had become a rendezvous for homosexuals, Matthew Saunders of Duke Street was one of the men taken up.[4]

A family that went on to play a great part in the Circus makes its first appearance with Jack Clarke, whom I have first noted at Norwich in 1815 when he was billed as "the celebrated equestrian of the Royal Circus". He was billed as "the Northern Wonder" when he played, with his seven-year-old daughter, at Astley's in 1822. By 1825 he had his own circus which attended the fairs round London for some fifteen years. He was affectionately remembered for his hot temper and warm heart; he would shout at his audience and brandish his stick at them if they misbehaved, and the boys delighted in teasing him. In his old age he was reduced to playing clown, but his descendants became some of the most brilliant circus performers of the century; a grandson founded the famous Clarkonian flying trapeze troupe, and his great-grandchildren became the champion jockey riders of the world.[5]

The greatest performer of the age was certainly Andrew Ducrow. His father, Peter Ducrow, billed as the Flemish Hercules, had been a leaper and strong man in various troupes from the 1790s. Andrew appeared with his father as an Infant Wonder from the age of three or four, and showed a precocious talent, being billed as the Little Devil on the tight rope and on horseback from the age of thirteen. But his genius lay not just in horsemanship but in mime, and he developed a remarkable series of acts in which he first posed as and then mimed various characters while standing on a horse's back while it cantered round the ring. This act was at first not fully appreciated in England, and in 1818 he embarked on a series of long engagements in Europe where – especially in France – he was greeted with an enthusiasm verging on idolatry. In 1823 he returned to England and – with financial assistance from West – took over Astley's, where he was now acclaimed as "the Colossus of equestrians", and from whence he toured and erected amphitheatres all over Britain. In 1841 the destruction of Astley's by yet another fire so unhinged his reason that his wife had him confined in a lunatic asylum. He died the same year.[6]

The characters that he personated included a Roman gladiator, a Chinese enchanter, a British tar, an Indian hunter, a Moorish warrior, and six figures from a Venetian carnival. In double acts with his partner and second wife, Louisa Woolford, they personated a Tyrolean shepherd and a Swiss milkmaid, a Neapolitan fisherman with a market girl of Portico, and similar duets. There were some fifty such acts in all. It is difficult for us now to appreciate the appeal of this combination of mime with equestrianism, but Ducrow must be regarded not only as a great circus artiste and horse rider but as a mime to be ranked with Deburau and John Rich, the elegant dancer who created the role of Harlequin in the English eighteenth-century pantomime, and in our own day with Marcel Marceau. The addition of mime to horsemanship was no mere gimmick but the creation of a form of true circus-drama that has never been achieved since.

At this time the family of Cookes, which dominated the British circus scene during the nineteenth century, began to make its mark. The founder was Thomas Taplin Cooke, a horseman, leaper and rope walker, who travelled to Lisbon in 1816 but he, too, lost his horses at sea on the return voyage. Undeterred, he built up a show again, assisted by his numerous children, of whom seven were sons who became noted circus performers themselves – Thomas, William, James, John, Henry, Alfred and George. By the early 1820s they were running the Olympic Circus in Liverpool, which they rebuilt in 1826. In 1836 they went to America, only to have two theatres burnt down around them, losing everything in a disastrous fire at Baltimore. Once again they started up from nothing, and in about 1840 they took over Ducrow's old circus in Nicolson Street, Edinburgh, which they ran successfully for many years with a chain of other circuses in Scotland; in the 1850s William was touring a Hippodrome, and in 1853 he took over Astley's for seven years. The list is endless. They inter-married

into almost every circus family in four continents.[7]

Another proprietor of Astley's was William Batty, who succeeded Ducrow in the rebuilt theatre. He is first heard of in the mid-1820s with an equestrian company which played in circuses up and down England and Scotland. In 1840 he was touring "a very elegant portable" in the south of England, and we have seen how quick he was to get his show under canvas three years later. In 1851 he took advantage of the presence of the Great Exhibition in Hyde Park to open a Hippodrome in Kensington opposite the Broad Walk, where he staged chariot races and similar attractions.

An apprentice and later manager of Batty's was Edwin Hughes. The son of a Birmingham toymaker, he became an expert polander, the first man, it was said, able to rotate his body round 360° without holding, while balancing on his head, probably on the single upright spar of a come-apart ladder. In 1843 he set up his own show, and after two seasons enlarged it into Hughes's Mammoth Equestrian Establishment. It mounted a particularly impressive parade with magnificent cars pulled by elephants and camels. He was said to be the first man to succeed in harnessing these animals. Hughes, himself, dressed like an oriental potentate, rode in one of the chariots. After only five seasons he had made a fortune, and he retired in 1847.[8] His chariots went to America, where they helped to create the superb American tradition of circus parade wagons.

Many circus proprietors began as equestrians, but Hengler, like Hughes, was originally an acrobat. The family of Hengler sprang from a rope dancer who is first recorded at the Royal Circus in 1803, when he was described as a pupil of Richer. Richer was a very

Andrew Ducrow in his most famous act as the Courier of St Petersburg, 1827.

famous rope dancer who had been a favourite at Sadler's Wells from the 1770s up to 1800. Hengler went on to become celebrated himself and to be billed as "the great French tight rope dancer", appearing with Cooke's, Price and Powell, and other companies. He had three sons who developed a touring circus from about 1850, but in 1860 they gave up tenting and concentrated upon performances in permanent buildings, building substantial circuses in Liverpool, Hull, Birmingham, Manchester, Bristol, Nottingham, Glasgow and Dublin. In 1871 Charles Hengler opened Hengler's Cirque in Argyll Street, on the present site of the Palladium, which became London's permanent circus for some forty years. A feature of the building was that the ring could be flooded with water for aquatic spectacles; this effect was introduced in 1891 and was copied at Astley's, the London Hippodrome, the Yarmouth Hippodrome, and the Tower Circus at Blackpool, where it still provides a magical finale to the programme.

Another builder of permanent circuses, mostly in the north of England, was James Newsome, who had started as a pupil of Batty in 1840. He was a good horseman but his wife, Pauline Hinné from Berlin, and his daughter, Ella, were outstanding equestriennes. He ran the Holborn Amphitheatre for a season in 1875.

Any survey of English circus proprietors of the nineteenth century cannot omit the Ginnetts, who claim to be the oldest circus family in Britain. Jean Pierre Ginnett was a French prisoner of war, captured at the battle of Waterloo. On his release he decided to remain in Britain; he bought four canaries, taught them tricks, and stood on the kerb at Ludgate Circus exhibiting them. He saved enough money to buy a pony, taught it to do fortune-telling tricks, and exhibited it at Barnet Fair. So the show was built up. By the 1830s he was appearing as the Horse Tamer of Corfu with the Infant Ginnett on horseback; on his father's death, this infant inherited circus buildings at Brighton, Belfast and Torquay, and a big tenting show; more circuses were built in Portsmouth and Southampton, and his own children carried on the tradition into the twentieth century.[9]

Members of the Ginnett family are still working in English circuses but they no longer own any circuses themselves. The only nineteenth-century English circus family to run a circus today is the Fossetts, recognised everywhere by their red hair and blue eyes. The first of these to have his own circus was Robert, who started, like Jean Pierre Ginnett, with performing birds in the street; he gradually built up a small family circus which was on the road by 1866 with five of his children performing. His son, Robert II, was acclaimed as the best bareback rider in the world and collected a great array of cups and medals as a mark of his prowess. His son, Robert III (1875–1948) was a fine horseman too, who originated the feat of running across the ring with his feet in wicker baskets and his head in a sack, and leaping onto the back of a cantering horse. I have seen his son, Robert IV, also performing this feat. The family circus has had its ups and downs, but it still goes on, with one branch of the family running a popular circus in Ireland as well as the "Sir" Robert Fossett show in England which may well be the oldest established circus in the world.[10]

The most famous circus proprietor of the nineteenth century was "Lord" George Sanger. His father, an ex-sailor, had showed a small peepshow and roundabout in the fairs; in 1848 George, in partnership with his brother John, set up on his own with a conjuring booth and some performing birds and mice. They went through very hard times, trying magic lantern displays and a penny theatrical gaff, and finally managed to make a little money out of a fake oyster smoking a pipe. With this they set up a small tenting circus with a learned Welsh pony, one ring horse, and a scratch company of nephews and nieces and just three circus artistes of any experience.

They began showing in the fairs in 1853 for an admission of one penny; threepence for reserved seats. Fortune and hard work favoured them, and by the end of the year they had some two dozen horses. They never really seem to have looked back. By 1856 they had sixty horses, and took on Howes and Cushing's American Circus on equal terms in a fierce battle of clashing dates and rival billing. In 1857 George added six lions to the circus, with his wife showing them in the ring. In 1871 he separated from his brother, who went on to run his own circus, and bought Astley's Amphitheatre, which he ran successfully until 1893. He put on seasons here and at the Agricultural Hall in Islington during the winter; he built or owned circus buildings in at least ten provincial towns; he had a vast tenting show touring Britain during the summer; and he took another, with 160 horses, 11 elephants, 12 camels and 230 people, to the continent for fifteen successive years. In 1897, when his business was made, temporarily, into a limited company, his profits were estimated at £14,000 a season.[11] In 1887 he had christened his show "Lord" George Sanger's, a self-awarded title arising out of pique in a legal dispute with Buffalo Bill's Wild West which he very properly lost. His brother, John, followed suit. In a similar style, the Fossetts knighted themselves.

George Sanger retired in 1905 and was killed, tragically, six years later. In his old age he had become lonely and eccentric in manner, adopting and discard-

Chariot racing at Batty's Hippodrome in 1851.

ing young men as his favourite companions in a somewhat wilful way. One of these, whom he had quite unjustly taxed with stealing some money, had been "informed on" by one of the domestic staff for sleeping with Lord George's grand-daughter. In a state of frenzy from being taunted, the young man became involved in a scuffle in the house, in the course of which he accidentally struck Lord George, who fell back into his chair. Apparently uninjured, he retired to bed some hours later where he shortly afterwards died – as much from the shock of the incident as from anything else. The young man had fled from the house, but when he heard what had happened to Lord George he committed suicide. A verdict of accidental death would really have been appropriate, but the background to the affair was hushed up at the inquest and the story was put out that the old circus king had been inexplicably battered to death by a madman.[12]

Sanger was certainly a great circus proprietor, but – unlike the other proprietors with whom we have dealt – he was essentially a showman rather than a circus performer himself. He came to the Circus from the world of fake freak shows and conjuring deceptions, and he never lost the taste for catching the public with vast spectacles and publicity stunts. Like Barnum, he didn't mind a little deception or a bogus sensation if it filled his theatres. In one sense he was the last of an old breed of fairground entertainers, but in another sense he was the first in a new breed of circus impresarios.

So little has been written about the early history of the Circus in England that it has been necessary to list these names, with their somewhat dry particulars, in order to provide a skeleton for what is to follow. But this list of names can do nothing to recapture the spirit of these early circus proprietors. We can catch a glimpse of their swaggering appearance in the description of old Saunders, who with "his scarlet coat, buckskin breeches, top-boots, spurs, white cravat and white hat ... add to this a long whip ... had a spice of the hunting squire after his rough fashion", and who, incidentally, may have set the fashion for the ringmaster's costume that still survives in some circuses today; or of old Jack Clarke at Croydon Fair "in a scarlet coat and white breeches, smacking a whip, and shouting 'This way for the riders! the riders'." We must try to picture, too, the artistes in their companies, with their long hair, often tied back with a ribbon, jack boots, flashy Birmingham jewelry and a comforter round their necks, smelling of lamp-oil, straw, orange peel, horse's provender and sawdust, penurious but flamboyant masters of their art.[13]

Behind the names and the dates and the few surviving playbills with their quaint woodcuts, lies a whole saga of horses and wagons plodding through the mud and rain or the choking dust of English summers, of grey dawns and wet soggy canvas, of empty bellies at supper time, of somehow eking out the long cold winter, of clashes with rival circuses stealing a march ahead to the next town, of rowdies from the village thinking it good sport to smash the circus up, of village folk taking their washing in and barring their doors because the Circus was coming.

It was a hard life for them all, and for some there were no material rewards – old Saunders and Pablo Fanque died destitute. But by the end of the century some quite considerable fortunes were being made by the big circus proprietors – Frederick Charles Hengler left £59,655 and Frederick Ginnett £32,139. George Sanger was reputed to be a millionaire.

A Pas de Deux on horseback unites the arts of ballet and equitation.

11
Horse Acts

WHAT THEN were the acts performed in these circuses directed by these proprietors?

Horse acts are an essential ingredient of Circus, indeed a show without horses has no right, in my opinion, to call itself a circus. The Circus had been brought into existence to accompany horse riding displays, and these continued to play an important part in it. But the tricks performed by Astley and Hughes were now regarded as somewhat stale, and were limited to rather occasional exhibitions of what was called the Old English Act of Horsemanship. In 1840, for instance, a coloured rider (though a native of Cork) called Pablo Paddington rode with his head on a quart bottle in Ryan's Amphitheatre in Birmingham and Lloyd's Olympic Circus at Croydon.

By the beginning of the nineteenth century the basic riding act had come to consist of the equestrian jumping over garters, or ribbons, that were held by the clown or ring attendants just above the level of the horse's head, or through hoops covered with paper, known as balloons. I can well remember, as a child at my first circuses, the excitement of seeing the rider burst through the paper and land on the horse's back again. Sometimes, more daringly, the hoops would be iron ones bound with tow which was soaked with paraffin and set alight. In 1845 M. Dumos stood facing backwards as he leaped the garters. Sometimes the horses leaped through balloons while the rider jumped over them. Another common act, popular with Ducrow, was the Fox Hunter, in which the equestrian straddled two horses cantering side by side and in this way jumped hurdles placed round the ring. A variant of this was the Jeux Romains, in which the rider, dressed in classical costume, straddled two horses while permitting others to pass between his legs; this might involve as many as six horses, as performed by Loisset

at Drury Lane in 1849. Or a man and woman, in classical ballet costumes, posed on a pair of horses in a Pas de Deux, one of the most graceful acts to be seen in the ring.

By the middle of the century American riders were leaping over flags 9 ft wide before alighting on their horses' backs again; and in 1855 J. H. Cooke developed an act in which he sprang from the horse's back on to a kind of platform stretching for 40 ft, a third of the way round the ring, ran along it while the horse galloped underneath it, and then – judging the right moment – jumped so as to land on the horse's back as it emerged at the far end. He called this Le Saut du Pont du Cirque.

An act popular with equestriennes was the Shawl Dance, in which the rider used a shawl or scarf or Spanish mantilla as a kind of skipping rope, passing it gracefully round her body and under her feet as she stood on horseback. This is recorded as early as 1806 at Saunders's Amphitheatre in Birmingham and was a favourite turn, especially with French riders, in the fifties and up to the end of the century. The long skirts of the early women riders were discarded in favour of a ballet costume, though a side-saddle riding habit was retained for *haute école*.

By the 1860s women riders were emulating men in the vigour of their voltige acts. A Victorian gentleman, Arthur Munby, who had a special interest in working women, has left some important descriptions of the performances of female riders and acrobats at this time in his, only partially published, diaries.[1] He gives an interesting account of the Holborn Amphitheatre in 1868: "The skill and daring of the female performers here is remarkable; they are all foreigners, and the place, which is admirably managed, has a continental air, which oddly enough seems to suit the staid English

Leaping through a paper balloon long remained a standard act of voltige riding.

The Jeux Romains, or Roman Games, have occasionally been revived in the century.

audience. One plump and comely damsel, Fanny Gaertner, leaped through hoops and played antics standing erect on her steed, with extraordinary vigour; another, Rosé Ethair, equally well-liking, stood on a barebacked horse at full gallop, and sat on its crupper, hanging on only by the curve of her knee. ... And lastly, the fair and graceful Pereira, the girl who hitherto has climbed ropes here and hung head downwards from the trapeze, smiling sweetly and virginally, appeared as a rider, drest in loose blue jacket and breeches, the hair en chignon, and riding (I never before saw it in England) upon a great horse *astride*, leaping on and off at full gallop, and finally hanging from the saddle by one foot à la Tartare."

Riders were, of course, always searching for more spectacular tricks to perform, and the most effective of these was to throw a somersault while standing on the horse's back. As early as 1787 at Swann's Amphitheatre, Birmingham, Master Smith was throwing a back somersault "as the horse is in a good three quarter speed – never attempted by any boy in the world but himself"; I fancy, however, that this was a somersault from the horse to the ground, for another bill speaks of him throwing "a somersault off the horse". The first person ever to throw a somersault on moving horseback in England is said to be the American rider, Levi J. North, in Batty's Circus at Henley in 1839; on this occasion the horse carried a

broad flat pad, but seven years later he accomplished the feat in America on a bareback horse – something that had never been achieved before.[2] The English acrobat, Lavater Lee, is said to have achieved a somersault on horseback at Batty's in 1842; and the American riders, Sweeney, Derious and Aymer, at the Lyceum, as well as W. Dale, with the Great American Circus, were throwing "back somersaults feet to feet on horseback" in 1843.

By the 1860s Hubert Meers was throwing twenty somersaults in succession on horseback. In about 1872 the American rider, Robert Stickney, is said to have managed a double somersault on horseback, and by about 1905 this feat was matched by John Frederic Clarke. The American, Oscar Lowande, and the French, the Lécussons, were throwing somersaults from one horse to another close behind by the turn of the century.[3]

An act that involved a group of acrobats standing with linked arms on each other's thighs and shoulders while on horseback was popular early in the nineteenth century. It was usually billed as The Walls of Troy or The Egyptian Pyramids. Ten men, for instance, presented this on three horses at Bridges' Circus in 1837. Later in the century it went out of fashion, but in 1900 the Frédianis in France achieved the perilous feat of a three-high on horseback, standing on each other's shoulders.

In the early years of the century circus riders used horses that were saddled and bridled in the usual way, but in 1820 "the young Austrian" at Astley's claimed to be performing his horsemanship without saddle or bridle and two years later this claim was repeated by several riders, including Mr Hunter, the Yorkshire Phenomenon, at Astley's. Twenty years later, however, saddleless riding still seems to have been unusual for Mr Moseley, who hailed from Dublin, was boasting that he performed his feats on a bare-backed horse – "a challenge to the whole profession". The saddle came to be replaced by a substantial pad on the horse's back when much standing was involved; this was sometimes quite a platform jutting over the horse's flanks, covered with silk and decorated with spangles, and a fringe, often marked with the artiste's initials. Simpler pads are still used by some performers, but it is more attractive to see the act performed on a bare-backed horse, and when this is done the horse's back is coated with powdered resin in order to provide a better grip for the rider's feet.

There is a curious story about Hunter that after he had returned from a successful tour of America he became "dissipated", and seems to have given offence to his fellow artistes. In 1839 he was performing in a company with Ben Stickney, the American rider, at the Liverpool Amphitheatre. Hunter accidentally took Stickney's coat, perhaps with some money in it. In order merely to frighten him, Stickney reported this as a theft to the police. But the law had to take its course, and Hunter was transported to Van Dieman's Land.[4] Circus was introduced to Australia at just about that time, but I don't know whether Hunter was responsible!

Finally riding, or voltige, acts developed into what came to be called the English Jockey or the Jockey of Epsom, as the riders – male and female – wore jockeys' costumes. As early as 1824 Ducrow presented an act

Skipping on a pad horse, as drawn by Heinrich Lang in "Cirkus-Bilder", 1879.

Lang's drawings of circus acts, made in German circuses, are among the best ever executed.

The Jockey Act. A Friedländer poster of 1908.

that he must have performed in France, called Le Jockeis Anglais aux Courses de Newmarket, and Tourniaire appeared as the English Jockey in 1843. The idea really caught on later in the century, influenced, it is said, by William Bell. In 1867 Alfred Bradbury performed a "jockey act" at the Holborn Amphitheatre, which was announced as for the first time in England, and by 1879 Mr Fredericks, in Newsome's Circus at Birmingham, was billed to "leap to a standing position on the horse's back without the aid of his hands while the horse is at full gallop". This developed into one of the most satisfying circus acts that there is, with sometimes four or five artistes leaping on and off a bareback horse, turning somersaults, cartwheels, and what have you as they do so. They sometimes make use of a "cushion", or small springboard, to assist their leaps; but some performers have boasted that they do not require any such aid.

A variant, but less common, form of voltige was the *voltige à la Richard*, which was named after an American, David Richard, who is said to have introduced it in 1860. In this act the "rider" runs alongside the galloping horse, clutching a handgrip fixed to its harness, and they leap obstacles side by side as they circle the ring. It is an exhausting and dangerous exercise, and Richard was, in fact, killed in a circus at St Petersburg in 1866.

A very good riding act, in which the riders work their way from one side to the other of a galloping horse, round its neck, under its belly, hanging from one stirrup, picking up handkerchiefs off the ground, and so on, is provided by a Cossack troupe. Joseph Hillier, the mulatto pupil of Andrew Ducrow, who took his company over after his death, was performing a riding act of this type in 1827. This was a solo act, but a Cossack troupe appeared at Ryan's Circus at Birmingham in 1836 and another at Astley's in 1844, but they do not appear to have been featured very frequently during the nineteenth century. Most equestrian acts remained solo turns.

Juggling on horseback was another popular feat –

more showy than difficult. Master Smith had juggled with three balls and had performed the feat of throwing an orange up and impaling it on a fork; M. Hinné, of the famous European circus family, was an equestrian juggler in the 'forties; and in the 'seventies two of the Cookes developed an act on two horses, in which one faced forward and the other faced backwards and they juggled balls from one to the other.

In the early part of the century, however, horse acts were dominated by artistes riding "in character" in the style orginated by Andrew Ducrow.[5] Many other equestrians copied the Ducrow characters up and down the country during his lifetime and for many years after his death, though none equalled him for grace and expressiveness. One act that seems not to have been conceived by Ducrow was that of Shaw the Lifeguardsman. This was popular with riders like Powell and James Cooke in the 'thirties and 'forties and was still being performed by Robert Fossett in the twentieth century. It depicted a hero of Waterloo, leaving his country village to join the regiment, drilling, marching, at the battle, firing, and at the last moments of his life throwing away his broken sword and fighting with his bare fists. Characters from Shakespeare – Richard III, Shylock and Falstaff – were being presented on horseback during the 'forties and 'fifties by the Cookes, Newsome and others, and characters from Dickens – usually the Pickwick Papers – were being enacted by George Cooke, Moseley and other riders up to the 'sixties.

A popular character for female riders was the Fishwoman of Newhaven, and in a more elegiac vein La Rosière or the Flower Girl, the Fair Circassian, and Amazonian Maid, the Chase of Diana, and the Female Hussar, all of which were enacted by Louisa Woolford.

Comic acts on horseback remained popular. Billy Button, the Taylor, continued to ride to Brentford – the last date that I have noted is 1845 at Cooke's Circus in Manchester, but the act went on being played by George Sanger and in country circuses up

Falstaff, Richard III and Shylock on horseback in Cooke's Circus, Edinburgh, in 1840.

A variant of Frolics of my Granny, in which the head and shoulders of the witch and the legs of Jim Crow are dummies. Ryan's Amphitheatre, Birmingham, 1839.

to at least the end of the century.[6] Variants of this were the Tipsy Peasant, performed by Crossman in 1799, and the Drunken Hussar, performed by Polaski in 1822. There were also three more elaborate comic equestrian acts that were played in many circuses during this time.

The Peasant's Frolic or the Flying Wardrobe was the best of these. During a display of classic equestrianism a drunken countryman clambers from the audience into the ring and tries to mount the horse; despite expostulations from the ringmaster he finally succeeds, swaying perilously on the horse's back. Then he throws off his overcoat, and then his jacket, and then a waistcoat, and another waistcoat, and another . . . , and then his trousers fall down and are sent flying as the horse canters on, so that he is left only in a long shirt. And then in a twinkling this is pulled off, and he is revealed as a handsome equestrian, clad in tights and spangles, who goes on to execute feats of skill and daring on the horse's back.[7] This act was performed by the young Ducrow at Astley's in 1812 and remained a favourite with touring circuses for over a hundred years; I can well remember seeing it at the first circus I ever attended, in about 1920 in a Hertfordshire village. It may owe something to the tradition of the gravedigger's waistcoats, a bit of funny business that low comedians used to introduce into *Hamlet* at the end of the eighteenth and early years of the nineteenth century.

Another comic act was variously described as the Humours or Metamorphosis of a Sack. In this a clown, or other performer in loose, baggy costume, was persuaded by some means to allow himself to be put in a sack which was placed on the horse's back. Off went

the horse round the ring with the sack bobbing and bouncing about on its back, till suddenly out sprang not the man who had got into it but apparently a smartly dressed lady. Crossman and Porter had performed this at the Royal Circus in 1793, Ducrow acted it as a young man, and Auriol was performing it in 1849.

A third such act was usually introduced as Frolics of my Granny or some such title. An old woman in bonnet and black bombasine skirt came riding in on horseback, while perched on her back was a young fellow waving his arms about with scant regard for the elderly grandmother on whose shoulders he was riding. After various manoeuvres and near tumbles it is suddenly revealed that there is only one rider after all; the young fellow's legs are dummies and so is the old woman. The rider is actually standing on horseback, but conceals the lower part of his body in a wicker frame dressed up to look like an old woman with a man's legs round her shoulders. The first appearance of this act that I have noted in England was at Astley's in 1822; it was taken up by many performers, including the Scotsman, Ord, in 1836 and the American, Stickney, in 1844; it was being played at Astley's as late as 1887. At some date it became combined with a comic knock-about in which a miller belaboured other members of the company with his sack of flour, smothering them with white in the process; an equestrian extravaganza on this theme, described as The Miller and his Men or My Grandmother on Horseback, was played at Astley's in 1829. Alternatively a coalman or a chimney sweep was introduced with a sack of coaldust. The miller whitened the coalman and the coalman blackened the miller, till they were colour reversed! My Grandmother on Horseback or The Sweep and the Millers was in Ducrow's programme at the Surrey, when it briefly reverted to a circus theatre after the fire at Astley's in 1841.

A "mythological equestrian scene" that introduced all the available children of the artistes in the company was called The Sprite of the Morning Star, or The Flight of Zephyr, or The Frolics of the Cupidons, or some such title. This consisted of an equestrian riding round a decorated ring and hoisting on to his head, his shoulders, round his waist, and wherever else he could carry them, as many little children as could be mustered. The idea seems to have been to portray the gentle west wind, father of the two marvellous horses of Greek mythology, bearing the infant god of love and his cherubic companions through the air, as if they were flying, while the night pales and the dawn comes up. This act was an elaboration of one of Ducrow's characters; it was being performed by

Bridges and Powell in the 'forties and was still being presented at Astley's in the 'eighties.[8]

The most famous horse act of the nineteenth century was the Courier of St Petersburg, which was originated by Ducrow in 1827. In this act the rider enters the ring standing astride on two horses, as in the Jeux Romains, but then picks up the reins of more and more horses as they pass between his legs till he is driving four or five in all. At one point he straddles all five, and then lies on their backs across them. The thin story that this is deemed to represent is that of a courier carrying dispatches to the Czar, and each horse carried a small banner and flag for the country through which he passed – France, Spain, Germany, England and Russia. The exact geographical route and the nature of the dispatches was left comfortably vague, but "the tinkling of the bells and other characteristics of the foreign Post House – the zealous ardour with which the Courier impels his horses – his reposing on their backs when he becomes fatigued – the chiming of the distant village bell – his stoppage at the relay, and his arrival at his destination . . . are strongly marked and cannot be misconceived."

This act, too, was copied by other equestrians and was still being performed at Covent Garden as late as 1890. It has occasionally been revived in this century. In 1833 Harry Adams introduced a variant of it as the Post-Boy of Antwerp with six horses, and in 1843 the fine French rider, Tourniaire, who had brought his troupe to England, was performing the Courier with twelve horses. In 1860 Marin succeeded in driving as many as seventeen horses at the Paris Hippodrome, standing on two of them and driving fifteen in five groups of three abreast by means of reins passing through rings attached to the surcingle of each middle horse.

The feats so far described have really consisted of acrobatics on horseback. The horse itself needed to be steady and reliable but not much more. The art of equitation, however, soon found a place in the Circus. *Carrousels*, or veritable ballets on horseback, had been popular in Europe since the seventeenth century, and *haute école* had reached a high standard by the end of the eighteenth century – the Spanish Riding School in Vienna, for example, dates from 1735; but the classic high school movements were, and still are, considered somewhat caviare to the general circus audience. Dancing horses had been exhibited since the time of Banks, and Astley showed some at the Amphitheatre in 1784, but in 1806 he conceived a way of introducing high school movements into the ring in a more effective manner by producing a cotillon or country dance, performed by eight mounted horsemen, accompanied of course by appropriate music, at his

Madame Klatt in haute école at Astley's Amphitheatre in 1845.

newly opened Olympic Pavilion. Horses that were said to dance to the time of music have continued to appear in circuses to this day. The claim has sometimes been made that they really do follow the music; Pablo Fanque, a coloured man and a native of Norwich whose real name was William Darby and who ran his own circus in the early 'forties, had a black mare which he rode at Astley's in 1847; it was said that "the steed dances to the air, and the band has not to accommodate itself to the action of the horses, as in previous performances of this kind." But this was nonsense. Horses can apparently recognize music, as I have been told that they show excitement in their stalls when the introductory music to their act is played by the band, but they cannot match their movements to the beat of the music. Perhaps that is why they are able to recognize the quietest verbal commands through all the blare of a circus band.

A visually exciting exercise, not strictly of the high school but sometimes combined with it, is the *baguette*, in which the horse leaps over a kind of skipping rope, usually made of thin willow, as it is swung by the rider.

An attractive variant of the high school riding act is the tandem manege, when a rider on one horse directs the movements of a second, or even of two more, by means of long reins. Miss Lilly Deacon was presenting this with two Spanish horses at Hengler's in 1878. Alternatively the "rider" may be on foot.

Learned horses continued to lie down on the word

The tandem manege, drawn by Heinrich Lang.

of command and refuse to get up for the unpopular tyrant of the time, and to pick out the prettiest girl or the biggest fool in the audience. These acts went well in small circuses, but as buildings and tents grew larger they inevitably dropped out. A new trick that became popular was for the clown to hide a handkerchief under the sawdust in the ring and for the horse to find it, sometimes with its eyes bandaged. The horse would scrape the sawdust away with its hoof, pick up the handkerchief with its teeth, and carry it to the ringmaster.

A popular act was for two ponies to be trained to sit down and take tea with the clown. This was originated by John Ducrow, Andrew's brother, in 1827 and was still being performed at Newsome's Circus at the end of the 'seventies. A contemporary engraving shows the two ponies with hats and bonnets sitting at tables, laid as for a tea party, while the clown – pretending he has become a pony – tries to stir his tea with his foot.

Ponies increasingly came to be used in circuses, sometimes being trained to work a see-saw, as with Newsome in 1887. Mules, too, were a popular intro-

duction, providing an entertaining act in which members of the audience are invited to try to ride them. They often came in pairs: Howes and Cushing, who seem to have been the first to introduce this act, had Pete and Barney in 1857; Newsome had Punch and Judy. This is an act you can sometimes still see today; I have never seen a spectator succeed in riding the mule round the ring, but sometimes the furiously bucking mule will stand as still as a statue when a tiny child from the circus is placed on its back.

Another comic act of unsuccessful riding by members of the audience is the riding mechanic. This useful device for training circus riders had been invented by an American, Spencer Q. Stokes, and had already been utilized in America as an act with spectators trying to ride by 1879.[9] I don't know when it was first used in this way in England, but it has certainly often appeared as the final act of a programme in English circuses in recent decades. The effect can be very funny, though I think it is a pity when the rider is lifted off the horse to go flying round the ring, arms and legs akimbo, before he has had a chance to show what he, or she, can really do.

60

Above: A horse at liberty. Below: A stooge from the audience on an unrideable mule.

Apart from the learned horse and pony acts, all the horse acts so far described were performed by a combination of horse and rider. No one had yet seen what is the glory of the Circus today – a ring full of liberty horses, wheeling, turning, reversing, circling, at the tiniest signal from their trainer without a hand touching them. The first step towards this was when a so-called dancing horse was shown without a rider, but with the trainer close by to guide its movements. In 1824 Powell was displaying his beautiful charger, Napoleon, in Newcastle in some kind of solo act; soon afterwards, in 1827, Ducrow introduced his dancing horse, Pegasus, wheeling and prancing with wings strapped on its back, while he stood beside it in the ring. One notices that star circus horses were always named on the bills in the nineteenth century. In 1835 the great French trainer, Laurent Franconi, brought his horse, Blanche, to Astley's, where it waltzed, fired a cannon, walked backwards up a flight of stairs, and struck "academic poses, quite unaided by reins or bridle"; in 1848 his nephew, Adolphe Franconi, appeared with his company at Drury Lane, and exhibited his celebrated horse, Atar Gull, *dressé en liberté*. This is the earliest usage that I have noted of the term "at liberty" in England.

In 1868 the Carré troupe came to the Holborn Amphitheatre with a European reputation; the English newspapers were ecstatic at the way in which four horses "without music to aid them, moved round the ring, backwards and forwards, changing places and positions on the instant at the word of command . . . implicitly obeying not merely the word but the look of the trainer". In 1893 and 1894 Wulff's Circus from Munich appeared at Hengler's with eight horses "in an entirely new class of performance", with numbered horses finding their way into the right order after being mixed up; the performance concluded with a superb Grand Tableau, or *Carrousel*, of sixty horses, with coloured lamps on their backs, circling round in concentric rings, each ring in the reverse direction to its neighbour, rising to a pyramid in the centre and with tiny ponies trotting round on the ring fence. The Liberty Act in perfection had at last arrived.

Liberty acts often end with the horses pirouetting as they leave the ring one by one, and then returning to execute solo turns or *da capos*, such as walking on the hind legs, or leaping on them – the courbette, or leaping horizontally with the hind legs kicking vigorously – the capriole. It is a pity that so few members of the audience today have any experience of trying to persuade a horse to obey even simple commands, or even trying to catch an unbridled horse in a field, so that they are unable to appreciate the degree of training involved in these horse acts of the circus ring.

The liberty horses of Circus Carré. A Friedländer poster of 1907.

The horses for liberty acts are usually Arabs or Lipizzaners, whose fine appearance and small size render them particularly suitable. The high school horse will usually be a bigger animal, such as a Thoroughbred or a Trakehner. The ring horse, or rosinback, is a plebeian broad-backed animal, a Percheron or Belgian, similar to the cart horse, and is often piebald in colouring.

12
Ground Acts

STRONG MEN still appeared in circuses, but they did not occupy a large part of the programme and were better seen in fairs, or later on the music halls. A typical "herculean feat" was for the performer to stretch himself horizontally from an upright pillar, or the king post of the tent, with his feet securely anchored in straps, and in this position to raise weights in his hands and teeth or support a couple of men or even a horse. Juan Bellinck, the American Indian prodigy, lifted a horse while hanging from a slack rope in 1823. These kinds of feats still go on; quite recently I have seen a strong man in a circus lift an elephant – admittedly, only a baby elephant.

Posturers were another link between the fairground booths and the Circus. They were sometimes known as indiarubber men, elastic incomprehensibles, or non-descripts; the name "klischnigger" was given to them from the 1830s, after an Edward Klischnigg, a famous ape performer in the theatres, who may have been an Englishman and certainly played at Covent Garden.[1] The modern term, contortionist, came in in the middle of the century. The most famous of these was Marinelli, who seems actually to have been an Englishman called J. H. Walter and who caused a sensation in the 'eighties; he was known as the Serpent-man, for he sometimes opened his act disguised in a snake's skin and his sinuous movements were certainly serpentine. He could bend backwards with his head looking out between his ankles, and a development of this posture in which the artiste lifts his feet off the ground and supports his body by clenching a mouth grip between his teeth is known as the Marinelli bend to this day. He earned large fees but lost most of them by gambling, and he put out a story that he had been obliged to sell his skeleton, for delivery after his death, for £1,000. He seems to have been a melancholy individual, and

once replied as follows to an interviewer who asked whether he was able to enjoy sexual activity and whether his remarkable bodily contortions were an attraction to women: "Sir, the chastity which monks do not always observe is forced upon an artist of my class. ... With regard to the point on which you question me, the greatest reserve is imposed upon me. I have all the appearance of a strong man; my chest is wider than your own, but beneath it I conceal the lungs of a child; they are stunted by the daily pressure of my thoracic cage. Consumption threatens me, and will carry me off very early unless I break my neck in the circus some evening, which I should certainly prefer."[2] His fears were groundless; he became a well known artistes' agent in America.

The greatest attraction that ground acrobats offered in the ring was leaping. As we have seen, this too had been a popular feature of the fairs. It was also a popular amateur sport in the north of England, with feats like jumping into a crate of eggs and out again without breaking any. The circus performers outbid each other in the claims they made: in 1799 Smith was leaping over six horses, twenty men, and through a balloon of real fire; in 1836 Pablo Fanque, described as "the loftiest jumper in England", was leaping over a post chaise placed lengthwise with a pair of horses in the shafts and through a military drum at the same time; in 1842 the clown Dewhurst was leaping over a garter 14 ft high, over ten horses, through six balloons, and so on; in 1858 the Cirque Impérial at the Alhambra staged a contest between the four Champion Vaulters of the Globe, with James Cooke clearing eleven big horses.[3]

When Dewhurst leaped over a garter 14 ft high it was specifically claimed that this was done without the assistance of a springboard; but this is not credible,

Bernhard Leitner, a famous strong man.

as it was not till 1876 that a high jump of even 6 ft was achieved in atheletics; either the height was grossly exaggerated or he made use of some kind of assistance in the take-off. For much leaping in nineteenth-century circuses the performers made use of a trampolin or a battoute; both of these were, at this date, terms for a springboard. I am not sure if the circus bills were very precise in differentiating between them, but the trampolin or *tremplin* was the kind of short springboard that is still used in gymnasiums, while the battoute or *batoude* or "trampling board" consisted of a length of planks, perhaps stretching for as far as 60 ft, leading down from a height of some 10 ft – perhaps level with the back row of benches in a circus tent – to ground level, where they met a short ash springboard sloping upwards. (It will be remembered that we met exactly this arrangement in the French fairground booths of the seventeenth century.)

There was great competition to set up a record for the number of successive somersaults that a performer could throw. In the 1830s Thomas Price, "the Bouncing Ball", claimed to have thrown fifty-six somersaults one after the other, but in a competition with the

A contortionist, elastic incomprehensible, indiarubber man, or klischnigger.

64

American, Levi North, in 1838 North emerged the winner with 414 somersaults over twelve days.[4]

Successive single somersaults were a test of endurance rather than a great technical skill, but many acrobats tried to improve on this by throwing double or even triple somersaults. These were displayed in the vaulting act that usually opened the programme. A group of all the available leapers would run down the battoute, one after the other, bound on the spring-board at the ringside, and throw a forward somersault to land on a big mattress placed in the ring. Then some horses would be brought in, the mattress would be moved further away, and the leapers repeated their vaults and somersaults over the horses; more horses would be brought in, the leapers would drop out one by one, until finally only the star was left, leaping over perhaps as many as twenty-two horses or even four grown elephants. For a final rally the horses would be taken out, the mattress would be brought closer, and all the performers would follow each other in rapid succession, throwing special twists and variations to the tune of a lively gallop from the band.

The first successful double somersault is said to have been thrown by Tomkinson at Edinburgh in 1835. It was a rare achievement, for in 1846 Mr Connor claimed that he was "the first and only artiste that has attained the certainty of this performance". If a performer failed to clear the horses the result was not too serious, as a horse broke his fall, but if he overshot the mattress the result could be dangerous, as he might easily land on his head and break his neck. An American artiste called Johnny Aymer, playing in a circus in the Isle of Wight in 1859, tried for a triple, achieved it at the rehearsal, but managed only two and a half on the night; he pitched on his face and was killed. Another American, William Hobbes, touring with the Howes and Cushing Circus, was killed in the same way at Astley's four years later.[5] Today, Don Martinez, the brilliant performer on the flying trapeze, likes to throw a double somersault from the ground, without a springboard, when he runs in for the final parade of the artistes at the end of the show.

A somersaulting, leaping and reversed pyramid-building act that never made use of a springboard is that of the Bedouin Arabs, who throw themselves about the ring in a wild flurry of foresprings, head-springs, lion leaps, flip-flaps, sideways leaps, and twists of every description. (The lion leap is a variant of handspring, a forward somersault but making use of the hands to help you over; the flip-flap is the reverse of this, with the hands assisting a back somersault.) The first troupe of Bedouin acrobats appeared in England at the Colosseum in 1836,[6] others followed in 1843 and during the 'fifties. Similar troupes have

A Bedouin Arab troupe builds a four-high column on each other's shoulders in London in 1843.

The Hollyoak troupe of acrobats acquired a European reputation towards the end of the century.

continued to this day to provide a very lively and energetic contribution to circus programmes. I have seen the bearer in one of these troupes support nine men in a circus recently.

The Bedouins were not alone in building reversed human pyramids. In 1868 Munby saw the Fillis Troupe of Female Acrobats at the London Pavilion. The troupe consisted of a tall man and four girls, aged from eighteen to twelve. Munby, upon whom these female acrobats exercised a curious fascination, records how "all five were drest alike, as male acrobats, in light fleshings, trunk hose, and close-fitting spangled vests. But the two young women were feminine above, i.e. their hair was long, and was arranged en chignon, and decked with flowers. I was struck by the personal beauty and attractiveness of the whole group. . . . There was a graceful unconsciousness in the looks of the elder girls and a childlike air about the younger which was refreshing in such a place, and was strongly in contrast with their mountebank dress and panto-mimic feats." The bearer, with an "almost Apollonian grace . . . made himself into a pillar of support, while the girls, one or two at a time, lightly leaped upon him, stood on his shoulders and his head, played skipping rope there, turned somersaults, or flung them-selves to the ground, or stood upon each other's head or shoulders, he sustaining all. Finally, the young woman of eighteen, with her sweet refined face and her ladylike hair, stood on his head and held out two of her sisters at right angles to herself, each of whom

hooked one foot behind her head – under her chignon – and planted the other on her hip or thigh; whilst down below, the youngest girl lay horizontal, curled round her brother's waist, face outwards, her head and her heels meeting. The British Public, who had applauded throughout, were enraptured at this feat, and the female acrobats, gracefully smiling, bowed and disappeared."

Juggling and balancing still found a place in the Circus, though these acts also appeared on the stages of theatres. In 1820 an Indian juggler, Ramo Samee, made a great sensation; his image was perpetuated as a marionette for many years afterwards, and Hazlitt was moved to raptures by his performance, writing of the balls revolving "like the planets in their spheres" or shooting up like meteors, "twining round his neck like ribbons", and summing up in words that could apply to all great circus acts: "There is something in all this which he who does not admire may be quite sure he never really admired anything in the whole course of his life. It is skill surmounting difficulty, and beauty triumphing over skill."[7]

The Indian juggler who so enchanted Hazlitt only kept four balls in the air at a time, and this total was to be greatly surpassed as the century progressed with totals of five, six, seven and eight being achieved, and even ten being claimed by the Hungarian, Chenko, in 1903.[8] An audience, however, does not appreciate the skill involved in juggling at this level, and there was a growing tendency for jugglers to make use of incon-gruous objects: an American, Kara, appeared in eve-ning dress and juggled with his hat, cigar, gloves, newspaper, matches and coffee cup; an Australian, Moritz Cronin, introduced Indian clubs, which have been used by innumerable jugglers since. The really great days of juggling belong to the music hall and the end of the century, with Cinquevalli who came to London in 1885 in the Covent Garden Circus. His incredible feats with billiard balls called for great delicacy, but he also displayed considerable strength, as when he caught a huge spinning washing tub on a spiked helmet on his head and kept it revolving, or caught a cannon ball falling from a height of 40 ft on his neck.

Cannon balls were made use of by other performers, including John Holtum who came from America and performed his sensational act for the first time at the Holborn Amphitheatre in 1871, when he caught a cannon ball that had been fired at him from a gun. At the first attempt he injured a finger, but undeterred he improved the apparatus, which was made to his specification by a Birmingham gunsmith, and went on to tour the world and collect a well-deserved fortune.[9]

As circuses became larger, the kind of balancing

acts with plates and knives that had figured in the eighteenth-century fairground booths were on too small a scale to be appreciated by the audience. In their place equilibrists like Lavater Lee in the 1840s stood on their heads on pyramids of decanters, or like M. Prince in the 1870s built pillars of chairs and perched precariously at the top. Chair balancing still excites wonder in circuses today; the balancer always seems to add just one more storey to his edifice than seems possible.

An act popular with some acrobats was the bottle equilibrist. In 1845 Mr Price's "Petit Son" (surely the offspring of an Anglo-French marriage!) walked on the necks of twelve bottles, stood on his head on a pyramid of punch bowls and bottles, and balanced on a bottle that was itself balanced neck down on another bottle. The famous clown, Auriol, was a master in this type of act.

An act that required no balancing skills but called for a well-developed physique was the Grecian Statues or Marble Groupings, in which male artistes in skin-tight fleshings posed in the attitudes of famous sculptures – Ajax defying the lightning, the fighting and dying Gladiator, and other such positions. Ducrow was performing this in 1837, and it was a speciality of the Boleno family in the 'forties. Later the performers coated their bodies with what looked like liquid

gold, and this is an act that can still be seen occasionally today.

Plates spun on canes don't really call for much skill if a small hole is drilled in the centre of the plate. They had formed part of the acts of Ramo Samee in 1820 and of Signor Malabar in 1824; in 1846 a Dutchman kept three going from hands and mouth while balancing on an arrangement of decanters, and it is indeed only as an extra to some other feat that they now justify their place in a programme. They were much featured by the Chinese troupes that began to appear in the early twentieth century, and these skilled performers had no need to rely on an indentation in the plate to help them.

The feat of balancing on a rolling globe became popular in the second half of the century: the earliest reference I have noted was in 1841 when Carlo Alberto, the German Tub Runner, demonstrated cask vaulting in Ducrow's company; in 1865 Signor Ethardo worked his way on a rolling ball up and down a steep spiral runway, and variants of this act were featured in many circuses.

Gymnastics on a single horizontal bar made their appearance by 1847 with Signor Le Tort in the guise of the Pole Sprite, who swung with his hands on the pole, turned in the air, and caught the pole on the other side. They had become quite popular by the

John Holtum.

John Holtum catching a cannon ball fired from a gun.

The Risley act was sometimes performed by carpet acrobats in the streets of London.

'sixties and 'seventies, and in 1885 feats on double and triple horizontal bars were demonstrated by the Americans, Lauck and Livingston, at Covent Garden. This act became something of a speciality of Romanian artistes, using sometimes as many as nine bars at differing heights. It is a kind of fixed trapeze performance at ground level, still to be seen in circuses today, with the artistes swinging and somersaulting from one bar to the other. It is a very strenuous act and a potentially dangerous one, for the centrifugal forces set up are considerable and there is nothing to prevent an artiste crashing into a bar or the ring fence if he loses his grip.

In 1843 the Strand Theatre in London announced "an interesting exhibition of Italian classical Gymnastics" by Mr Risley and his son, who was said to be "little more than six years old". A contemporary journal reported that "they display a variety of gymnastic feats, the most difficult of which appeared to us to be that of a youth's throwing a number of somersaults in the air and alighting on his father's hands". The next month they were at the Surrey, with increasing public acclaim – "no description, however vivid, can convey even a faint idea of the grace and elegance

of their hitherto unequalled performance . . . in which the son, flung from the upraised hands of his father, alights upon the feet in like manner upraised." Here, on September 11, they added a new feat to their Classical Gymnasia and Aerial Dancing, for "the Little Wonder . . . standing on the feet of his father throws from thence a somersault and alights in the same position again". One of the classic feats of circus acrobatics was born.

The basic idea of this feat was not entirely new, for as long ago as 1777 a Signor Colpi had appeared at Astley's in an act that involved him lying on his back with his feet in the air and balancing up to four children on them in various attitudes and combinations. But Risley, who was actually an American called Richard Risley Carlisle, brought something of an infinitely higher order to the concept of a child and an adult in a double acrobatic act, in which the child's movements seemed to weave a veritable poem in space as he was launched from his father's strong arms or legs and received safely back again. Later that year Risley added a second "son" to the act, and went on to tour Europe with great success, giving his name to what is called the Risley act in English but the Icarian Games in European languages.

Risley did not perform in a circus in England, but circus artistes were soon copying his act. In 1847 H. Lupino was performing it with his seven-year-old son, who added an extra touch by putting a French cocked hat on his head in mid-air while somersaulting from his father's feet; a street performer boasted in 1856 that his young brother could turn over fifty somersaults one after the other from his feet;[10] and the London-born Cottrell brothers were touring the act in Germany with sensational success in the 'fifties.

Foot juggling is, naturally, performed more easily with inanimate objects than with living people, and had appeared slightly earlier. In 1841 Felix Carlo was billed as the French Antipodean Professor, and in 1843 Herr Duval and Mr Kemp were presenting what they called the Magic Pole at Astley's, dancing the pole on their feet. The objects used in this way have usually been poles, barrels, Maltese crosses, and even giant bottles of champagne, and I have seen the act performed with large dolls. When lying on one's back with one's feet in the air, it is necessary to have some support for the hips. It is not certain what aid Risley and the earlier antipodean acrobats employed, but in 1843 an American, Mr Derious, whom we have already met somersaulting on horseback, appeared in Van Amburgh's and Sands' Circus with what he called the Tranka Hispaniola. The *tranka* or *trinka* is, in fact, the name given to the kind of cradle on which a foot juggler lies to support his back and

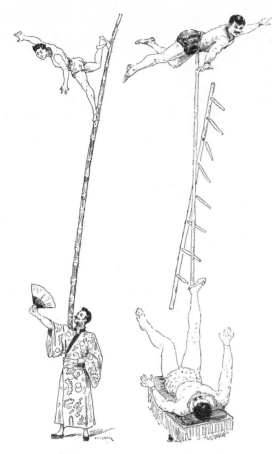

Two varieties of the perch act, one with a break-away ladder.

Bicycle and unicycle acrobatics were popular by the end of the century. A Friedländer poster of 1913.

hips, and the act was known by this name for a few years. Even with inanimate objects a trinka act can be very attractive, especially when two or three jugglers toss their objects from one to the other, but when performed with an agile child the effect can be breathtaking.

In the early years of the century dancing and acrobatics on stilts was sometimes introduced into circuses. A family called Jellini was particularly noted for this. This now only survives as a clown run-in between acts, but the Sloan family have performed it very effectively in recent years. An English performer, Harry Yelding, claims a record by walking on stilts 22 ft high.

Another act that brought variety to circus programmes in the middle of the century was called à la Perche – what we now call a perch act. The bearer balances a long pole on his shoulder or in a pouch fastened to his belt or even on his forehead, and a mounter, often a girl or young boy, climbs up it and performs various balances and head stands at the top. This act was a feature of the Japanese troupes that were seen in Europe from the 1860s, but they did not originate it for it was being performed by Lavater Lee

in 1849; the Siegrist Brothers, who were at Astley's in 1852, claimed to have invented the idea, and no less than three circuses were presenting it in London with different performers in 1853. A normal perch might be some 24 ft in length, but in 1855 one act was using a perch 40 ft high. The first perches were fir poles, whose weight was a great physical strain and possible danger to the bearer; the Japanese used bamboo poles, and nowadays lightweight steel or aluminium alloy is used. Perch acts are featured in many circuses today and are very effective; they are the kind of act that really keeps the spectator's heart in his mouth until the mounter is safely back on the ground.

The invention of the bicycle introduced a new type of circus act. A "Bicycle Circus" was exhibited at the Agricultural Hall as early as 1869. Exhibitions of advanced technique, often on a unicycle, were being given in the 'eighties by performers like Letine and the Selbinis.[11] Minting was being billed as the Champion Cyclist of the World in 1892, performing on the bicycle, one wheel, cart wheel, and half wheel. Bicycle and unicycle acts have remained popular in the Circus ever since, with some remarkable feats being achieved.

A fast-moving circus act that is sometimes seen

today is roller skating on a small circular platform. A roller-skating ballet had been choreographed by Paul Taglioni as early as 1849, and ball-bearing skates were introduced in 1884, but I have been unable to find a nineteenth-century reference to this act in the Circus. Possibly the temporary boards laid over the sawdust for cycling acts did not provide a firm enough surface for roller skating.

A pattern of development for the ground acts in the Circus during the nineteenth century should now be apparent. The first half of the century was dominated by the simple, primitive displays of the leapers and carpet acrobats; during the second half of the century acts employing apparatus and requiring more delicate skills, like the globe, the bars, the perch and the trinka displaced them and are with us still. I am not alone in believing that audiences today would enjoy seeing the leapers return.

13

Aerial Acts

ROPE DANCING, which had played such a great part in the pre-Circus entertainments of the fairs, still held its own in the ring. Many of the famous equestrians were tight rope performers as well; specialization did not really come in until the second half of the century. One rope dancer, who was indirectly responsible for a notable contribution to American history, was a Portuguese known as Il Diavolo Antonio. He is recorded at various places between 1816 and 1824, and in 1821, when he was performing at Liverpool, he became involved in a quarrel with the eminent actor and rival of Edmund Kean, J. B. Booth. Booth, who had a quick temper, assaulted him and injured him fairly seriously. To avoid any prosecution, Booth fled from Liverpool, England and his wife, and taking a flower-selling girl with him he emigrated to America, where he founded the great line of actors that bore his name, including the assassin of President Lincoln.[1]

The simple act of dancing on the rope, however, now needed some variety, and this was often provided by two dancers performing a kind of duet on parallel ropes. Double ropes, one above the other, had been introduced at Astley's in 1796, but it was more usual for them to be rigged side by side; Mr and Mrs Ferzi gave a double operatic performance on the ropes in 1814, which I suppose included singing; a double tight rope ballet was performed by Ducrow and Louisa Woolford in 1832 in which a pair of Hungarian peasant woodcutters were transformed, by a lightning change of costume, into the characters of Zephyr and Flora without quitting the ropes. Sometimes triple rope performances were given, usually with a rustic or pastoral ballet of action as their theme: "Lubin and Annette, or The Wandering Pedlar" and "The Rivals, or The Jew of Lubeck" were, for instance, being performed in various places during the 'twenties and 'thirties. I suppose that a girl danced coquettishly on the middle rope, while the rival lovers struck attitudes, advanced and retired on either side; perhaps the disappointed lover fell off the rope at the end. The Jew of Lubeck was the eponymous hero of a popular melodrama, who had been driven into concealment and disguise by the profligacy of his son. His daughter effects a reconciliation. How this story could have been transferred to rope dancing baffles the imagination.

A famous rope dancer from Paris who appeared at Astley's in 1816 was Madame Saqui; despite her masculine figure she attracted great attention, especially when she performed, surrounded by fireworks, in Vauxhall Gardens. There was, indeed, an increasing tendency for tight rope acts to be presented in large open places, like pleasure gardens and, later, the Crystal Palace, rather than in circuses. In 1853, for instance, a tight rope was erected in St Helena Gardens that was 80 yd long and 100 ft high. The supreme exponent of this kind of exhibition was Blondin, who created a sensation when he crossed the Niagara Falls

Miss Cooke at dinner on the tight rope in the family circus at Edinburgh in 1842.

A double tight rope act in 1852. Such acts might portray dramatic sketches in mime.

on a tight rope in 1859. Blondin was a great showman, and varied his act by carrying a man on his back, cooking an omelette on the rope, walking with chains or baskets on his feet or on stilts, but most of his feats lie outside the strict boundaries of circus performances.

Blondin was followed by half a dozen or more rope walkers across Niagara, but this was really a feat of endurance and nerve rather than of exceptional skill. In the Circus the emphasis was shifting from the grace of rope dancing to the skill of balancing. In 1842, for instance, Miss Cooke was sitting on a chair before a table and pouring a glass of wine from a decanter on it, all on the rope. The wire increasingly came to replace the rope, and from 1858, when strong thin copper wire became available, we read of performances on the electric wire, on the telegraph wire, or on the invisible wire. In 1886 an Australian, Ella Zuila, walked blindfolded, stood on a chair, and rode a bicycle on the wire.

One popular act was for the performer to make several changes of costume while on the wire, and George Sanger devised an amusing finale to the high-wire act performed by his grand-daughter, Georgina. A volunteer from the audience was invited to allow himself to be carried across the wire on the lady's shoulders; when a bold volunteer came forward and the journey was safely accomplished, Georgina turned round, returned across the wire, and quickly descended the rope ladder, leaving the unfortunate volunteer stranded at the other end of the wire with no means of descent. He was obliged to try to walk back across the wire himself, and of course invariably fell into the net beneath.

Some performers, like J. M. Hengler in the 1850s, were now abandoning their balance poles and ladies

sometimes carried only an open parasol, which provides some assistance in balancing. An Italian boy, trying a spin on the rope without a pole at Astley's in 1829, fell 10 ft to the ground. This was the usual height of rope acts in circuses at that time. As tents became larger, so high-wire acts began to appear in travelling circuses as well as in pleasure gardens. Balance poles are usually, but not invariably, used in these acts, and they do greatly facilitate tight rope balancing. Indeed, I remember an occasion at the Festival Pleasure Gardens in London when some accident obliged the funambulists to descend in the middle of their act, leaving their bicycles behind, which remained perfectly upright on the wire thanks to the long, dipping balance poles lying across them.

Just as a somersault on horseback was considered a great achievement, so a somersault on the rope or wire was a goal much sought after and infinitely more difficult to achieve. In 1811 Astley's announced that Mr Wilson on the tight rope would "throw a back somersault and alight on the slant of the rope, never attempted by any other person whatsoever". I am not sure just what "the slant of the rope" means. Perhaps the rope was at an angle, for journeys from the stage to the gallery were quite often featured at this time; in that case a rope at a slant would have facilitated a backward somersault, but it is difficult to believe that anyone could have landed on their feet on a slanting rope. I suspect this was a somersault from feet to crutch. Four years later, in 1815, Mr Cunningham was performing on the tight rope at Newcastle, "concluding with his astonishing summerset, in which he has no competitor". Was this a somersault from feet to feet on the rope, or was it perhaps merely a somersault from feet to crutch on the rope? Or from the rope to the ground? In 1816 we read of something even more sensational, when Andrew Ducrow was billed to perform "a double Somerset" on the rope exactly above the pit of the Theatre Royal, Bath.[2] If this means a true double feet to feet somersault I, frankly, don't believe it at that date, although it is a feat that has been achieved since. Possibly what Ducrow performed was a couple of hand-assisted somersaults, or foresprings. The next year Mr Wilson was billed to somersault on the rope while firing two pistols at the same time, so this, at least, could not have been hand-assisted. Bridges gained great applause by turning a somersault on the rope at Astley's between 1825 and 1830, and Frost thinks he was the first to achieve the feat. It was certainly being performed in 1841, when Master J. Hengler was advertised to "throw backward and forward summersets on the tight rope, a feat that astonishes those in the profession, much more so those that pay a visit to the arena". This was the son of the original rope-dancing Hengler, and the same feat was in the repertoire of his brother, Edward Henry, usually billed as Herr Hengler. A forward somersault on the rope is even more difficult than a backward somersault, as the performer cannot even glimpse the rope as his feet come down. By the 1880s the young Lloyd brothers were performing on the double tight ropes, playing violins and turning somersaults while doing so without losing a note.[3]

A somersault on the wire is even more difficult than on the rope, but as early as 1781 at Sadler's Wells Abraham Saunders had performed "a continual Summerset on the Wire, while Fireworks are playing from different parts of his body". I am sure that these were hand-assisted somersaults. In about 1885 Juan Caicedo achieved a true somersault on the wire in Paris; it was claimed that he did this in spurred Mexican boots and without a balance pole, but the photographic record fails to support this.[4]

The slack rope or wire was still a popular act; Signora Riccardoni drank tea on a swinging wire in 1787; in the 1850s John Henderson achieved a head-stand on a swinging wire that was "only like a piece of thread".[5]

A variant of the slack rope was the Flying Rope act, in which an artiste is usually described as standing on it and spinning rapidly round. In 1818, for his last appearance in public, Mr Smith announced that he would "draw himself up 20 ft high by his neck, and will stand on the rope and turn round like a fly on a jack"; in 1842 William Cooke displayed vaulting on the flying rope "by standing erect on the cord and revolving one hundred times . . . the chef d'oeuvre of rope vaulting". The rope in this act is sufficiently slack for the performer to grasp it in each hand while resting his feet on the dip between them. An act of this type is now known as a cloudswing number.

In the 1830s there are various references to the *corde elastique* which must, I think, have been a bouncing rope, attached to springs; this device is used by some artistes today, and it permits some very effective bounds. French terms were common in this speciality: we also have the *corde roide* (the tight rope), the *corde volante* (the slack rope) and the *corde lisse*, which is a rope hanging vertically, often with a wrist hold attached.

Superb performers on the *corde lisse* were the three Foucart sisters. They were the daughters of a French teacher of gymnastics, and under his training developed exceptionally well-developed shoulder muscles and biceps. One of them could climb a 60 ft rope with her hands alone. They appeared in England at the Crystal Palace and at the Alhambra in 1870, and won a challenge cup against competition from the best athletes in the British Navy.[6]

A development of the *corde lisse* is when two vertical ropes end in rings – called the Roman Rings – or are linked by the bar of a trapeze. These pieces of apparatus came into use in gymnasiums by the second half of the nineteenth century, and they soon found their way into circuses. Nathalie, the eldest of the Foucart sisters, was a particularly fine performer on the trapeze and the Roman Rings. Munby has left a detailed description of her act at the Alhambra in 1862 when she was only ten years old; unfortunately it is too long to quote here, but the climax came when she locked the bar of the trapeze between her shoulder blades and her arms, which were clasped over her chest and in this position revolved rapidly around the bar in both directions. This painful exercise was called the "muscle grind" or "Hindoo punishment" in circus slang.

A special variant of trapeze is named after the American artiste, Keyes Washington, who introduced it to Europe in 1870; this now usually has a small metal saucer screwed to it, so that the performer can

Juggling on the slack wire. From a drawing by Heinrich Lang.

balance himself on his head, while the trapeze makes long swings above the ring. I do not know of anything that looks more dangerous, for the artiste must, of course, continually alter the inclination of his body to maintain a vertical line as the trapeze swings to and fro. An artistic connoisseur of circus acts, like George Strehly, may with justice complain that the position of the body, with arms and legs spread sideways, is inelegant, but the act is certainly a heart-stopper.

An act that was sometimes combined with the trapeze was for a performer – usually a woman – to support herself, or another artiste, by the teeth – what is called an Iron Jaw act. In the 'sixties, for instance, Leona Dare, the Queen of the Antille, hung from a trapeze by her knees while she supported a man revolving in the air below her by means of a rope attached to his belt that she apparently clenched in her teeth. Whatever the illustrations may show, however, I think it is fairly certain that such performers did not actually clench the rope in their teeth but held it in a mouth grip.

The single trapeze can be a very attractive act when presented by a skilled artiste, but it has been somewhat overshadowed by the invention of the flying trapeze.

In the 1850s there was a gymnasium in Toulouse run by a teacher of physical education called Jean Léotard. A model of it can be seen in the Toulouse city museum, with its ropes and other equipment and a single trapeze hanging above a pit in the floor level. In this gymnasium the son of the owner, Jules, was in the habit of practising. At the age of twenty-one he had perfected the feat of swinging from one trapeze, letting go at the right moment, flying through the air, and catching the bar of another trapeze. He is said to have practised this over a swimming bath. This feat was seen by some visiting circus artistes, and Jules was invited to present it in Paris. He first performed it in public on November 12, 1859, at the Cirque Napoléon, now the Cirque d'Hiver. You can read a commemorative inscription on the spot to this day. It was a historic moment in the history of the Circus.

News of this sensational feat spread rapidly round the circuses of the world, and a couple of English gymnasts then performing at the St Petersburg circus determined to achieve the same effect themselves. Their names were Richard Beri and James Leach. After practising and becoming proficient in it, they offered the act to the well-known agent and impresario, Mr Van Hare. Van Hare put them on as the star billing in a circus at the Alhambra in London, with a good programme that he built round them. This was in 1860. Léotard himself came to London and performed at the Alhambra in 1861. By this time it had been converted from a circus into a music hall, and Léotard flew above the spectators seated at the tables below, with a row of mattresses to break his fall if necessary.

Léotard was a performer of really star quality. When he entered the ring, we are told, he resembled a Roman gladiator; then, as he began his leaps from one trapeze to another, while the band played the lilting music of a popular waltz, he resembled a tropical bird leaping from branch to branch and leaving in the dazzled eyes of the spectators a brilliant but confused impression of its bright plumage.

Munby saw him at the Alhambra and has left a remarkable, and curious, account of his technique. Instead of "taking off" from his trapeze, as one would expect, as it neared the highest point of its upward swing, he let go on the downward swing just *before* it reached its lowest point. From that point he "flew" in a dipping and soaring flight path, first slightly downwards and then rising to seize the next trapeze as it swung towards him. This may, of course, have been an optical illusion, but it was the impression made upon a careful observer.

The first woman to perform on the flying trapeze appeared under the name of Mlle Azella at the Holborn Amphitheatre in 1868. *The Illustrated London*

Lulu, the boy trapezist who passed as a girl for many years. A photograph taken in 1871.

A sketch by A. J. Munby of Mme Senyah (Mrs Haynes) on the trapeze in 1868.

News was "doubtful if such an exhibition can be in good taste", but observed that she was "graceful in form, with well cut features and ... makes her appearance in a costume suited to the exigencies of the occasion"; Léotard had introduced the close-fitting costume to which he gave his name, and female performers had of necessity to wear something similar. There was plenty of interest in her proposed "flight across the Arena of 100 ft terminating with a somersault at an elevation of 30 ft from the Platform", but the actual performance was rather a disappointment as the somersault was merely turned as she fell to the mattress. In 1871 Lulu, who was actually a man disguised as a woman, gave a trapeze performance at the Holborn Amphitheatre in which "she" turned a triple somersault; but this, also, was not between bar and bar but between the trapeze and a net. This would appear to represent the earliest use of a net in a circus ring.

Incidentally, Lulu was not the only case of a man passing as a girl in the Circus. Several gymnasts in Europe found this advantageous. Among equestrians, Alfred Clarke appeared as Mademoiselle Isabella in the 1880s and Alfred Johnson as Miss Beatrice in the 1930s; the most remarkable was Ella, of whom more later. In the twentieth century the trapezist and wire-walker, Barbette, has been the best known.

Léotard and his next imitator, Victor Julian, had thrown single somersaults between bar and bar, but

soon performers were achieving double somersaults. Niblo, the stage name of Thomas Clarke, who first appeared at the Canterbury Music Hall in 1868, claimed to have been the first, and both Onra and Bonnaire were throwing doubles between bars at the Holborn Amphitheatre in 1869.

At about this date the act developed into a double act with a flyer and a catcher. This is marginally less difficult, as the catcher can slightly adjust the swing of his trapeze to grasp the flyer, and the partnership between the two is very satisfying for the spectator to observe. This is now the usual arrangement, but acts in which the trapezist flies from bar to bar can occasionally still be seen.

The earliest instance that I have noted of a catcher being used is in 1870; once again Munby provides the evidence, and his description is so interesting that it is worth quoting almost in full.[7] It provides what is so rare in circus literature – a detailed description of exactly what happened during a performance; and it gives, moreover, a fascinating insight into the suppressed sexual emotions of a middle-class Victorian gentleman at the sight of a female acrobat in the scanty costume appropriate to this act. So, on an evening in June, the diarist visited the Oxford Music Hall to see the performance of an acrobat described as Mlle de Glorion. "She came forward to the footlights hand in hand with two male acrobats; she was drest much like them; and she made a bow, and not a curtsy, to the

Léotard on the flying trapeze, assisted by his father.

spectators, as they did. A very pretty English girl, she seemed to be, of 18 or 20 years; trim and slight and shapely, standing about 5 feet 4. The only clothing she had on was a blue satin doublet fitting close to her body and having very scanty trunk hose below it. Her arms were all bare; her legs, cased in fleshings, were as good as bare, up to the hip; the only sign of woman about her was that she had a rose in her bosom, and another in her short curly hair.

"She began the performance by placing the nape of her neck in a noose at the end of a rope that hung over a pulley aloft; then, hanging so with her head thrown back, she cleverly hoisted herself up, by hauling at the other half of the same rope, to the triple swing or trapéze, some twenty feet above the stage. There she sat, side by side with her two male companions; and went through the usual gymnastics; hanging head downwards, hanging by one leg or one knee; sliding down headforemost over the body of one of the men, and then catching her feet under his armpits, and coming up again by grasping his body between her knees and his leg with her hands, whilst she brought her head & shoulders up by a strong muscular effort;

and lastly, balancing herself on the small of her back upon the trapéze, till at a given signal the two men, who were hanging head downward on either side of her, each seized one of her ankles, and pulling her so by main force from her perch, flung her bodily forward and downward, and so held her upside down in the air, her limbs all sprawling apart.... She was rewarded with great applause by the crowded hall, as the men dropped their hold and left her to grasp and slide down a loose rope alone.

"But this was not all: for the chairman got up & said 'Ladies and Gentlemen, Mlle de Glorion will now take her daring leap for life, along the whole length of the hall.' And the fair acrobat went down from the stage among the audience, alone, and walked, half nude as she was, through the crowd, to the other end of the long hall, and there went up a staircase into the gallery. She passed close to me; taking no heed of any one; her fair young face all crimson with heat and wet with perspiration; and climbed the rope ladder that led up from the gallery to a small platform, just big enough to stand on, which was suspended high up under the ceiling ...

The catcher on the flying trapeze was sometimes precariously held by hooks on his shoes.

"Two strong parallel ropes were stretched from hooks in the roof, fifty feet off, to the platform where she was: on the stage, far beyond that, one of her mates was hanging inverted from the trapéze, awaiting her; but he was wholly hidden from her by two great discs of paper stretched on hoops, which were hung near him, one behind the other, above the footlights. And she had to swing herself, high over the heads of the crowd, across that great space of eighty feet or so, and leap through the two discs and alight in his inverted arms, which she could not even see. A fair girl of eighteen, preparing in sight of all men for such a feat as that; perched up there, naked and unprotected, with no one to help her; anxiously testing the ropes, chalking the soles of her feet, wiping the sweat off her hands and her bonny face, and trying to smile withal . . .

'She did it, of course; she leaped into the air, and in leaping, left the ropes that swung her, and dashed through the two hoops, and was seen hanging in the arms of her mate, grasping his body, her face against his breast. A moment more, and she had lowered herself by the loose rope to the stage, and was bowing and smiling amidst thunders of applause."

This act took place in a music hall, but it could have been – and no doubt was – equally well performed in a circus. Munby estimated that there were sixteen female acrobats appearing in England at that time. This act was not really the flying trapeze act as we

know it today – easier because there was no return to the launching platform, more difficult because of the paper discs. Similarly, the double act of the Rizarelli Brothers, as seen at the Holborn Amphitheatre in 1871, differed from the classic flying trapeze in that the flyer took off by leaping from an elevated springboard to grasp his partner's hands. By 1875, however, the Silbons were certainly working as a flyer and catcher in the now accepted way.

The Rizarellis worked with a safety net. This was a very necessary piece of equipment, as a trapezist called Majilton was killed at the Canterbury Music Hall in about 1870 and another called Artois was killed at the Star Music Hall in Dublin twelve years later; the music halls refused to allow the act to be performed after this. Even a net is not a complete guarantee against injury, however, for it is only too possible to miss the net in falling, and even if you fall into it you must land in the right way. A girl called Zaeo was so badly disfigured after a bad landing at the Alexandra Palace that she always had to be carefully made up before performing in public afterwards.

Zaeo diving to the net. Her scanty costume caused an uproar in some quarters.

The first tenting circus to present a flying trapeze act was George Sanger's with the Carl Mora troupe, who performed a double somersault while four men held a flimsy piece of canvas below that could hardly have been of the slightest use if one of the Moras had fallen. Nets are, of course, now always fitted in tenting circuses for flying trapeze acts.

The flying trapeze act went on to become the supreme acrobatic glory of the Circus, with artistes like Alfred Eugene Cooke, Mme Senyah (Mrs Haynes spelt backwards), the Americans Romah and Gonza, and Edmond Rainat. The Hanlon-Voltas were claiming treble somersaults by 1881, when the programme at the Royal Aquarium promised "La Voltige Aerienne, comprising ... double and treble somersaults and the great dive by Robert Hanlon, the originator of this feat". Robert Hanlon was "little Bob", who had been an apprentice with the famous Hanlon-Lees acrobatic troupe, and he had teamed up with two brothers, old boys of an English public school, called Volta.[8] They created a fine act of combined fixed and flying trapeze and were noted not just for the difficulty of their tricks but for the grace and sureness of their execution, but one of them later bounced out of the net in falling and was killed. If the claim at the Royal Aquarium is accepted, the Hanlon-Voltas are entitled to the honour of achieving the first triple somersault on the flying trapeze, but I think this may have been thrown from the perch to the net. A triple somersault from bar to catcher was, however, certainly achieved in 1897 by a Russian girl, Lena Jordan, in Sydney, Australia.[9]

At the turn of the century the Fortmans of Leeds, who were billed as the Cee-Mee family, were one of the finest troupes, giving a wonderful display in which the flyer flew 20 ft through the air before being caught, which caused King Alfonso of Spain to toss his top hat on the floor and jump on it in his excitement. The "20 ft" may be an exaggeration, but it is certain that the trapezes for this act when it was first performed were further apart than they customarily are today. In modern circuses the distance between the swing paths of the trapezes is, I estimate, about seven or eight feet. That gap is, of course, more than halved by the catcher hanging from one bar, so the actual direct flight path – if we are to keep to aeronautical terminology – is only about three feet. This is quite insufficient space to allow multiple somersaults, so the flyer must swing up high into the roof and let go at the apex of his swing, falling almost vertically downward to reach the catcher on a gentler swing below him. Léotard, on the other hand, flew on a more or less horizontal flight path, perhaps ten feet or more through the air, swinging, in Munby's estimate, in a grand

Robert Hanlon somersaulting from bar to bar, as depicted in the "Strand Magazine", 1895.

combined arc of 40 ft or more. His act was simpler than the flying trapeze as it has developed since, but it was closer to the idea of flying.

Since those early trials and errors the act has been enhanced with a whole repertoire of passes and pirouettes. It has been performed blindfold, and in ultra-violet light. But however it is performed, the moment when one human being flashes through the air to the safe harbour of his partner's hands is, for me, one of those magical moments in life when skill, courage and beauty meet together in one unity.

There are two other aerial acts introduced in the nineteenth century that should be mentioned here. One is walking upside down "on the ceiling". The earliest example of this was in 1806 when Sanchez demonstrated it at Sadler's Wells; the advance billing made this sound sensational, but in fact all he did was to insert his boots, that were fitted with iron bolts to the toes and heels, into iron staples driven into a board about 12 ft long. Even then, at the first attempt he managed only three steps.[10] In 1862 at the Alhambra a performer called Olmar walked upside down some 90 ft above the floor by hooking his feet into a series of large rings; "the performance was really fearful to behold."[11] The next year Munby saw a twelve-year-old girl called Corelli repeat the same feat, but in such "a cautious, perfunctory way that it was painful to witness". In 1853, however, Richard Sands, the American equestrian and circus proprietor, had demonstrated how to walk head downwards on a slab of polished marble with the aid of suction cups on the soles of his shoes.[12] (There was a strong but apparently baseless rumour among the English circus fraternity that Sands had killed himself doing this in America, and that it was his assistant impersonating him who came to England.) Some English performers later made out that they were walking by suction in the Sands manner, but actually inserted iron plates hidden in their boots into concealed traps in the marbled board serving as a ceiling.[13]

The other new effect was the man or girl shot from a cannon. Lulu was catapulted 25 ft into the air by a powerful spring at the Holborn Amphitheatre in 1871, but the first appearance of the act in its fully developed form was in 1877 at the Westminster Aquarium, when a girl calling herself Zazel was shot into the air, to land safely in a net. She eventually missed the net, broke her back, and spent the rest of her life in a steel corset; some of her imitators were killed. The gun was, of course, actuated by a spring, with a fake flash and explosion to accompany its release.

This act has been repeated many times over the years, and a family called Zacchini made a speciality of it. It really belongs to the category of sensation rather than skill, but it certainly provides a good, though brief, spectacle, but more effective, I think, in big arenas than in the small area of a circus ring.

A man shot from a cannon to grasp a trapeze bar above the net in 1893.

14

Animal Acts

P ERFORMING DOGS and monkeys had appeared at Astley's in the eighteenth century, but, apart from horses, it was only gradually that animals were introduced into circus programmes.

Dogs are easily trained and clearly enjoy performing. They appeared on the stage in several dog dramas, notably the famous *Dog of Montargis* of 1814, and it is surprising that it took so long before they found a regular place in the Circus. By the 1850s Moffat and Henry Cooke were billing dog acts, and the showman, Van Hare, had the bright idea of pitting his star dog,

Napoleon, against human leapers in a contest for the Champion Vaulter of the World. They still provide acts that are much enjoyed by audiences, and one of the most popular in this century has been that of footballing dogs, who leap with enormous enthusiasm to head a balloon football towards the opposite goal; Riccoboni's dogs had been performing that act with a leather football in 1900.

Many clowns have found willing and intelligent partners in dogs, and a particularly charming example of such an act is that developed by Pat Freeman, John

Sanger's grandson. He billed himself as Old Regnas (Sanger spelt backwards), an old coster with a donkey cart, whose work was constantly thwarted by the playful antics of his canine companion. This act can still be seen today, performed by Pat's son, Michael, and it seems to bring back something of the atmosphere of the Victorian Circus.

Cats, on the other hand, are very difficult to train, but some clowns succeeded in introducing them into their acts. Laurent, a clown at Astley's at the turn of the century, was one; another was Dickie Usher, who somehow persuaded these independent creatures to pull him in a little cart round the ring, like a four in hand. He was demonstrating this in the 'twenties and 'thirties, and in about 1850 another clown, Boswell, drove eight cats in harness from the top of the New Cut to Astley's Amphitheatre, which must be nearly a quarter of a mile.[1] I am prepared to bet that these carts were really pedalled, with the cats being pushed ahead rather than pulling them!

By 1882, however, a Dutchman called Bonetti had trained a cat to play with mice and canaries without harming them, and Leoni Clarke had a "Baldwin" kitten that climbed up a rope and then descended in a parachute, and a troupe of cats who played "Home Sweet Home" on sleigh bells – though they probably just shook them while the band played the tune. In the 1930s the circus writer, Antony Hippisley Coxe, succeeded in training a troupe of cats, and he has given us a fascinating description of how this was done.[2]

Bonetti was a specialist in training "happy families", and he persuaded dogs and foxes to appear with geese, ducks, hens and ravens in apparent amity in the ring. This kind of act was first exhibited in the streets in 1820;[3] it still sometimes appears in circus programmes; I have seen a cat jump through a hoop surrounded by pigeons and then "kiss" one of them.

Farmyard animals appearing in circuses included geese, rams and goats. The most popular was the pig. Bradbury, the clown at the Royal Circus, had introduced business with a porker; Astley had showed a learned pig in 1784 and there was another in 1823, but the "learned" animal type of act was losing its capacity for exciting wonder and was somewhat slow and small-scale for the tempo of a true circus programme. In 1887 J. Rosco, described as the great American pig performer, was presenting the only performing pigs in Britain in Newsome's Circus in Edinburgh. About the same time, however, James Lloyd had trained two pigs to each draw a carriage, in harness, with a clown in it. They used to race round the track as if they were in earnest, squeaking like mad, and often collided, upsetting the clowns. It must

The dogs most easily trained for circus tricks are usually mongrels.

have been a very funny act. One of the pigs used to cheat by cutting corners so as to win the race.

Another farmyard animal that began to appear in circuses was the bull; in 1859 Dan Castello introduced a performing bull into the American circus at the Alhambra,[4] and by 1860 there were three different bulls in various circus programmes, one of whom, trained by Colin, stood on a barrel while he stood on its head. They have continued to make rather occasional appearances in circuses ever since, though their range of tricks is fairly elementary. When I worked on a farm as a young man I noticed how lively the heifers were and tried to train them to follow a few simple directions; I never got as far as exhibiting them, but I notice that the Moscow Circus in 1977 introduced an act with cows, which were described as "clever, tender, understanding, beautiful and adaptable".

Monkeys on horseback always make an amusing act, as was well known to the Elizabethans; they were appearing in Ryan's Circus, Birmingham, in the 1830s; and in the 1860s and later baboons dressed as jockeys were trained to ride on horses and donkeys, to jump through hoops, turn somersaults, fall off, climb up the donkey's tail, and so on. Van Hare trained a monkey to walk on the tight rope with another monkey on its back, and in 1869 he brought a gorilla (at least, he says it was a gorilla) back from Africa, called it Hassan, and persuaded it to wear clothes, turn somersaults and walk on the tight rope.[5] I can't help feeling that the baboons – and probably the gorilla – were actually chimpanzees, which are

Zebras were successfully trained by Ducrow. A bill for his appearance at Birmingham in 1833.

surely the best performers of all the ape family. In 1913 Hagenbeck presented chimpanzees in a delightful turn on roller skates, and these animals perform some marvellously entertaining acts in circuses today. One that always brings the house down is when the chimpanzee goes to bed, squats on a chamber pot, and then puts it on his head!

It will be recalled that Astley had led a zebra round the Circle in 1780, and in 1832 Ducrow introduced four of these animals in a wild zebra hunt, drawing a chariot in harness, and standing unflinching while fireworks exploded all round them. Batty had zebras in 1836, and they still appear from time to time to give variety to a simple liberty act.

A bear had been introduced into plays at Astley's in 1822, but it proved incapable of performing the feats intended for it. Another appeared at Usher's benefit in 1837, but it was not until nearly the end of the century that there was much development in the training of these genial-looking but dangerous and untrustworthy animals. In 1889 Hengler's showed a bear that rode a horse, leaped through a balloon, and – reversing the pattern of the Elizabethan bear gardens – played with an English mastiff. By 1890 Permane's Siberian bears were sitting at table and drinking out of bottles, walking on a globe and swinging on a swing. Bears have a good sense of balance and they now often ride bicycles in circuses; I have seen a bear foot-juggle a burning pole as in a trinka act, walk on its fore-feet round the ring, and do a hand-stand on another's back. Polar bears are less versatile and did not appear till later; the earliest reference I have noted in England is to a performing group in Bostock and Wombwell's menagerie in about 1904, but they were appearing with Krone in Germany by 1888. In 1909 seventy polar bears, trained by Hagenbeck, performed at the London Hippodrome.

A Peruvian llama had appeared with Ducrow; camels had been introduced into a play at Astley's in 1822; a baby hippopotamus, not much larger than a pig allowed a clown to ride on its back at the Alhambra in 1860; and a kangaroo had been persuaded to go through the motions of boxing by the 1880s. All these animals can still be seen in fairly elementary routines in circuses today. But the great attraction was, of course, the big cats.

Lions and tigers had been shown in menageries from the eighteenth century and earlier, and these menageries continued to be extremely popular throughout the nineteenth century until the growth of zoos made them superfluous. George Wombwell started the most famous of the English menageries in 1805, but Polito's was already on the road by then and it was followed by Atkins', Hilton's, Manders', Bostock's, and many others. A famous menagerie was run by Cross at Exeter Change in London. The usual arrangement was for the cages to be drawn up round a square, and at first it was sufficient simply to display the strange and exotic animals behind their bars. But gradually an attempt was made to produce a performance of some kind, and keepers – one can hardly call them trainers – ventured into the cages of the largest animals.

By 1825 Atkins' Menagerie was showing quite an ambitious performance. The keeper entered a cage with a lion and a tigress, who posed on either side of him and then jumped through a hoop; he put his head in the lion's mouth, and then lay down on the floor with the two of them "and the trio gambolled and rolled about like playful children on the floor of a nursery."[6]

In 1831 Henri Martin, a menagerie owner who had been exhibiting his lions in France, appeared in a lion-drama at Drury Lane called *Hyder Ali, or The Lions of Mysore*. In the course of the action he vanquished an "untamed" lion in single combat and appeared in a triumphant procession with the conquered lion at his feet. Martin and the lion performed behind a strong wire net on the stage. The next year he appeared at Astley's.

This further demonstrated the possibility of a man venturing into the same cage as "the savage king of the jungle" without being torn to pieces, and a number of intrepid performers took up the challenge. In 1832 Winney, the trainer at Atkins' Menagerie, appeared at Astley's; the animals leaped through hoops "as when pursued by the Indians", and Winney (who was billed as Zoomkantorah, the Indian tiger tamer) struck attitudes as Daniel in the den of lions and Hercules conquering the brute. A contemporary journalist commented that the tricks were "passing strange, but we

Polar bears did not appear in circuses before the end of the century. A Friedländer poster of 1909.

confess we lack the taste essential to the enjoyment or even just appreciation of them".

This is a reservation that some people have expressed about big cat acts ever since, but it is a minority view and the acts have always proved popular with the bulk of the public. People certainly flocked to see them in the middle of the nineteenth century. The most famous trainer of wild animals was an American, Isaac Van Amburgh, who arrived in England in 1838 and presented his lions, tigers and leopards at Astley's; later in the year he appeared with Ducrow in a magnificent production of *Charlemagne* at Drury Lane, in the course of which a lion and panther were persuaded, in the biblical phrase, to lie down with a lamb. Something of the awe with which these animals were regarded at that time can be sensed from the theatre manager's highly coloured account of Queen Victoria's visit to see the beasts fed after a performance.

"The rolling of the tiger's eye, while he was devour-ing the massive lump of meat and bone, clutched between his forepaws, seemed to possess the brilliancy as well as the rapidity of lightning; and was only diverted by a tremendous and sudden spring of the lion, who, having demolished his own portion, seized upon what was left of this ferocious neighbour's fare. The dash against the sides of the den sounded like the felling of huge trees, and was enough by its force and fury to shake the strongest nerves."[7]

Victoria witnessed Van Amburgh's performance no less than seven times, and left a very interesting description of it in her Journal. She noted that Van Amburgh "is a very strong man and has an awful squint of the eyes. . . . [The animals] all seem actuated by the most awful fear of him . . . he takes them by their paws, throws them down, makes them roar, and lies upon them after enraging them." At a later performance she seems to have qualified her estimation of the animals' fear, for she noted: "He threw himself down on the ground with the Lioness over him; and

81

then half lying down, allowed the Lioness to come *behind* him, and then pushed his head into her mouth; she also licked his hair (all the time behind him) like a dog would your face." Victoria added, "It's quite beautiful to see, and makes me wish I could do the same." If she had been permitted to fulfil her wish, the spectacle of the queen of England as a lady lion tamer would indeed have added a notable chapter to circus history!

A year or so later Van Amburgh began touring his collection of lions and other animals round England, and in 1844 he went into partnership with Richard Sands in a combined circus and menagerie. In 1848 he performed in a new lion-drama at Astley's, based on the story of the Wandering Jew, called *Morok the Beast Tamer*, which introduced a rare black tiger which was probably actually a panther. He had achieved great fame by this time, was the subject of a vast number of popular prints and Staffordshire chimney ornaments, and was painted in the midst of his beasts by Sir Edwin Landseer.[8]

A rival to Van Amburgh was "the American lion king", John Carter, who appeared at Astley's in 1839 and continued to perform in England for about six years. He drove a lion harnessed to a chariot, fought

A detail from the painting of Van Amburgh with his animals by Landseer, in the Paul Mellon Collection.

An anonymous painting of Maccomo in the menagerie.

82

with a "Brazilian tiger" (which was probably a jaguar), and was hoisted with a leopard in a balloon basket from the stage to the gallery. He appeared with Van Amburgh as a double attraction in a play called *Aslar and Ozines, or The Lion Brothers of the Burning Zaara* at the Lyceum in 1843, and one can see that most of these early performances with the big cats were dressed up in a dramatized form. The critics, however, didn't think much of the play nor of the acting ability of the "brute tamers".

The menageries, however, were now presenting acts of straightforward animal training. In about 1845 the first woman lion trainer, Polly Hilton, ventured into a cage, and she was followed in 1847 by Ellen Chapman in Wombwell's Menagerie, where she was billed as Madame Pauline de Vere, the Lady of the Lions. She was the first woman to put her head between a lion's jaws and she soon showed a mixed group of lions, tigers and leopards. She was once clawed in the cage, and the long-term results were believed to have led to hallucinations and her death after being happily married to George Sanger for many years.

Another woman trainer at this time was Ellen Bright, who was killed in 1850 by an angry tiger whom she had struck with a whip when it failed to perform a trick. Among men trainers a man known as Manchester Jack made his mark with Wombwell; he used to sit on a lion's back and open its mouth. Another equally daring trainer was a Zulu called Maccomo, who had worked briefly in America and then joined Manders' Menagerie in 1857 as the African Lion King; he once succeeded in separating two tigers who were fighting in their cage, though he was badly lacerated in the process. Maccomo was succeeded by an Irishman, Macarte, who had an arm torn off on one occasion and lost his life in 1872 while presenting a noisy act with a sword and pistols, in imitation of a so-called lion hunt; he was probably not quite sober at the time.

By 1840 big cat acts were beginning to appear in the programmes of travelling circuses. Batty's was presenting a spectacle called "The Council of Clermont" in which trained lions and leopards were introduced, and Mr Needham, "the tiger tamer", was

Julius Seeth with his mixed group. A Friedländer poster of 1906.

appearing with lions, tigers and leopards, "his couch formed on the backs of the wild forest herd – the native wildness and ferocity all subjugated to man's will and courage, the Lord of Creation". At first the big cats appeared in their living cages, which were drawn into the circus ring for their performances. This involved a restricted type of act, in which the trainer had to work close to the animals and not much movement was possible, but there was one act worked in a small cage that was all movement and enormously exciting, even terrifying, for the audience. This was known as the Bounce, and involved a lion, or sometimes two lions, leaping round the bars of the cage with the trainer apparently missing death by inches as they bounded past him. The act is believed to have been discovered by accident by Tommy Purchase in about 1898, and only a few trainers ever succeeded in performing it. As well as cool nerves it required an animal that could be trained to leap round the cage, and only some lions – usually lionesses – ever mastered it.[9]

The ring cage, encircling the whole ring, was not introduced until near the end of the century. In the Drury Lane Circus of 1889/90 a huge cage was erected in sections round the ring, and this is now the normal practice. The first lion cage to be built up in the ring of a travelling circus is said to have been for John Sanger in 1890, but Sydney Howes, the oldest lion trainer working today, believes that arena cages were not in general use before Chapman's Circus toured with one in the early 1930s. The time involved in erecting and dismantling the ring cage has always presented a problem to circus owners: often it is covered by an aerial act; some circuses hold competitions between two teams of ring boys as to which can finish its side first; at the London Hippodrome in 1900, when Julius Seeth presented twenty-one lions together, a steel grill was raised round the ring by hydraulic rams, and in some big circuses in this century, like Bertram Mills and Krone, a strong wire mesh has been housed in the ring fence that can be raised and lowered rapidly.

Trainers for these acts seem to have entered their hazardous profession as much by accident as by anything else. In 1852 one of the lions in Batty's Menagerie broke loose and no one dared to approach it, till a little boy who had run away from home two years earlier and had been given a humble job about the place, calmly walked up to it and fixed a collar round its neck. Mrs Batty fainted and her husband gave the boy a sound spanking, but he was soon billing him as "John Cooper, aged 12, the youngest lion-tamer in the world". Cooper went on to become one of the best-known lion trainers in the business, with a reputation all over Europe. His performance was always of the "quick and superior" order, as opposed to the kind of bounding, whip-cracking, wrestling acts, known as *en ferocité*, which impressed ignorant spectators. Cooper taught several leopards to jump from a shelf on to his head and shoulders, an act requiring complete confidence both in man and beast, for the least shrinking would have called out the animal's long claws with the most frightful consequences.[10] Anyone who has ever caught a domestic cat jumping from a height will know that the animal's instinctive action on landing is to cling on with its claws, and Cooper's training must have been of a very high order; but I have seen a similar feat performed with a black panther by the German trainer, Gert Simoneit Barum, and the English trainer, Dick Chipperfield.

The trainer with George Sanger's Circus was James Crockett, who was a bandsman in the orchestra but had to give up trumpet blowing because of a chest complaint. When Howes and Cushing's American Circus arrived in England in 1857, Sanger was determined to match anything they could put on, so he quickly obtained six lions and installed Crockett as their trainer, on no better grounds than that he was a tall, handsome man of imposing appearance with a full beard.[11]

None of these trainers escaped without scars, and fantastic stories are told of their bravery. Once in Brussels, with Myers' Circus, a fight broke out in the cage between a lion new to the group and one of the old ones. Cooper took his whip to quell the disturbance, but in striking at the old lion, who should have known the discipline of the group, he inadvertently gave a smart cut to the new one, who immediately flew at him, clawing the flesh from his left shoulder and breast and then seizing his right arm in its teeth and baring it to the bone. The other animals, as is often the way, joined in, biting his legs. Incredibly, he managed to assert his authority, whipped the brutes into subjection, and made good his exit from the cage. Three months later he was back at work, and the lion which first attacked him developed into one of the most faithful and intelligent animals he ever had to deal with. On another occasion, Timothy Newsome, brother of the circus proprietor, who worked as a lion trainer with various circuses and menageries, received twenty-five wounds from a lion that attacked him, scarring his body all over, but he managed to kill it with a blow from the butt end of a musket.

It was indeed a hazardous profession, though the press agents rather tended to exaggerate the dangers. Van Amburgh and Cooper died in their beds. Comparatively few trainers have been killed actually in the circus ring. Nevertheless the list of trainers who have been clawed by their animals is a long one. They can

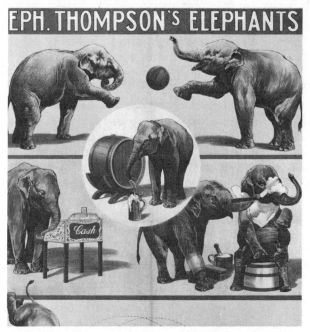

Elephant acts, as illustrated on a Friedländer poster of 1908.

THE ELEPHANT'S FEAT, ASTLEY'S.—(SEE NEXT PAGE.)

An elephant's two-foot stand at Astley's Amphitheatre in 1853.

never feel entirely safe. As I write these words a very experienced young English trainer was killed by his lions while rehearsing with them in Ireland.

The actual feats performed by lions and tigers have remained fairly elementary, being limited to various leaps and groupings, rolls over, and by-play with the trainer. They are not natural performers. A remarkable achievement of training was recorded in 1889, however, when the Covent Garden Circus exhibited one of Hagenbeck's lions riding on a horse's back. In 1892 Frank Bostock persuaded a tiger to ride on the back of its jungle enemy, an elephant; this act is featured by Louis Knie and Gunther Gebel-Williams today, and in 1972 Freddie Knie presented something quite unique – a tigress riding on the back of a rhinoceros. In all these cases, of course, a pad was used.

The other animal, beside lions and tigers, that attracted the greatest interest in nineteenth-century circuses was the elephant. It had, of course, been known for some time that this animal could be trained to execute simple actions, and a "sagacious" elephant had, for example, appeared in a melodramatic spectacle at the Olympic Pavilion in 1812, but the earliest example of strictly performing elephants that I have noted are in Wombwell's and in Atkins and Gillmore's menageries in about 1820. In the latter the animal would take a sixpence from the floor and place it in a box for the keeper's benefit, bolt and unbolt a door, take its keeper's hat off and replace it, and so on. An elephant appeared in the Circle at Astley's in 1827, but the great breakthrough, as with lions, came from a production in the theatre.

In 1829 a spectacle called *The Elephant of Siam* – like *Hyder Ali*, taken from the French – was produced at the Adelphi in London. The title role was taken by an elephant called Mademoiselle D'Jeck, who sat down to banquet, rang a bell when she was ready for the next course, rescued her master, snatched the royal diadem from the villain's head, placed it on her master's, and walked wonderfully caparisoned in the final procession.[12] This production was toured all round Britain the next year, and Mademoiselle D'Jeck appeared at Astley's, where she not only played in *The Elephant of Siam* but gave her "sagacious performance" in the Circle.

Elephants now began to be in great demand for circuses. By 1833 Hilton's menagerie had obtained specimens and in 1836 there was one at Batty's; Van Amburgh added an elephant to his travelling exhibition and equipped it with shoes and a coat to wear as it walked from place to place; Hughes had two elephants by 1845; Cooke had elephants in the 'fifties and so did Sanger in the 'sixties.

We are not told a great deal about the feats these elephants accomplished. In 1843 the elephant at the Lyceum stepped delicately over the prostrate body of its trainer, Mr Jameson, and carried him on its tusks. In 1853 an elephant at Astley's was balancing itself on its two front feet; the one-foot stand was to come later, and is still a rare accomplishment. Some elephants rang a tune on the bells by pulling ropes; an elephant was playing the organ and the harmonium at the Holborn Amphitheatre in 1870; this trick is still being presented, though the animal shows little feeling for the rhythm of the music it produces. The greatest feat of elephant training was certainly reached in 1846 with an elephant that walked on a double tight rope at Astley's; elephants will walk along a substantial narrow plank readily enough, or from one giant bottle top to another, but a trainer has to give it a great deal of confidence before it will venture on to anything as insubstantial as a swaying rope. This act was withdrawn after only a fortnight, and I suspect that the performance proved unreliable. Similarly a baby elephant advertised to perform this feat at Covent Garden in 1885 vanished rather quickly from the publicity. I confess that I was at one time sceptical about the possibility of this feat, although several classical authors record it in the first century A.D., but my doubts were banished when I discovered a photograph of a young elephant performing exactly a walk on a double tight rope in Circus Knie in 1941.[13] Circus Knie produced this feat again in 1976.

In 1852 a group of elephants appeared at Astley's "who had been taught to run in the Circle as horses"; this seems to have been a very elementary routine, but it probably represents the earliest presentation of a group of elephants working together. Cooke was presenting four elephants together in 1856; but the first trainer to present a group in a well-trained act was the lion trainer, John Cooper, who trained six in a combined act for Myers' Circus; by 1876 he was presenting a group of eight, walking on rolling barrels, while one carried him in its mouth and rode a tricycle. Famous elephant trainers from the 1870s were George and Sam Lockhart who presented separate acts; it was difficult to know which was the better, but it was Sam who trained two elephants to play skittles while a third kept the score.[14] George was killed by one of his elephants while transferring them from railway trucks. A very amusing act, shown by George Sanger and still performed by the Richters today, is the elephant barber who lathers the face of a volunteer from the audience and then "shaves" him. Elephants have remained popular in circuses to this day and, even when they don't do much, audiences love to see them in the ring and watch them exit in a long mount, each with its front feet resting on the back of the animal ahead. Some circuses dress the act up with girls riding on the elephant's heads, but though this can look very pretty it is quite unnecessary if the animals have been trained in a good fast routine.

Performances by amphibious animals did not come in until near the end of the century. In 1859 a seal had been exhibited in a big tub in London; it kissed its trainer's face and was supposed to talk. A sea-lion was giving performances at Cremorne Gardens in 1865; and by 1879 a seal was ringing bells, banging banjos, and climbing a ladder at the Royal Aquarium; but the first trainer fully to appreciate the remarkable balancing abilities of these creatures was Joseph Woodward. His sons adopted Canadian nationality and developed a famous act; by the 'nineties they were exhibiting six seals and six sea-lions, who balanced leather footballs on their noses, caught clown hats thrown to them from the balcony, and tossed up and caught drum-majors' batons and even lighted torches.[15] Reptiles, snakes and crocodiles have also been featured in the ring from time to time, but the interest really lies in watching the performer handle them rather than in anything they do.

Performing amphibians, as illustrated on a Friedländer poster of 1901.

It is not easy to make a satisfactory circus act with birds, but fan-tail pigeons and doves can be trained to fly at command, and a very pretty act is one in which a flight of these birds settles upon an equestrienne as she rides round the ring. This turn was featured by Ernestine Rosa Cooke and by Jennie O'Brien, for instance, and it can sometimes still be seen today.

At this point we should, perhaps, consider the whole question of whether cruelty has been, and is, involved in training animals to perform feats (I dislike the word "tricks") of this kind. It is a question about which some people feel very strongly, and I will try to limit myself to historical evidence.

As early as 1785 a writer to the *Morning Post* expressed the view that "the increase of learned animals of the brute species, as horses, dogs, pigs, etc. must touch the feelings of every humane heart, when it is known that the tricks they perform are taught them by process of the most excruciating torture". Some people still believe that today. But on the other

Trained pigeons, "like a mantle streaming in the wind", added a touch of beauty to some acts.

hand, Philip Astley, who knew what he was writing about, gave this advice in the book that he wrote on breaking horses: "A little obedience from a horse is very great, therefore if somewhat tractable the first morning, take him into the stable and caress him; for observe this as a golden rule, mad men and mad horses never will agree together."[16] Some seventy years later the trainer of a "happy family" of cats, rats, birds, dogs, hawks, and mice maintained that "it's principally done by continued kindness and petting, and studying the nature of the creatures".

In fact, nineteenth-century animal trainers treated their animals very much in the same way as they treated their children. They loved them, they cared for them, but they expected them to be obedient and if they weren't they were punished. In an age when boys were whipped for almost any laziness or naughtiness it is not really surprising that animals were sometimes treated in the same way. After all, dog whips and horse whips are still commonly used as the only sure way of telling the animals that they are doing wrong.

Some nineteenth-century trainers were certainly a bit rough and ready in their methods. Van Hare wrote in 1888 about his experience with a group of lions: "I felt at once I was their master; I placed the hoop against the iron bars for them to leap through; the first came up with a growl. I gave him a good cut with a whip, which he answered pretty quickly by flying through the hoop." The trainer who taught a lion and a bear to ride on horseback in 1889 described his methods as follows: "You have to try and attach the animal to you, for by cruelty no wild animal yet was trained. . . . But unless their affection for their trainer is mingled with a certain dose of fear, you can do nothing with them. The one fact which it is necessary to impress upon them is that you are their master, and that punishment awaits them if they do not try to work. Cruelty would be as unwise, or unwiser than, petting, but a judicious mixture of wholesome dread and attachment is the best. . . . Mr Hagenbeck, my principal, and I trained him [the lion] together, but I had to punish the pupil when he would not obey orders, and every whipping he received during his school days he has remembered against me."

Cooper, one of the best trainers, spoke in much the same terms: "A cut of the whip is a necessary thing on proper occasion, but it needs a forbearing discrimination to tell when the proper occasion arrives"; he was clear that the animals must respect, even fear their trainer, but "it is not the sort of fear which is engendered by brutal whipping and driving. . . . Of course it must be remembered that with a wise trainer, who loves his animals, the animals soon learn to return the affection. . . . It *is* all done by kindness – of a wise and severe sort. For it must be remembered that with all their affection the brutes still remain dangerous and treacherous in their nature and variable in their moods."

One hears the voice of a stern but understanding Victorian headmaster in all this. But just as methods of teaching children have changed, so have methods of training animals. An animal trainer today (I dislike the term "tamer", which is an inaccurate description of what he does) would not speak like Cooper nor act on quite those principles. But it still remains true that the trainer must be recognized as master, a mastery exercised by loving care, rewards, and infinite patience.

Some trainers in the past have been cruel in their treatment of their animals; for all I know some trainers today may be; some parents are cruel to their children today; but almost all parents are kind and considerate to their children, and almost all trainers have known that the only effective way to train an animal for performance is by rewards, not by punishment. A thorough investigation into the training of performing animals and the cruelty, if any, that was involved in it was carried out by a Select Committee appointed by the British House of Commons in 1921. Evidence was heard from trainers and from people who were convinced that much cruelty was used. The Report of the Committee summed up its conclusions as follows: "Your Committee are convinced that . . . best results obtained in training are effected by kind and patient treatment. . . . Generally speaking, the evidence tends to show that there has been a marked improvement in the care and treatment of animals during recent years, and that the growth of the humanitarian spirit in this country is being extended to animals with advantageous results."[17] That growth has certainly continued to the present day.

The grosser charges of cruelty made against circuses by some well-meaning but totally misinformed people today are easily refuted. But one question does nag in the mind. Are we really justified in taking an animal away from its natural environment and forcing it – even if only by bribery – to entertain us with unnatural tricks?

The charge of "unnatural tricks" is easily answered. Animals are – can be – only trained to perform actions that *are* natural to them. They may be developed, dressed up a bit, and so on, but all the so-called tricks are simply extensions of what the animals do of their own accord. Moreover, there is some evidence that the modest exercise, the variety, and even the applause of the public that circus performances involve, lead to healthier animals. Certainly it seems a better life than the aimless existence in a zoo.

But are we – men – justified in using animals at all just for our pleasure? This is the nub of the problem. I can only answer that throughout recorded history we have taken animals away from their natural environment and forced them to pull our carts to fight in our battles, to provide the basis for a gigantic gambling industry, to guard our houses and our sheep, to guide the steps of our blind, to hunt foxes and criminals and escaped slaves, to catch our mice, to sing to us in our homes, and to solace our loneliness. Compared with all that and much more, is it an insult to their dignity, an infringement of their nature, to take them into the circus ring, there to display their own skills in company with skilful and courageous men?

15
Clowns

THE ENGLISH CIRCUS clowns used to observe a pleasant custom of laying a wreath on the grave of Joey Grimaldi – a ceremony at which I once had the honour of joining them; they still honour his memory by meeting once a year for a memorial service to the man who is regarded as the founder of their art.

One does not want to disparage so filial a tribute, but the historian must point out that, though Grimaldi certainly influenced the development of clowning in general, he never appeared in a circus himself, and clowns were performing in circus rings before he ever appeared on a stage.

We have seen that Astley had introduced burlesque acts of horsemanship in his very first season in 1768, and by 1780 he was billing a clown on horseback in his programme. Clowns have remained as essential to the Circus as horses ever since.

Two important clowns who helped to mould the tradition of circus clowning in its early years were Delpini and Dubois. Carlo Delpini had already enjoyed a distinguished career as a Pierrot and as a deviser of pantomimes on the English stage when he was engaged to succeed the elder Grimaldi at the Royal Circus in the 1780s. Here he became noted for the catch phrase "What you please" – meaningless catch phrases of this kind have always been the trademark of comedians.[1] In 1798, when he was past his prime, he went on to devise entertainments at Astley's. He may have brought the tradition of the Italian Comedy to the circus ring; he certainly brought some of the business of eighteenth-century pantomime.

More important was Baptiste Dubois, who had been a principal performer and stage manager at Jones's Amphitheatre in Whitechapel from its opening; he was a dancer and leaper, appeared in feats of strength as the English Hercules, danced on the rope

with two boys tied to his feet, performed burlesque horsemanship on a donkey, and introduced a comic riding act called the French Post Boy's Journey from Paris to London, in which he effected a change of costume (and probably sex) while inside the post boy's bag. He was performing this in 1786, and it is the earliest example of the act subsequently known as the Metamorphosis of a Sack. He had been billed as clown at Astley's by 1780, and as far as I have been able to discover he was the first to be so named there; he also appeared as clown with great success at Sadler's Wells, the Royal Circus, Drury Lane, Covent Garden, and the Edinburgh Equestrian Circus.

Dubois was a particular favourite at Sadler's Wells, where he played for many years as clown to Richer's performances on the tight rope; during this act he would dance a reel with a set of conical hats, which he set spinning like tops on the stage floor, and then kicked them up one by one – up to thirteen it is said – to catch them on his head.[2] This trick became a favourite with circus clowns. It was here that he invented an act described as "rope dancing by Mr Dubois and his Grandmother", which must have been something like Frolics of my Granny, with a dummy old woman perched on his shoulders. He was performing this as early as 1792, thirty years earlier than the earliest appearance of the act on horseback that I have noted.

Dubois used to dress as a rustic booby, with a red wig and a ruddy face, and brought to the Circus the tradition of the pre-Grimaldi clown, the English comic yokel, a type deeply embedded in folk literature and drama. He originated several of the most popular clown acts of the nineteenth-century Circus, and it is on his grave – alas unknown – that the circus clowns really should be laying their wreaths today.

A clown to the ring gazes in dumb adoration at the beautiful lady rider.

The tradition of the nineteenth-century pantomime harlequinade was brought to the Circus by several clowns who had experience of both mediums. The most famous of these was Tom Matthews, often regarded as Grimaldi's successor, whose work was really in the theatre but who once appeared in the ring at the Alhambra in 1860 in a burlesque of the Sayers versus Heenan prize-fight and as a tamer of a "prancing steed" which was in fact a real miniature horse, so small that it could be carried into the ring wrapped up in the clown's handkerchief.[3] But the arts of circus clowning and stage clowning are very different; the clever clown at Hengler's in the 'seventies, Little Sandy, proved not half so funny on the stage as when he was fooling in the sawdust, and the great circus clowns, Grock and Antonet, found they had to fundamentally alter their act when they began to appear on variety stages in 1911.[4] If I may be allowed to introduce a personal experience here, I discovered the same thing when a big English circus allowed me to try out in the ring a clowning act that I had performed with success in the atmosphere of intimate theatres, but which went for nothing in the setting of a huge circus tent.

Clowns were used in the early circuses as foils to the more serious artistes, and to provide a little breathing space for them between the different feats within their acts; a riding or a rope dancing act would last much longer than is usual today, and would be broken up by comic skits contributed by performers described as "clowns to the ring" or "clowns to the rope". One of the clown's jobs was to hold one end of the garter or length of cloth over which the equestrian was to jump; he would make a mess of getting this to the right height, pull the groom who was holding the other end over, and when at last he was told he'd got it right he'd say "I'm glad of it", drop the garter and walk away with his hands in his pockets. When the equestrian had finished his display, he'd exclaim "Now I'll have a turn myself", fall flat on his face, dribble some sawdust over his head, and say "See how my nose is bleeding." If it was a lady equestrienne he would throw himself into absurd attitudes of lovesick adoration, stammering out "What can I come for to go, for to fetch, for to bring, for to carry, for to do, for you, ma'am?" When the rope dancer appeared he would chalk the rope or the artiste's shoes to prevent him slipping, and then chalk his own nose; he would make a great show of trying to stand the balance pole upright in the sawdust, and then carefully pick up a piece of straw so as not to fall over it.[5]

The clown, or Mr Merryman as he was often called, engaged in a repartee of traditional wisecracks with the attendants, telling the groom "to rub the horses well down with cabbage puddings, for fear they should get the collywobbleuns in their pandenoodles". His choicest repartee was with the ringmaster. "I say, sir!" begins the clown; "Well, sir?" answers the ringmaster; "Did you ever happen to hear I was in the army, sir?" – "No, sir." – "Oh yes, I can go through my exercises, sir." – "Indeed, sir." – "Shall I do it now, sir?" – "If you please, sir." But the clown takes his time over adopting a suitable posture, and the ringmaster with a "Come, sir, make haste" gives him a cut with his long whip which produces a yell and an immediate commencement of activity. The "exercises" consist of the clown throwing himself on the ground and going through a variety of gymnastic convulsions, doubling himself up and untying himself again, to the vociferous delight of the audience. But the equestrienne has rested long enough and it is time for her next appearance.[6]

On failing to execute some acrobatic feat the clown may complain that his calves are weak. "How does that come about, sir?" asks the ringmaster; "My shoes were too large for me", he answers, "so I stuffed them with hay, and the calves came down to eat it and forgot to go up again." The ringmaster then asks for a pint of stout; the clown brings it in a pewter mug; the ringmaster requests it to be served, more elegantly, in a tumbler. The clown promptly drinks it down, throws a somersault, and says "Here it is, in a *tumbler!*"[7] On his first appearance he would bound into the ring with a "Here we are again"; and on his exit, on making to precede the ringmaster, that dignitary would say "I never follow the fool, sir", on which the clown lets him go first and then follows him with the parting cry "Then I do!"

Not all the clown's witticisms were in dialogue. Sometimes he delivered comic monologues. A mock election address was a popular item, and here is part of a disquisition on the horse by Charlie Keith, a clown who played all over Europe in the second half of the nineteenth century: "The horse is one of the most noble of animals, for like man it can walk, trot, and run, and I have seen a horsefly. . . . I have never seen a green horse, but I have seen a horse reddish. . . . I may be a little hoarse at times, but women are perfect nags." This kind of thing was to be much developed at the end of the century by the music hall comedians.

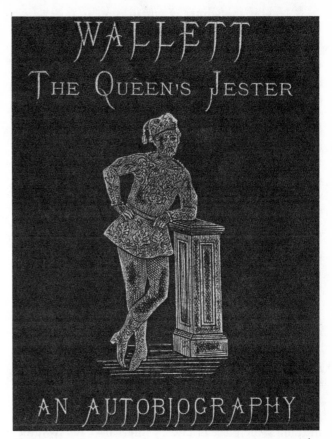

Wallett, as depicted in medieval costume on the cover of his autobiography, 1870.

Much – too much I would say – of these clowns' humour was verbal. It was delivered, we are told, in "a twang that generally characterizes circus utterances". It may have gone over well enough in the small booths and intimate circuses of the early nineteenth century, but there were few fresh ideas and by 1867 *The Era* could complain that "there is a sad lack of originality in the sayings of circus clowns generally". In the middle of the century there was a vogue for what were called Shakespearean clowns; a clown called Charles Marsh, who worked with Batty and Holloway, claimed to have originated the style; the most famous exponent was W. F. Wallett, who took the title of "the Shakespearean jester" some time in the mid-'thirties and wrote an interesting autobiography, though maddeningly short of dates. It is not clear how Shakespearean these acts really were. In the humblest circuses they amounted to no more than the clown pretending he had a dreadful toothache and declaiming "To draw or not to draw, that is the question". Sometimes clowns introduced parodies of familiar speeches, for this was a style of comedy then very popular in theatrical burlesques; one example that has been recorded starts like this:

Now is the winter of our discontent –
We have not enough money to pay the rent.[8]

At their most loquacious the Shakespearean clowns seem to have indulged in word play reminiscent of the fools of Shakespeare. One of Wallett's speeches ran as follows: "Three or four hundred years ago was the time to be a fool, when kings and queens used them in their palaces. In those days fools were great men, but now great men are fools. In those past days fools were well fed and paid, but now so many people make fools of themselves for nothing." This is in the spirit of Touchstone's, "The more pity that fools may not speak wisely what wise men do foolishly."

By 1857 Wallett was spouting a bit of word play that became traditional with circus clowns in some such form as, "Whether the weather is cold, or whether the weather is hot, we shall always have weather, whether we want it or not."[9]

At times the Shakespearean clown stepped right out of conventional clowning into an almost surrealistic black comedy. There is an extraordinary description of James Boswell, a Shakespearean clown at Astley's in the 'fifties who became all the rage in Paris and was greatly admired by Théophile Gautier; we are told that he would sometimes pause in the middle of his fooling as if yielding to some macabre fantasy, and draping some piece of tawdry finery over his costume, assume a tragic expression upon his white-painted face and run round the ring declaiming the most frightening lines of Shakespeare in a shrill and raucous voice.[10] Boswell fell dead from a stroke in the middle of a performance.

Not all the humour was verbal, however. One of the good old tricks was "the headless man". A very tall man, with a mask-like impassive face, walks into the ring. The clown speaks to him, but receives no answer. In irritation, the clown knocks his hat off, and the head falls off too. While the clown is trying to put the headless corpse in a coffin it gets up and runs out of the ring. The trick is, of course, a false head loosely mounted above a short actor's real head. This turn was being played by Harry Croueste at the little circus in Vauxhall Gardens in the 'fifties, when it was already recognized as an old favourite, and I have seen it performed in circuses today. Another trick that was already old by the 'eighties was for the clown to mistake a scrap of paper tied to the end of the ringmaster's whip for a white butterfly, and chase it in a ridiculous way round the ring. Charlie Keith had a clever trick in which he dived through what appeared to be a paper hoop and emerged wearing a long nightgown.

A popular piece of clowning was balancing a peacock's feather. Jimmy Chipperfield recalls how his

Auriol in his bottle dance. He was an expert acrobat as well as a clown.

father "would blow the feather into the air, wait as it came slowly down, and then catch it on his nose, his foot or his chin. That was all he did – but I have seen him tear the people up by doing it. I've seem them crying with laughter, just at this feather. All on his own he made the tent sound like a football ground at the climax of a match."[11]

In small family circuses like Chipperfield's, the audience was often persuaded to provide the comedy themselves. There might be a tug of war with an elephant in which a score of the locals were invited to take part; the elephant simply pulled the lot of them over, into the sawdust and out of the ring. Or two men were invited to play blind man's buff with the clown; the first to hit him would win a quacking duck he was carrying under his arm; but it always ended up with them hitting the king pole or each other.

These clowns were not just comics. They could all perform feats of skill as well. For instance, Mr Porter, clown at the Royal Circus in 1801, leaped through a hoop surrounded by fireworks, firing two pistols as he did so. The great French clown, Auriol, who appeared in England at Drury Lane in 1848, was as famous as an acrobat as a clown; he could dance on a ring of bottles, and throw a somersault out of his shoes and land back in them again. Such examples could be duplicated almost endlessly, up to Charlie Rivel in our own time, who needed to be an expert acrobat before he could pretend to be Charle Chaplin on the trapeze.

As the century went on there was a tendency for clowns to specialize as talking clowns, equestrian clowns, musical clowns, or augustes. The Price brothers, John and William, who achieved enormous popularity in France in the 'sixties, combined acrobatics with music; they balanced on unsupported ladders over 10 ft high while playing a flute and a violin, and they played a violin duet while throwing somersaults.[12] The Daniel brothers, who were in the opening programme at the Holborn Amphitheatre in 1867, had a similar act, in which they performed all kinds of double acrobatics, the bow of one Daniel sometimes playing on the strings of his brother. The tradition of musical clowning has been greatly developed by European clowns since that time; Grock was a master on the concertina, and most European clowns today play at least a trumpet or saxophone.

Meanwhile, the tradition of acrobatic clowning developed in a most curious way, reaching its apogee with the troupe of the Hanlon-Lees. The six Irish Hanlon brothers had been trained by "Professor" John Lees, and developed into a well-known team of trapeze and carpet acrobats, retaining Lees' name in their title even after his death in 1855. Ten years later they met a juggler called Henri Agoust in Chicago, under whose inspiration they devised a series of acrobatic pantomimes, of which *Voyage en Suisse* was the most famous. They took London and Paris by storm in the 'seventies and 'eighties; French audiences, in particular, were fascinated by this style of clowning. Edmond de Goncourt wrote of the "kind of working-class poetry and fantasy which English clowns use a great deal in their performances", and "England is the only country in Europe which has succeeded in introducing true imagination into its feats of bodily strength. . . . Great Britain has developed an entirely new form of satirical comedy, largely created by unknown performers. . . . It was as if the Italian comedies had been rediscovered. . . . In recent years the art of the English clown has developed a sinister quality . . . the clown's art is now rather terrifying and full of anxiety and apprehension, their suicidal feats, their monstrous gesticulations and frenzied mimicry reminding one of the courtyard of a lunatic asylum."[13]

The performances of the Hanlon-Lees were presented mainly in theatres, and so lie outside the limits of a history of the Circus, but the roots of this *genre* lie in the acrobatic clowning of the circus ring. It is a form of popular theatre that has as yet been all too little studied.

Within the circus ring the art of clowning seems to have declined in England in the last quarter of the nineteenth century. The best talent, both in comedians and acrobats, was drawn to the music halls which were springing up everywhere. During this time, however, English clowns were making great reputations on the Continent, so much so that even French and German clowns were obliged to adopt an English accent. It was here that a repertoire of *entrées*, or comic sketches, was being built up that have delighted circus audiences ever since. Here is one of the earliest to have been recorded, "The Duel", performed in the 1850s by James Boswell and young Price.[14]

The two clowns try to perform an acrobatic trick, but Price keeps on making a mess of it and knocking Boswell over, so much so that Boswell gets angry and complains to the ringmaster. The ringmaster suggests that the only way to settle their dispute is to fight a duel, and they are presented with pistols. Their eyes are bandaged, but both of them shift the bandages and then complain that the other can see. When the pistols are eventually fired, each one falls down as if dead. Boswell rises cautiously to his feet, asks Price if he is dead, to which he answers "Yes". The ringmaster warns Boswell that he will be charged with murder. Boswell in a panic fetches a sack, puts Price in it, and staggers off to throw it in the river. Meanwhile, as in the old equestrian comic act of The Humours of a Sack, Price wriggles out of his clown costume in the sack, falls out of the bottom, and emerges as a woman who chases Boswell out of the ring.

This entrée was seen in England when Little Sandy and James Holloway performed it at Astley's in 1875, but it is a tragedy that so few of these delightful entrées, of which something like one hundred and fifty are known, ever found a place in the rings of English circuses. Some of them borrowed basic situations from earlier comedies: there was the marvellous Broken Mirror entrée, the plot of which can be found in a seventeenth-century Spanish farce (and the best performance of it that I have seen was by Spanish clowns); the Dentist and the Barber Shop entrées, which repeat funny business from the Comedia dell' Arte; and the Living Statue entrée, whose basic situation can be found in eighteenth-century English pantomime. Others were created directly for the Circus, and can be seen fairly frequently today: like the William Tell entrée, with the auguste eating the apple that he is supposed to balance on his head; or the Catching the Bullet entrée, in which the auguste is supposed to catch the bullet fired by the conjurer in his mouth; and then there are entrées like the Boxing Robot, the Restaurant Dinner, and the Wallpaperers, in which broad slapstick has replaced any element of pathos or subtlety. Perhaps the most popular entrée today is some variant of You Can't Play That Here, in which the clown is trying to play some serious music and is continually thwarted by the discordant interruptions of his partners.

The costume of the circus clown was never entirely standardized; it was influenced by that of the pantomime clown but developed its own particular features. The most distinctive of these was a round conical hat, such as Dubois must have used as a spinning top; a popular act was for a clown to throw these hats across the ring for another clown to catch, one on top of the other, on his head. This act was being featured at Hengler's and Newsome's in the 'seventies and 'eighties, and Antony Hippisley Coxe recalls still seeing it in about 1950. Some performers followed the pantomime tradition by wearing annulated breeches ending above the knees, but it was more common in the Circus – especially later in the century – to wear Dutch-like baggy trousers fastened near the ankles, which might be of one piece with the shirt. A frill often went round the neck. The wig was sometimes in the form of a cock's comb, the traditional mark of the medieval fool, rather than the three-tufted style that had been made familiar by Grimaldi. Wallett wore the costume of a court fool, copied from a

medieval miniature, but I don't think anyone else followed this archaic example.

Loose-fitting costumes of this kind were all right for talking clowns, but were not good for tumbling clowns, who wore close-fitting shirts and tights or skin-tight breeches; but whatever the cut of the garment it was normally striped in bright colours or decorated with circles, lozenges or other devices. The Price brothers embroidered a delightful design of butterflies over their violet costumes.[15]

The highly spangled costume, with loose calf-length trousers, that has become the uniform of continental white-face clowns today, did not evolve until the twentieth century, when it seems to have been introduced by Antonet, Grock's master and partner.[16] But there had been a constant tendency to decorate and prettify the clown's costume throughout the nineteenth century, and in reaction to this a new type of clown made his appearance. This was the auguste, dressed in absurd clothes, much too large or much too small for him, with a ludicrous wig and make-up, who began to feature in the ring in the 1870s.

There are various and contradictory theories as to who invented this character and when. Some books give the credit to an English clown, James Guyon,

Clowns often trained animals to take part in their acts. Here a pony has seized the clown's shirt tail, but it will probably turn out to be a length of cotton stretching for about 10 yards.

An elegant white-face clown at the end of the 19th century. By this time the clown's costume had become too ornate for slapstick comedy.

Billy Hayden, an English comic, made his mark in France at the same time in the newly developed style of an auguste.

but the most widely accepted story is that Tom Belling, an American acrobat in Renz's Circus in Berlin, was dressing himself up for fun in some ridiculous clothes when Renz saw him and sent him straight into the ring (in another version he was running away from Renz and found himself in the ring). Arrived on the sawdust, he fell flat on his face, and the audience greeted him with roars of laughter and cries of "auguste".

I must say that I have always regarded this anecdote with a good deal of scepticism, though it is based at second hand on Belling's own account.[17] It does seem to be a fact that the auguste, as a name for this type of clown, originated in Berlin. But why on earth should the audience have fixed on this name? Some books state that *August* was Berlin slang for any ridiculous person, but the truth seems to be that the slang term was named after the clown, and not *vice versa*. By 1882 a dictionary of Berlin slang noted that "*Aujust* (also a term of abuse) has become very popular

from a clown in the Circus Renz who played the role of a stupid booby."[18]

If this was the case, who was the original August? One nearly contemporary source hints at a ring boy in the Renz Circus of that name,[19] but there is surely another possibility. The Agouts were a family of circus performers of French origin whose names crop up on both sides of the Atlantic in the second half of the nineteenth century. In 1885 what I take to be two members of this family, billed as Les Deux Agoust, were actually appearing in the role of auguste clowns in the Covent Garden Circus, wearing "a kind of burlesque evening dress". Could one of this family have given his name to this type of clown in Berlin? Here is a problem that lies outside the scope of this book, but I leave it for circus historians and etymologists to work on.

It cannot be said, however, that any one "invented" the auguste. It is surely an immortal type that can be found in the clowns of the Elizabethan theatre and the eighteenth-century fairs, and had already, in essence, appeared in the Circus as early as Dubois, with his florid make-up and old-fashioned, *outré*, servant's uniform. The type certainly made a comeback in the 'eighties, and clowning acts tended to develop into double turns, with an elegant white-face clown and a disreputable auguste as partners; it was always the auguste who got drenched with water, or hit on the head, or whose trousers fell down, and it is the auguste who has almost monopolized clowning in the circus ring today.

The most famous of these double acts was that between Footit and Chocolat, which achieved enormous popularity in France at the end of the century. Powell, Footit and Clarke's Circus had been touring England in the 'sixties, with Funny Footit as clown introducing his wonderful performing hippopotamus. His son, George, became a clown, too, but – like many of the best English clowns – he found more appreciative audiences in France, where, in 1889, he teamed up with a dark-skinned Cuban who adopted the stage name of Chocolat and together they created the classic clown–auguste partnership. Later commentators have seen something sadistic and racially degrading in the relationship between the immaculate, haughty, white-face clown and the foolish, battered, humiliated Chocolat; but this is surely to view their act with hindsight from a later age.

The double act became a trio in the persons of the Fratellini brothers, originally a burlesque acrobatic act, who were asked to fill a gap in the programme by appearing as clowns at the London Hippodrome in 1902. It was here that Albert, wondering what costume he should wear, wandered through what he described as "these dark streets shrouded in fog, which made of London a kind of city of the moon, vague in outline and enveloped in mystery, where one expected some strange adventure at every turn".[20] Attracted by the sound of a sentimental sing-song, he entered a pub in Whitechapel, and among the crowd of dockland prostitutes and shabby riff-raff of the quarter he saw a man dressed in an ancient frock coat, green with mildew, its tails dragging the ground and its sleeves hanging below his finger tips; beneath it his trousers billowed around his belly and fell in concertina folds to his feet. Suddenly Albert saw in this the costume of an auguste. He bought the clothes on the spot, and created a marvellous make-up to go with them, consisting of an enormous red mouth curving upwards, a huge bulbous nose, and fantastically high arched eyebrows, all strongly etched against a white background. From this moment of inspiration the act gradually took shape, with his brothers, Francois, as the mischievous white-face clown and Paul as the

black-coated straight character who formed a link with Albert, the bewildered grotesque. They went on to become the idols of Paris in the decades between the wars.

A type of clown that is even more shabbily dressed than the auguste is the hobo or tramp clown. This is mainly an American speciality and originated on the vaudeville stage towards the end of the nineteenth century, sometimes as a tramp philosopher, sometimes as a tramp juggler, among whom the greatest exponent was W. C. Fields. The most famous hobo circus clowns have been Emmett Kelly and Otto Griebling, both of whom acquired star status between the wars. The many circus imitators of Charlie Chaplin, of whom Charlie Rivel was the cleverest, are cast in the same mould. Their act is essentially more sympathetic and less grotesque than that of the auguste, and at its best a great deal cleverer.[21]

Female clowns have always been rare in the Circus. Munby recorded a clowness at the London Pavilion in 1862 and another at the Metropolitan in 1869, but these were playing basically in the spirit of the harlequinade. Today, Annie Fratellini upholds her family tradition in a performance of some charm and zany humour, but she cannot really persuade me that the circus clown is a unisex role.

The clown's facial make-up was subject to two opposing influences. On the one hand the tradition of Pierrot, brought to the Circus by Delpini, led to the clown with a white face, an effect originally achieved with the aid of flour but later, more dangerously, with dry white lead,[22] or, more expertly, with oxide of zinc, lard and tincture of benzoin; this tradition must have been reinforced by the influence of Deburau and the French pantomimists of the boulevard du Temple. On the other hand, the bucolic red-cheeked appearance of Dubois, stylized by Grimaldi and the clowns of the English pantomimes and then exaggerated by the augustes, led to grotesque effects with huge crimson mouths, enormous eyebrows, and so on. Eventually there was a tendency for these elements to combine, producing exaggerated features upon a white-face base. Tom Barry's make-up in 1842, for instance, consisted of a white face with a small, delicately outlined red mouth, formalized red triangles on the cheeks, greatly exaggerated black eyebrows, and a bald wig.[23] Clown make-up has developed into quite an art, and today any circus clown worth the name has evolved his own style of make-up, which the profession accepts as his copyright.

The clowns in a circus supply a necessary element of anarchic foolery to balance the discipline of the acrobats and the obedience of the animals. Where everything else is neat and controlled, they are wild and unpredictable. They are needed not just to make us laugh, but to provide a contrast to the rest of the programme, and even if they are not very funny they

still have a part to play in creating a genuine circus atmosphere.

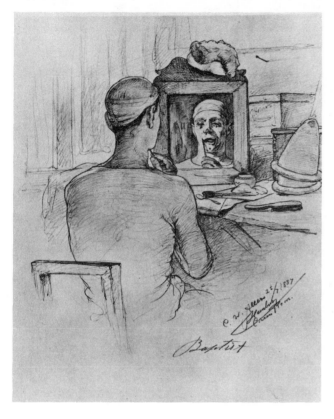

A clown makes up before a performance. From a drawing by C. W. Allers.

The pointed white hat, the brilliant costume, and the delicate make-up of a white-face clown.

16
Ringmasters and Others

ANY PROPER CIRCUS ought to commence with a splendidly attired gentleman stepping into the centre of the ring and proclaiming in ringing tones the first item on the programme. Alas, today it is too often an insignificant fellow, or even a girl in tights, talking into a microphone whose discordant amplification makes whatever is said incomprehensible to most of the audience. Indeed, quite apart from any inadequacies of the equipment, the reliance upon microphones, not only by ringmasters but by clowns, even in quite small circus tents today, is scandalous.

It is quite possible to be heard in a tent of moderate size if one speaks properly; I recently attended a performance of Peter Brook's famous production of *Ubu* that was actually given in a circus tent. One could hear every word perfectly. Of course, these were proper actors. But ringmasters and clowns should be proper actors too. In the nineteenth century the worlds of the Theatre and the Circus lay close together. Today they are miles apart. It would be of value to both of them to learn a little from each other.

The office of ringmaster, or riding master, has a

The ringmaster plays an important part in keeping the performance moving smoothly.

proud tradition. He may often have been required to engage in dialogue with the clown or lend a hand in a clowning entrée, but his chief job was to announce the turns and "keep the horses up" – that is, to stop and start the horse in a voltige act and keep it cantering at a steady pace while the equestrian performs on its back.

He was an imposing figure, sometimes dressed in a theatrical costumier's fancy version of military uniform, though some riding masters in modest circuses sported only a nankeen dressing gown with brown frogs; by the end of the century evening dress with tails was common. French ringmasters – traditionally called M. Loyal after a mid-nineteenth-century forbear – usually wore a blue tail coat with gilt buttons. The custom of wearing hunting kit – scarlet tail coat, white buckskin breeches and black riding boots – which is sometimes seen today, was introduced, or perhaps revived, by Bertram Mills in 1921. However dressed, the ringmaster's badge of office was a long whip, used of course to cue the horses not to strike them, though he might pretend to whip the clown with it.

A famous ringmaster at Astley's was Mr Widdicomb who held that office from 1819 to 1853. He also played the Dandy Lover in the harlequinades and was renowned for his superior-toned voice, though this was sometimes made fun of; he was said to talk with a plum in his mouth, pronouncing good as "gud", for as "faw", cattle as "kettle", and so on. With advancing years he dyed his hair so as to maintain his exquisite appearance. He was fond of a drink and was once taken up for drunk in the streets, but all accounts agree that he cut a very noble figue in the ring, though Dickens was rude enough to write that he reminded him of a fowl trussed for roasting wrapped up in a tablecloth.[1]

However fallen from his former glory, a ringmaster is still essential in a circus. The job of keeping the horses up is now usually undertaken by someone belonging to the equestrian troupe, but the ringmaster has the important task of keeping the turns following one another smoothly and promptly by blowing a whistle as a signal for changes and overseeing the work of the ring boys. In the circuses of the early nineteenth century changes were signified by ringing the manager's bell – like the prompter's bell that was used as a signal to stage hands in the theatres of the time.

The earliest displays of trick riding had been accompanied by music of some kind, and many circuses presented horses that were supposed to dance to music, so a band was soon recognized as an essential element in any circus. Gradually a repertoire of suitable pieces was built up. By the end of the century it was commonly accepted that the flying trapeze, balancing and Risley acts called for waltzes; weight lifting and strong man acts should be accompanied by military marches; the fixed bars, springboard and ground acrobatics needed a gallop; and horse acts a quadrille.[2] The actual selection of pieces was a good deal wider than is generally realized today, with composers like Johann Strauss and Waldteufel well represented; an overture of light classical music was sometimes listed in the programme; at Hengler's in the 'seventies this might be selections from Rosini's *William Tell*, from Balfe's *The Bohemian Girl*, from Bousquet's *La Favorita*, or at the Holborn Amphitheatre the overture to Hérold's *Zampa*. A march called "The Entry of the Gladiators", composed in about 1900 by Julius Fucik, a kind of Czech Sousa, become almost a signature tune for the opening parade of any circus. Other popular pieces that became inseperably associated with the Circus were Sousa's "Esprit du Corps" for a cage act, Berlioz' "Rakoczy March" for an elephant act, and Lehar's "Gold and Silver Waltz" for the flying trapeze.

Later bands have, of course, drawn upon popular music of the day. At the present time one of the best flying trapeze acts in the business, the Flying Cavarettas, has used music ranging from *Jesus Christ Superstar* to an arrangement of Beethoven's Fifth Symphony, and Katja Schumann performs her High School act to music made famous by Edith Piaf. Other acts pick up tunes from the latest movies. There is, however, a clear affinity between the traditional kind of circus music and the business in the ring, and bands which ignore this render a great disservice to the art.

The job of circus bandmaster is not merely that of playing appropriate music. He often has to adjust his music to follow the tempo of the artistes' routines or the horses' movements, or bring his players to silence at some moments of special daring. Today bands have unfortunately disappeared from all but the largest circuses, driven out by recorded music and union-imposed fees for musicians, but some small circuses do keep the spirit of live music with an electric organ or with a drum and cymbals.

At the beginning of each act in a good quality circus, the male members of the company who were not required in it would line the entrance to the ring, wearing a special uniform – perhaps a gilt-buttoned tunic and gold-striped trousers – to act as a kind of guard of honour for the artistes making their entrance. This is a feature that has quite disappeared from present-day circuses, but circus artistes are still expected – and readily agree – in the time-honoured phrase, "to make themselves useful", and circuses still advertise for "useful people" today. There are no trade union demarcation disputes within a circus tent.

When not in work, circus artistes, with actors and music hall performers, tended to congregate in the area of London along the south side of the river between Waterloo Road and Vauxhall Bridge. Here, too, were to be found the equestrian and theatrical agents, like Martini, the man-monkey before retirement, Roberts, and Maynard, who came to fill an important link between the performers and the managers.

A key member of any travelling circus was – and is – the advance agent. He was responsible for booking a field for the tent, ordering horse meat, hay and other food for the animals, straw for litter, and for supervising the bill posters. The billing of circuses developed into quite an industry; early posters were similar in style to theatre playbills, though they were often illustrated with crude but wonderfully effective woodcuts; with the development of colour lithography from the 1870s a new era opened. The big shows had their own designs, and firms like Stafford of Netherfield and Allen of Belfast provided a wide range of ready-printed colour-lithographed posters of circus subjects, on which individual shows needed only to add the place and date of performance. Stafford's catalogue of 1894, for example, offered a choice from 166 posters, ten slip bills, and seven window bills, ranging from pictures of "a performing bull with legs outstretched and balancing on his head his keeper seated on a chair", in three colours 22 by 35 inches, to a circus interior flanked by lions performing on one side and elephants performing on the other, in four colours, the three posters put together making an 8-sheet streamer 306 by 60 inches. It was the use of stock posters like these that gave the Circus a well-deserved reputation for advertising acts that never appeared in the ring!

Another of the advance agent's duties was to book lodgings for the principal artistes. The proprietors of travelling circuses had acquired handsome living-carriages by mid-century, and tentmen and minor employees must have often dossed down in the straw, but throughout the nineteenth century most circus artistes seem to have stayed in digs in the towns they visited. The idea of each family of performers having its own living caravan which travelled with the circus had been introduced by the 1870s, but it does not seem to have become general until the advent of motor transport and the growth of a commercial caravan industry. It is important to remember that circus artistes were not gipsies, and did not live like them; their way of life was closer to that of strolling actors.

A duty of either the advance agent or of the proprietor himself was to try to secure the patronage of the most important gentleman of the district. If he agreed to bring a party, this would be proudly stated in the bills. Alternatively the patronage of the colonel and officers of a regiment that was stationed in the locality might be obtained, as for instance by Quaglieni's Italian Cirque at Sheffield in 1868. This soliciting of "a bespeak" had been a feature of the life of strolling players in the eighteenth century and earlier; it was not confined to the travelling circuses, and circuses as permanent and important as Cooke's in Edinburgh in the 'forties were proud to announce the patronage of the Lord Provost and the magistrates.

The circus proprietor's nightmare was to find that he was following close after the passage of another show through the same area. Everyone had seen "the circus", and they didn't want, or couldn't afford, to see another. For this reason proprietors kept their advance routes secret, and still do. It makes the task of a circus enthusiast trying to see tenting shows very difficult! If a clash seemed inevitable a good deal of skullduggery went on in the nineteenth century: once two menageries fought a pitched battle on the high road; sometimes a circus would paste its own bills over its rival's; or the marks left on the roadside by one circus's advance wagon to indicate the route to the next site would be turned round by its rival, so that the bulk of the transport went off in the wrong direction. It was a hard and sometimes an unscrupulous profession.

Another danger was an attack by village rowdies. In some areas the circus was regarded as fair game by any gang of toughs spoiling for a fight. Tent ropes would be cut, canvas slashed, and even wagons overturned. Time and again the circus people had to defend

The horse-drawn circus and menagerie wagons move to the next tober.

their livelihood and their homes with fists and iron staves; and it must be said that they usually gave as good as they got.[3]

Circuses were, of course, transported by horse wagons, but as early as 1859 an American circus proprietor, James Myers, who was touring in England, is said to have bought an agricultural Bray steam traction engine for pulling some of his loads, and to have decorated it with carved wood and bright paintwork, creating a style in showland decoration that has survived to this day.[4] These road locomotives came to be used quite extensively by fairground and circus proprietors, pulling trains of seven or more wagons slowly but powerfully along the roads;[5] I can well remember, as a boy, gazing with fascination as these monsters made their way down the Hertfordshire lanes in the early 1920s. Occasionally elephants lent a hand in pulling a wagon out of a muddy field.

A small travelling circus making one-day stands in the nineteenth century might move only some twelve miles each day. It would be on the move by six in the morning at the latest and would aim to arrive at its new site by nine. Here stakes were driven in, the centre or king pole erected, the canvas pieces laced together and hauled up round it, "quarter poles" placed to hold the tent out, and by midday all should be ready, with a dressing tent, a mess tent and stable tents erected at "the backyard", and a ticket wagon in position at the front. At about one o'clock the parade took place, with every performer and attendant required to dress up in costume and ride a horse in a grand procession through the streets, preceded by the band in a special wagon and interspersed with the menagerie animals in cages when they could not be allowed to walk. In 1835 Ducrow mounted, in Hull, one of the earliest street parades to have been recorded.[6] By 1846 Hughes's Mammoth Equestrian Establishment was mounting a particularly impressive parade with fifty horses, of which thirty-two were driven in hand, the Sacred Egyptian Dragon Chariot pulled by four camels, and the Burmese Imperial Carriage and Throne pulled by two elephants. These had been designed by Wallett, the Shakespearean Jester, who had had some experience as an artist and carver when he worked for a time with Maffey, the French marionette showman, and later with Calver.[7] He reckoned that they were "the first and best ornamental carriages that ever travelled with circus tents". The Egyptian Dragon Chariot cost £750, a great sum of money in those days.

These parades grew more and more elaborate as the century went on, with elaborately carved and finely gilded wagons carrying tableaux of allegorical characters depicting themes like Victory, Peace or Plenty.

In George Sanger's parade there was a three-tier tableau of Britannia, depicted by Mrs Sanger holding a shield and trident, attended by a Life Guard in glittering cuirass and white-plumed helmet, while at her feet lay a full-grown lion and a lamb.[8]

The parade made its way back to the tent, where the afternoon performance was due to begin, hopefully drawing most of the crowd after it. Between the performances the artistes would eat in messes of six or seven people each, which were given fancy names. The proprietor's mess was often called "the Rumcull". Then the evening performance, rather longer than that of the afternoon, and as soon as it was over the gear had to be packed, the tent taken down, and all made ready for an early start the next morning.[9]

In return for his work the performer might expect to be paid something between one and three pounds a week in a small circus in mid-nineteenth-century England. This was better than actors got in small strolling companies, and circus artistes regarded themselves as somewhat superior to humble barnstormers. In a good but tight-fisted family circus like Powell and Clarke's or Cooke's the leading artistes might not earn more than £6 a week;[10] Tom Barry, the clown at Astley's, got £10 a week in the 'fifties, but less rated performers were poorly paid, "I reckon Astley's is the worst money for any man", was the opinion of one performer, "if a fellow wants to be finished up, let him go there."[11] American proprietors paid better and Wallett earned £20 a week, with a carriage and horse thrown in, with Van Amburgh. Occasional stars could command much higher salaries. Tom Sayers, the boxer, was paid £55 a week for appearing with Howes and Cushing's American Circus in 1861, after his fight with Heenan had made his name a household word. In the same year Léotard was paid £180 a week at the Alhambra, but that was in a music hall not a circus. The best talent was being attracted away from circuses to the music halls all through the last quarter of the century.

The performers in circuses could often hope for a benefit; in circuses this sometimes merely meant that the artiste could keep the value of any tickets he sold personally. As with a bespeak, eminent patrons were solicited to support such evenings, and we find, for instance, that Mr Alfred Norton, manager of Ginnett's Circus at Portsmouth, was able to secure the presence at his benefit of, among others, H.R.H. Prince Edward of Saxe-Weimar and the Superintendent of H.M. Dockyard.

The taking of benefits was the usual practice in the theatre of the time, and there are many references to it in circuses up to at least the 'eighties. The latest that I have noted in England was at Sanger's Circus at Reading in 1885, but as late as 1919 Bostock's Royal Italian Circus gave a benefit at Shanghai for its clown, Little Spuds, and as recently as 1978 a benefit performance was staged by Circus Courtney in Dublin for the widow and children of Gordon Howes, a lion trainer who had been killed by his animals. This custom is a further indication that the world of the Circus and its artistes in nineteenth-century England was not quite the self-contained community into which it has later developed, but all part and parcel of that larger community of actors and performers in every type of entertainment. As in ancient Greece and in medieval Europe and in the eighteenth-century fairs, they were all just players.

Hughes paraded the streets in a Burmese Imperial Carriage pulled by two elephants in 1845.

17
The American Invasion

THE CIRCUS is an international art. The foreign names that have already spattered these pages are evidence of the flow of artistes from all over Europe who came to England to perform in English circuses during the nineteenth century. We have seen that Astley had put a German tumbler in his programme as early as 1768; Italian and Spanish acrobats were on the bill in 1773; by 1847, for example, the programme at the Amphitheatre included a Belgian juggler, a German voltigeur, a Dutch equilibrist, a Polish equestrian, a French equestrienne, and "an African Wonder". The greatest circuses of Europe provided acts for English audiences: in 1860 the Astley's programme included performers from the Franconi Circus and the Cirque Impériale in Paris, Circus Renz and Circus Wollschläger in Berlin, and the Imperial Circus in St Petersburg. At the same time English circus artistes were performing all over Europe.

But there was one country that was pre-eminent in the quantity and quality of the performers it supplied to English circuses. It may surprise many people to know that this was the United States of America. The Circus had been brought to America by English performers. Now the debt was repaid with interest.

The first Americans to appear in an English circus ring were two Indian Chiefs from the Catabaw nation, whom Astley introduced into the programme at the Amphitheatre in 1796. They were dressed in real Indian habits and performed a variety of exercises with tomahawks and the Indian bow and arrow, together with renderings of a war dance and song. Perhaps this was hardly a display of circus skill, but the next American performer was also almost certainly an original native of the continent, for in 1806 "the youthful Indian" was displaying horsemanship in

Saunders's company at Birmingham; another Indian Youth, nine years of age, was performing on horseback in Powell's company in 1822; six years later a "Flying Indian" was performing on the slack rope at Astley's. I think that these must all have been American Indians, not Asian Indians; Asian Indians have displayed great skill in juggling, but they have never been noted for dexterity in other circus arts.

In 1822 a man who was certainly an American Indian appeared at Astley's; he was Juan Bellinck, described as "the American Indian prodigy and flying rope vaulter", who had already made a reputation for himself and his "sable family" in Europe, where he was known as Le Diable Superbe. He performed on a rope stretched at a height of 100 ft from one side of the theatre to the other. For a special performance he put on a double act with Il Diavolo Antonio, who had been involved in that fight with J. B. Booth the previous year. All rope dancers liked to call themselves "the Devil" something or other.

The first white American circus artiste to cross the Atlantic appears to have been a woman, for in 1816 a "profesora americana" appeared as an equestrienne with William Southby's company that was then touring Spain.[1] The first American to receive star billing appeared at Astley's in 1819; he was Mr Blackmore, usually described simply as "the young American", but there is some doubt about his American provenance though he came to England from performing in America as he may have been playing at the Royal Circus as a youth in 1803.[2] In Birmingham he ascended on the rope from the stage to the gallery, blindfolded and tied in a sack. One must reluctantly guess that he made use of an old circus trick by slipping the bandage off his eyes when he put the sack over his head, and pulling it on again when he lifted the sack off; the

Young Hernandez, as portrayed in 1849. The artist probably exaggerated his youthfulness.

sack of rough hessian or other coarse weave allows the performer to see through it fairly clearly. Blackmore also rode with his head on the neck of a quart bottle. He was still performing in various provincial circuses in 1829.

In 1830 "the celebrated American rider", Benjamin Stickney, appeared at Astley's, and remained in Ducrow's company for the next fourteen years or so, specializing in character acts ranging from the Youth of Olympus to Jim Crow and his Grandmother. He toured Germany with the company Hillier took over after Ducrow's death. Stickney was the first of the great American equestrians to demonstrate their skills across the Atlantic. He was followed by "the American wonder of grace and activity", Levi J. North, who was vaulting in Ryan's circuses between 1838 and 1840. The lion trainers, Van Amburgh and Carter, arrived in 1838 and 1839, and the sensational gymnasts, Professor Risley and sons, in 1843. I have already described their acts, and the impact they made on the English Circus. In 1849 perhaps the greatest American rider of all, young Hernandez, appeared at Astley's. He was said to be "scarcely fourteen years of age", and the English press raved about his performance. There was nothing very sensational about the feats he achieved: he sprang from the horse's back while standing and kneeling; he skipped with a small hoop or riding whip, passing it three or four times round his body in one leap; he leaped over flags spread three abreast, nearly 9 ft in breadth, facing both front and back; he stood on one foot, with the other in his hand and on his head. But it was the manner in which he

presented it that made his performance so remarkable. Every feat was cleanly and successfully accomplished at the first attempt – something quite unusual with riders at that time. And he did it all "with a beautiful smile upon his countenance ... and a singular gracefulness. ... All that we have seen achieved by Ducrow ... are transcended by Hernandez ... undoubtedly the greatest living equestrian. ... What Cerito is as a dancer, he is as a rider." In those days there were critics capable of appreciating the *style* of a circus performance! Hernandez was last seen in England in 1885 at the Internationale Cirque at Covent Garden and at Hengler's.

An equestrian more noted for his acrobatics than for his grace was "the champion American somersault rider", Frank Pastor, who first appeared at Astley's in 1857, and was back at the Holborn Amphitheatre in 1868.

These are, of course, only a few of the individual American artistes who worked in English circuses in the nineteenth century. We have met the names of many more already in this story. There were riders like Thomas McCollum who opened the Holborn Amphitheatre in 1867, and women riders like Lizzie Keyes in 1875, vaulters like E. O. Dale in 1843, jugglers like Master Belong in 1826, contortionists like Manuel Woodson in 1894, equilibrists like W. Roberts in 1894, aerial voltigeuses like Ella Stoke in 1852, flying trapezists like the Senyahs in the 1860s, gladiators and living statues like Robert and William Gilfort in 1878, Risley acrobats like Professor Conrad and sons in 1875, clowns like W. H. Dodd in 1853, and black-faced banjo minstrels like E. R. Harper in 1845.

The greatest impact of the American Circus upon England, however, came not from the individual performers but from complete American circuses visiting the country. The first of these to tour England was brought by Richard Sands in 1842; we have already seen how he was the first person to introduce the use of a tent for a major circus in England; he also introduced a parade of "twenty-five caparisoned horses" and a brass band in a carriage drawn by ten horses driven in hand; these were small enough features by later standards, but they were apparently original innovations at the time. His company included Camille Leroux and L. J. North; in 1843 he joined with Isaac Van Amburgh to put on a show at the Lyceum, and they then presented a combined circus and menagerie which toured for a year or so before they split up and returned to the United States.

The next American circus to tour England was that of Madame Macarte, "late of the Grand Circus, New York", who went into partnership with Richard Bell, "the greatest horseman in Europe"; their company included Madame Isabelle, of Franconi's Circus, and Tom Barry, the clown from Astley's. In their parade Mr Samwell drove a coach pulled by twenty horses in hand – again, something that was to be exceeded later but a sensational achievement for its day. There are references to this circus touring between 1850 and 1861. Although it was billed as Macarte's American Circus I do not think that this was a complete American company, but rather a troupe made up on the European side. Madame Macarte's name was originally Macarthy and some American sources refer to her as "the English equestrienne".

In 1851 a joint American–French equestrian company was formed under the direction of Thomas McCollum, which presented a three-month season at Drury Lane. The American star was Eaton Stone, a brilliant bareback rider, and the French stars were the graceful Caroline Loyo and Baptiste Loisset. The

equestrian acts were varied with a strong man, a contortionist, and Chinese bell ringers.

The next year Hernandez went into partnership with Eaton Stone and Welch. Hernandez was billed as the star performer; Stone, "who had the wild Indians for his tutors", presented the Wild Horse of the Prairies; and the company they gathered included Arthur Barnes, "champion vaulter of the world"; James and Pauline Newsome, the excellent English riders; and George Ryland, juggling on horseback. They toured the West Country, the Midlands and the North, and in 1853 put on a programme at Drury Lane. The show seems to have split up after this; I think it, too, must have been an *ad hoc* company, formed from artistes who were available in England at the time.

Among the artistes in the Hernandez–Stone company was Little Ella, described, in typical circus hyperbole, as "the American Wonder . . . the most

ELLA

Ella, as she appeared in 1857. Mystery still surrounds "her" sex. "She" was probably male, but possibly a true hermaphrodite.

accomplished Female Equestrian in the World". She made such an impression that she headed an American and Continental Troupe at Drury Lane in 1857, where she was starred alongside the Shakespearean clown, W. F. Wallett. She was then said to be seventeen years old, a Creole born in Louisiana, who had appeared to rapturous applause in Berlin, Vienna and Turin since her previous London engagement. She leaped through fifty or sixty papered hoops in succession with a display of stamina that was unique for a girl rider. No wonder! "She" was later revealed to be a man, though it is now thought that she was actually a true hermaphrodite.

The biggest American circus yet to visit England arrived at Liverpool in 1857. This was Howes and Cushing's Great United States Circus. The company included Rose Madigan, "sylphide of the ring"; James Madigan, "vaulting, riding, daring acts"; David Richards, "wild rider of the Prairies"; James Robinson, "somersaults upon a naked horse"; George Bachelder, "wondrous leaping star"; Frank Rosston, with "high trained Indian horse"; Murray and Holland, gymnasts; Joe Pentland, "Yankee fun"; Jem Myers, "clown of clowns"; the Bedouin race, "agile and active"; a Tribe of Red Men, "Nature's untaught child"; and the mules, Pete and Barney.

In 1858 and again in 1859 they put on strong programmes at the newly-opened Alhambra in London's Leicester Square, and they toured the country until 1864, returning for a second visit in 1870. At one time they apparently split into four separate units. It was a really big show; the parade seemed to go on for ever, with J. P. Paul driving a musical chariot, or Apollonicon, pulled by forty cream horses driven in hand. This was actually an organ, decorated with paintings of the landing of Columbus on the western shores and a buffalo hunt.

The show's programme was refreshed from time to time with new talent from the United States. One of these was Dan Castello, a leaper, equestrian, animal trainer and clown, who had a great reputation in America and arrived in England in 1859. One of the acts he showed in England was a bison, which he "played" in the manner of a bull fighter. In Sheffield the animal tossed and gored him. Castello recovered, but the bison was taken out of the bill.[3]

The English circus proprietors liked to make out that they could out-match these invaders. Hengler's Circus was resident in Liverpool when Howes and Cushing arrived, but despite all the bally-hoo the local press considered that Hengler's had a far superior show.[4] During their second English tour Howes and Cushing had a clash of dates with Sanger; Sanger's advance agent placarded the towns the Americans

were visiting with his own bills as if he was coming the day after; most of the public waited to see the second show; then he got ahead of the Americans and scooped the market before they realized what was happening. At least, that was Sanger's version of what happened.[5] The truth of the matter is, I think, that Howes and Cushing helped British circus proprietors to think big. It was their competition that shook English circuses out of their reliance upon the traditional mixture of riding acts and acrobatics that had made up their programmes for so long, and forced them to bring elephants, lions and other big cat acts into the ring.

The next American circus was that of James Myers. He is said to have arrived in England in 1851, and to have worked with Howes and Cushing for a time as the "clown of clowns".[6] He set up his own show some time in the late 'fifties, and we have seen that he was enterprising enough to obtain a steam road locomotive for it; there are references to him touring round England during the 'sixties; he was touring in Germany in the 'seventies, played in Paris, and was the first American circus to visit Europe. In England he showed his circus for the most part in the large multi-purpose exhibition halls that were being built at this time, like the Crystal Palace at Sydenham and the Agricultural Hall in Islington, and he engaged some good performers like John Cooper with his lions and elephants, and the Madigans – one of whom he married – in a chariot race. This was another example of an American proprietor forming his circus company in Europe. Myers sold up in 1882.

Robert Stickney with James Robinson came to London in 1867 with the Great American Circus, that had been formed by the Flatfoots to play at the Exposition Universelle in Paris. They put on a season at the recently opened Holborn Amphitheatre. Stickney threw a double somersault from a battoute, and Robinson rode standing on horseback with the tiny Robinson junior standing on his head while they jumped through balloons together.

And finally, at the end of the century, Barnum and Bailey's Greatest Show on Earth came to London to play in the new hall at Olympia in 1889. More than just a circus, with a menagerie, a display of human and animal freaks, as well as three rings and two raised stages in the circus proper, this was the ultimate in American showmanship. They brought 450 performers, 300 horses, 21 elephants, 32 cages, and 35 parade and baggage wagons; and a vast spectacle entitled *Nero*, employing 1,200 in the cast, was mounted by Imre Kiralfy. Unfortunately the authorities in London would not allow the huge parade to drive through the streets, so the great wagons and

Howes and Cushing's American Circus at the Alhambra in 1858.

some 200 horses to pull them had been brought over for nothing. Barnum managed the publicity with his usual genius; the circus was launched with a banquet attended by much of London's high society – Lord Kilmorey presided, and the guests included Lord Randolph Churchill and Lord Charles Beresford. This was a stunt to be repeated by Bertram Mills in later years. The Prince of Wales came to see the show, and the Olympia season played to packed houses for three months.[7]

In 1897 Barnum and Bailey (though Barnum was dead by this time) came to England again for an extensive tenting tour. Winter quarters were built at Stoke on Trent, and a seventy-car circus train was ordered from the railway company. No circus had ever travelled by train in England before, and the 60-ft-long trucks needed were something quite new on British railways. The Americans were somewhat contemptuous of the slowness of the British workmen and of the inadequacy of the English food, but they put their own men in as job overseers, and with a good deal of American drive and hustle the work was completed in time.

The show ran in a transformed Olympia, seating 10,000 people, for three months, and in the spring of 1898 it set out on a tenting tour that was to take it as far as Scotland. Despite the rain and mud of an English summer, the vast tent and equipment was successfully moved, with 840 people, 420 horses and 105 wagons. Parades were held almost everywhere; the procession was three miles long, with five big band wagons, scores of animal dens, hundreds of mounted riders, twenty elephants, and a steam calliope; it took twenty minutes to pass any given spot, and blocked all traffic for the best part of an hour. The biggest band wagon, the Columbia and Four Seasons, was pulled by forty horses driven in hand by Jake Posey.

Barnum and Bailey met with such success in England that they set up a special British limited company, Barnum and Bailey Ltd, which declared a ten per cent dividend for the first half year. After another Christmas season at Olympia, the show set out on its second tenting season, including the South and West Country. Success was again phenomenal; the tenting complex, with its associated attractions, could accommodate something like 11,000 people at a time; excursion trains, with circus entrance combined with the rail fare, were arranged to draw people in from surrounding areas, and when they played at a small town like Llandudno, for instance, which by itself could not justify the visit of such a large outfit, 15,000 people were brought into the town on sixty-two special excursion trains.

After a winter lay-off, the Greatest Show on Earth embarked at Liverpool in 1900 for a tour of Europe that was to occupy it for the next two years. All England had now seen the biggest circus that America had to offer. There has never been another opportunity.

This American invasion of the English Circus had brought some fine performers and had introduced some impressive feats of skill and organization. The first major use of a tent for a travelling circus in England was by an American show, Richard Sands; the first major circus parade seems to have been by this show, too; the first circus to use a road locomotive was the American, James Myers; the first circus to travel by train was the American, Barnum and Bailey; it was an American, Levi North, who first threw a somersault on horseback; it was an American, Richard Risley, who first trained a boy to throw a somersault from his feet in the Icarian Games; it was an American, John Holtum, who first caught a cannon ball fired from a gun; it was the Americans, Lauck and Livingston, who first introduced the triple horizontal bars; it was an American, Keyes Washington, who first made possible a head stand on the swinging trapeze; it was an American, Isaac Van Amburgh, who first developed lion training into something like a scientific display of skill; it was the Americans, Howes and Cushing, who first introduced unrideable mules; it was an American, Dan Castello, who first trained a bull to appear in the ring; it was an American, J. Rosco, who first presented performing (as opposed to learned) pigs.

All this is not to belittle the contribution of English performers and circus proprietors. It was an Englishman, George Sanger, who first put three rings in a circus in 1860; it was an Englishman, Hughes, who first used carved and gilded wagons in a circus parade in 1845; it was an Englishman, Philip Astley, who first successfully combined horse acts with acrobatics to create the modern Circus; it was an Englishman who first took a circus to America; it was an Englishman who first presented displays of trick riding there.

Each country competed with and complemented the achievements of the other. By the end of the nineteenth century every element of what we now recognize as Circus had been introduced into the ring. Improvements lay ahead, but no fundamental changes. It is time to shift our gaze to the other side of the Atlantic to see how the Circus had developed in the United States.

Opposite: Ringling is the greatest name in the American Circus. A poster of 1895.

IV
THE CIRCUS IN AMERICA

18
The Beginnings

THE ELEMENTS that were brought together to form the Circus in Europe may be found, also, in America. From early in the eighteenth century the hard conditions of the early settlers were increasingly alleviated by the entertainments offered by showmen of all kinds – acrobats, puppeteers, actors, animal exhibitors, and so on.[1]

In 1724 a troupe of rope dancers was performing in Philadelphia with an act in every way similar to what was being presented in the fairs of London and Paris at that time, with a woman dancing on the rope with baskets and iron fetters on her feet, wheeling a wheelbarrow, and spinning with swords, accompanied by the clowning of a Pickle Herring. In 1753 in New York a recent apprentice of the Grand Turk, Anthony Dugee, was swinging, juggling, and balancing on the slack wire as well as on the tight rope; this was only three years after Mahomet Caratha had introduced the wire into England. Dugee's wife also appeared on the bill as the Female Sampson; and it is of some interest that a Negro boy and an Indian assisted him in his performance. It will be recalled that American Indians appeared as tight and slack rope performers in the early English circuses.

Among other troupes, Alexandre Placide and Paul Redigé, whom we have already met in Paris and London, brought a company of tumblers and rope dancers to Boston and Salem in 1792. Their visit had an unfortunate influence upon the children of New England, who tried to emulate their feats while balancing on fences, but invariably slipped down, "wounding themselves in every quarter".

Exhibitors of animals appeared early on the American scene, from the first lion imported in 1716 to the first elephant in 1796. Some of these were trained to perform tricks, and we read of a performing monkey in 1751, performing canaries and dogs in 1788, and a learned pig in 1798. Most of these animals, however, were simply exhibited as curiosities in themselves, and from 1781 travelling menageries began to be formed; these developed into quite considerable undertakings, culminating in the establishment of the Zoological Institute, founded by June, Titus and Angevine, which acquired permanent winter quarters in the Bowery, New York, in about 1820.

Jacob Bates was exhibiting trick horsemanship in America in 1772 and 1773.

An important step towards the creation of the Circus came from exhibitions of trick riding. As we have seen, Charles Hughes claimed that he visited America in 1770, though no records of this visit have yet been found. In 1771 Mr Faulks, who claimed that he had performed before royalty and nobility in Great Britain, was exhibiting horsemanship in Philadelphia and in New York; and in the same year John Sharp, late from England, was in Boston and Salem; their feats were very similar to those of Johnson, Price and Sampson, who were performing in London at the same time; they rode standing on two or three horses, vaulting over a single horse while at full speed, and so on. Jacob Bates was performing in Philadelphia in 1772 and in New York in 1773; he introduced, for the first time in America, "the burlesque on horsemanship, or The Taylor riding to Brentford", which had been invented by Astley five years earlier. In 1785 Mr Pool was exhibiting horsemanship, enlivened with the antics of a clown, in Baltimore, Boston and Philadelphia; the next year he was in New York and in 1787 in Georgia. His clowning included an adaptation of the familiar equestrian burlesque as "The Taylor Humorously Riding to New York" – John Wilkes was quite forgotten! Mr Pool described himself as "the first American that ever exhibited the following feats of horsemanship on the Continent", meaning the continent of America; but Pool, too, was English in origin, for he had been exhibiting his feats in the Windward Islands and Jamaica between 1774 and 1784, when he was described in the local records as "le Sieur Pool, Anglais". Ten years' residence in the West Indies, and an eye for what would sound well in a newly independent country, no doubt suggested a change of nationality.[2]

Shows and exhibitions of all kinds had suffered during the Revolution and they were formally forbidden by an Act of Congress in 1774. After the end of the War of Independence a new period of peace and stability was ushered in by the first elections under the new Constitution in 1788; life could begin to resume its normal pattern, and entertainments could again play their part in the life of the people. America was ready for its first circus.

19

The First Circus

IN 1792 JOHN BILL RICKETTS opened a riding school in Philadelphia at the corner of Twelfth and Market Streets. During the next few years he presented his "equestrian exercises" in the chief cities all down the eastern seabord: at New York in 1793, at Charleston and Baltimore in 1794, and at Boston and Hartford in 1795.[1]

Ricketts had served his time as an apprentice with Charles Hughes at his Riding School by Blackfriars Bridge in London; he had shown himself "the first rider of eminence" at Jones's Equestrian Amphitheatre in Whitechapel;[2] and in 1790 he had joined the company at the Equestrian Circus in Edinburgh. Now from Scotland he came to try his luck across the Atlantic. His portrait by Gilbert Stuart, in the National Gallery at Washington, shows a strikingly handsome young man, with curly hair parted in the centre, gazing steadily from the unfinished canvas at the New World he had come to conquer.

The performance he presented owed a great deal to his British origins. At New York in 1793 he leaped from his knees on horseback over a garter 12 ft high, threw a somersault from the horse at full speed to alight on his feet, and presented a young pupil as the Flying Mercury – that is, a two-high classical pose on horseback, many years before Ducrow was performing a similar act. He also introduced some of the semi-dramatic equestrian acts from the English repertoire: the Peasant's Frolic – which is actually the earliest reference to this act that I have noted – with a complete change of clothes, concluding with a hornpipe on horseback; and our old favourite, the Tailor's journey to Brentford.[3] Both were to remain popular in America for many years; the Peasant's Frolic came to be known as the Canadian Peasant or the Pete Jenkins act.

This was not all, however. In the same programme he threw a somersault – certainly from a springboard – over thirty men's heads and over six horses; one of his company presented the polander's tricks, including drinking a glass of wine while hanging upside down; and Mr McDonald, the clown, performed a row of flip-flaps with his feet tied together.

In subsequent years Ricketts was picking up four handkerchiefs from the ground at full speed, and rode blindfold in a sack, emerging in a totally different costume and sex – the old act of the Metamorphosis of a Sack. His horse, Cornplanter, purchased in New York in 1794, ungirthed its saddle and picked up a hidden handkerchief. Signor Spinacuta, who had been a famous rope dancer and animal trainer in the French fairs and at London, joined Ricketts in 1793 as a rope dancer and clown to the tumbling.

With this mixture of equestrianism, acrobatics, rope dancing and clowning the Circus had indeed arrived in America. It received high patronage; President Washington visited it in Philadelphia and sold Ricketts one of his horses.

As in England, these circuses were presented in permanent, if hastily constructed, buildings. The first structure in Philadelphia was replaced in 1795 by the Pantheon, or Ricketts' Amphitheatre, in Chestnut Street. This was built like a huge circular tent of wood, 97 ft in diameter, with white walls, straight for 18 ft and then slanting upwards to a conical roof 50 ft high. It included a stage and seated 600 to 700 persons.[4] In New York Ricketts erected various amphitheatres in Greenwich Street and the southern end of Broadway, in 1797 incorporating a coffee house in the amenities of his New Amphitheatre. The site of this, Ricketts' most ambitious circus building in New York, must lie at the southern tip of Manhattan, just by the exit of the Brooklyn–Battery tunnel today. The entertainments of Broadway have now moved more up-town, but even in the eighteenth century Broadway was a main street for the location of theatres and circuses.

Stage performances came to play an increasing part in the programmes, as was the case in England. At first these were slight sketches in the eighteenth-century pantomime tradition, with titles like *Harlequin Statue, Vulcan's Gift*, or *The Triumph of Virtue, or Harlequin in Philadelphia* (it became *Harlequin in New York*, with appropriate scenery of the local townscape, in New York); later ballets, dances, shadow shows, and various kinds of burlettas were added to the bills, including a piece entitled *The Independence of America, or the ever memorable Fourth of July, 1776*.

Ricketts had come to America accompanied by his brother, Francis, and perhaps one or two horses, but apparently with no regular company of his own. He was anxious to recruit performers, and in Philadelphia he saw an artiste called John Durang performing on the tight rope and slack wire, whom he invited to join his company; two years later Durang took the offer up for a salary of 25 dollars a week plus a benefit in

This romantic engraving of John Bill Ricketts indicates the esteem in which he was held in America.

each town visited. In later years Durang wrote a fascinating account of his life and of his experiences with Ricketts' circus.[5]

By this time other performers had joined the company: Mr Sully, from a family well known in Charleston theatricals; Mr Franklin, a noted equestrian and clown from the Royal Circus in London; and others. By 1795 the small troupe of four or five artistes with which Ricketts had commenced his performances had grown to seventeen, of whom seven performed in the horsemanship in the ring, plus two painters, two carpenters, and an orchestra. This was really too large to be economic, and Ricketts himself seems to have realised "that an equestrian performance blended with dramatic performance would never agree. . . . The public's taste is only to be gratified to see dramatic performances at a regular theatre. . . . A circus within its own sphere, well regulated . . . must succeed and please." This is a lesson that the American Circus learned long before the Circus in England and Europe.

Consequently Ricketts cut his company down and split it into two. In 1797 Francis, with three performers and seven horses, went off to Lancaster and Baltimore, where he went broke and had to sell the horses; John, with four performers, set out for Canada. At Albany they built a temporary circus in a week, with the boxes on one side of the ring under cover and the pit on the other side open to the sky. They moved on to Montreal, where their success was so great that Ricketts decided to stay for the winter. He built a more permanent circus of stone, with a roof and skylights over the ring, a circle of boxes, and the pit beneath them. The orchestra was placed over the entrance to the ring. The interior was gaily painted with the dome in light blue, cupids bearing garlands of roses round the circle, and the boxes rose pink with white panels and festooned with blue curtains; the ring fence was painted to represent posts linked with gold chains. At Albany there had been a portable stage that could be moved into the ring, but at Montreal this was a fixture, with a curtain, stage doors and scenery.[6]

From here they moved on to Quebec, where they played for two months, and then retraced their steps to Philadelphia.

Durang has left a good account of what he performed during this Canadian tour. "My business was the Clown on foot and horseback, and obliged to furnish all the jokes for the ring, and to ride the Tailor to Brentford, with the dialogue which I was obliged to speak in French, German and English (the principal inhabitants are French, a great many Germans, a few merchants and British soldiers English). I rode the foxhunter, leaping over the bar with the mounting and dismounting in full speed, taking a flying leap on horseback through a paper sun, in character of a drunken man on horseback, tied in a sack standing on two horses while I changed to woman's clothes; rode in full speed standing on two horses, Mr Ricketts at the same time standing on my shoulders, with Master Hutchins at the same time standing in the attitude of Mercury on Mr Ricketts' shoulders forming a pyramid. I performed the drunken soldier on horseback, still vaulted, I danced on the stage, I was the Harlequin in the pantomimes, occasionally I sang a comic song. I tumbled on the slack rope and performed on the slack wire. I introduced mechanical exhibitions in machinery and transparencies. I produced exhibitions of fireworks. In short I was performer, machinist, painter, designer, music compiler, the bill maker, and treasurer."

This account tells us a great deal about the nature of circus acts at that time. The Foxhunter act, which I have not seen recorded in England before the time of Ducrow, was here being presented in America in about 1797, only four years after Ducrow had been born. The paper sun was, of course, the same as the balloons which were popular everywhere. The Flying Mercury act is the earliest three-high on horseback that I have noted. The Tailor to Brentford and the Metamorphosis of a Sack remained popular old favourites; the earliest appearance of the latter that I have noted was in 1793, a year after Ricketts had left England. It must be older. The Drunken Soldier was

Ricketts' Circus in Philadelphia. A drawing by D. J. Kennedy in 1870, but based on an original of 1797.

a similar act to the Drunken Sailor that Hughes had originated, or to the Drunken Hussar that was being performed at Newcastle in 1822. It is interesting to see that both the rope and the wire were being used at the same time in this modest little show.

On his return to Philadelphia in 1799 Ricketts suffered the disaster of seeing his circus burnt down. A drunken carpenter left a lighted candle in his workshop, and a fire broke out during the display of horsemanship in the ring. They managed to save the horses, the scenery, the wardrobe, and even the proscenium of the stage, but the building was a total loss.

After this tragedy Ricketts moved to Baltimore, where he left Franklin to run a show which did not last long, and himself made a tour to the south as far as Georgetown, running up circuses in each town and usually selling the structure for half price when he left. It is typical of the shortage of material and the initiative of showmen in those days that when he ran out of paint, Durang found that he could make some kind of substitute by mixing charcoal with a local hard red chalk. On their return to Philadelphia Ricketts tried to perform in the roofless ring of Lailson's collapsed circus, but the candles provided only a feeble illumination for night performances. He lost heart for his American enterprise and decided to try his luck in the West Indies; perhaps he had heard of Pool's success there. In 1801 he set sail with his brother, one boy performer, a groom, a stable boy, and his horses, with sufficient lumber to build a circus at his destination.

He may have been making for Jamaica, but his ship was captured by a French privateer and taken as a prize to Guadeloupe in the Leeward Isles. Here he was lucky, for his groom (the same man whose carelessness had ruined him by setting his theatre on fire) managed to hide his silver-mounted sword and pistols beneath some horse manure; with the funds these realized, Ricketts persuaded a local merchant to buy the horses and circus equipment on his account. He performed with success here and in some of the other islands, but two of his company died of yellow fever, and Francis was jailed for deserting the native-born girl he had married. In about 1803 John Bill Ricketts felt he had had enough. He sold his horses for a good price and set sail for England. The ship foundered in the Atlantic and no one was saved.

That is the story of America's first circus proprietor.

A newspaper advertisement for Ricketts' first circus in Philadelphia, 1793.

POSITIVELY THE LAST NIGHT *of Mr. VILALLIAVE's Company, at* HATHAWAY'S
HALL, *on* MONDAY *evening next, the 17th of August, 1818.*

THE PERFORMANCE WILL COMMENCE BY THE

TIGHT ROPE,

WITH BALANCE POLE.

1st *Performer.*	The *Little Chinese.*
2d.	The *Young Spaniolet.*
3d.	The *Young Roman.*
4th.	Mrs. *Vilalliave.*
5th.	Mr. *Vilalliave.*
6th.	Mr. *Begodes*, in the character of a *CLOWN.*

Among the great variety of Feats which they will perform, Mr. VILALLIAVE will dance on the Rope

A GROTESQUE DANCE,

With a BASKET *tied to his Feet, and his Hands and Feet chained.*

THERE WILL LIKEWISE BE EXHIBITED,

The Dance of the Double Rope,

BY THREE PERSONS, *(as represented in the Plate above.)*

They will afterwards perform a great variety without the Balance Pole, too numerous to be inserted.

BENDING FEATS,

BY THE CHINESE AND YOUNG SPANIOLET.

TUMBLING,

BY THE COMPANY.

Strength of Hercules,

OR,

The Egyptian Pyramid;

Performed by Mr. VILALLIAVE.

The Publick are respectfully informed, that there will be no pains or exertion spared, to give a brilliant Exhibition.
₊ Doors open at half past 7, and the Performance to commence at 8 o'clock, precisely.
August 15, 1818.

Villalliave's company performed what may be the earliest two-high ever achieved on the tight rope.

20
Early Circuses

RICKETTS did not enjoy a monopoly of Circus for long. Indeed, the year before he arrived in North America a Spanish troupe of equestrians, vaulters and clowns had appeared in Mexico City.[1] Two years after Ricketts' arrival, in 1794, Thomas Swann announced an exhibition of horsemanship at the Circus, near the Battery, in New York, probably in Ricketts' Amphitheatre. This may represent the earliest use of the term "Circus" in America. The programme here included horsemanship by Miss Johnson, "a native of the city of New York" and so the first American equestrienne and, indeed, the first named American circus rider of either sex. Also on the programme was General Jacco, a monkey on the rope, who seems to have been the first animal other than a horse to appear in an American ring.[2] This had been the name of Astley's performing monkey ten years earlier.

Swann was probably the man who had had an Amphitheatre in Birmingham in 1787, and so another English immigrant. His season in New York cannot have been very successful, for he moved to Philadelphia where he ran an orthodox riding school for some years.

In 1796 an equestrian company of French riders and acrobats, headed by Philip Lailson, landed at Boston. They had been in Sweden a year or so previously. They were in New York the next year, by which time the company included the first named American male rider, Mr Langley, "the American equestrian" who threw "a lofty back somersault on a horse at full speed". One must assume that this was a somersault from the horse to the ground. The company also featured a Miss Venice, described as the first woman rider in America, a false claim unless it meant "the best in quality" rather than "the first in time". The programme also included a Grand Indian Dance. President Adams attended a performance.

American Indians are occasionally recorded on the circus bills at this time, but always in tribal-type dances or similar displays. It is curious that while American Indians appeared in several English circuses in the first quarter of the nineteenth century, there seems to be no record of them performing basic circus feats in American circuses. It may be that the Indians who appeared in England were, in fact, half-castes and that the presence of such performers did not call for any special notice in the United States.

Lailson went on to Philadelphia, where he erected an elegant circus and mounted some much-praised pantomimes; the show was noted for the brilliant trappings of the horses and the splendid wardrobe of the company, and they would ride in equestrian procession through the streets of Philadelphia to advertise the show. Sadly, the snow in winter lay heavily on the hemispherical dome of Lailson's circus and it fell in. It was on a Sunday and nobody was hurt, but his career in Philadelphia was ruined. He left for the West Indies.[3]

European circus artists were now flocking to America. Lailson was followed by another French company, who came on from a tour of Spain. It was directed by Pepin, who was a French Canadian by birth, and Breschard. They played the east coast towns from 1807; in 1810 the company split into two, and one group, with their star performer called Cayetano, was performing in New York in 1812. On this occasion an elephant made its first appearance in the ring of an American, or any, circus. The advertisement claimed that "it will draw a cork from a bottle, take an apple from his keeper's mouth, pick a handkerchief from a man's pocket and put it on his head, open his mouth at the word of command and show his teeth,

117

and smack a whip with ease". This show also boasted that its company included "Mrs Redon, being the first American lady that has ever attempted the art of horsemanship". Clearly Miss Johnson and Miss Venice were soon forgotten!

Another act featured by Pepin's company was a horse trained to stand still in the midst of a cascade of fireworks. This had been one of Astley's popular turns. As presented by Durang after Ricketts had left America, the rider wore a suit of armour, with a visor over his face, and the firework was actually fastened to the top of his helmet while the horse was galloping round the ring. The firework ended with a big bang, which so frightened the horse that it jumped over three benches of the pit and threw Durang off. He was not seriously hurt, but he gave up circus performances after that.

In 1814 Mr Vilalliave's company appeared in New York and was about, usually in halls, for the next fifteen years. Its main strength was in rope dancing, and they presented a dance on the double rope which differed from the double tight rope acts being performed in England at that time in that only one rope was used, two performers stood on it with a bar linking their shoulders, and a third artiste balanced on the bar. I have not seen any earlier reference to this feat, which later became a feature of several high-wire acts.[4]

In 1816 a complete troupe of riders and horses from England, directed by James West, arrived in America and performed with success in the towns of New England. The company included Mr Blackmore, who was to star at Astley's two years later. In New York in 1822 the clown in this show, Mr Williams, leaped over a stage wagon with six horses, and over an elephant and a camel. This was hardly a performing camel, but it does seem to be the first camel to appear in a circus ring.

James West had appeared at Astley's in 1801 before forming his own troupe. In 1814 he had supplied the equestrian company when the Royal Circus briefly resumed circus performances. In 1822 he sold his American interests and returned to England. He came back from America a rich man,[5] and went into partnership with Ducrow at Astley's in 1825.

The purchasers of West's outfit were the theatre managers, Price and Simpson, who engaged Mr Hunter, the Yorkshire phenomenon from Astley's, with his bareback riding act; he was billed as the first man to ride a horse "in the rude state of nature". In 1826 he was playing in Hartford, Connecticut, when he was prosecuted for breaking the state's anti-Circus law, which had been strengthened in 1798. The description of his offence is of some interest: he rode without saddle or bridle, leaped through a hoop from horseback, turned a somersault from a horse, walked on a slack wire, danced a hornpipe on the rope "accompanied by a display of colors", and turned a somersault from the rope. Hunter returned to England in 1829, to meet the dismal fate already related.

In 1824 the first American-born circus proprietor appears on the scene, with Bancker's New York Circus. James W. Bancker was to enjoy a long career in the American Circus until the 'sixties. With his appearance we may say that the Circus in America was now firmly established as a native form of entertainment.

It has seemed worth while to tell the story of Ricketts and these early circuses in some detail in view of their Anglo-American interest; but similar companies were now springing up all the time. In 1828 advertisements for seventeen companies have been recorded. I cannot tell the history of them all here. The story of the Circus in America has already found its historians.[6] Here I can do no more than indicate the main lines of its development, and draw especial attention to those fruitful interchanges between the circuses of the United States and of Great Britain that had so much influence in both countries.

21
A Performance

BEFORE WE PROCEED with the chronological story, with its necessary strange names, and dates, and facts and figures, let us pause for a moment and take our seats at a performance of Pepin and Barnet's Olympic Circus during a far-flung journey to the West. We are at the city of St Louis on the Mississippi on September 20, 1823, and the bill announces, in French and English, a performance for the benefit of Miss Payne, the equestrienne. Seats cost one dollar in the boxes, 75 cents in the pit, and people of colour are admitted for 50 cents.[1]

The programme opens with a Grand Carousel of four horsemen dressed as Turks, riding in various formations, engaging with each other in mimic combat with swords and lances, and as a finale catching ribbons on the points of their lances as they gallop at full speed round the ring. This is followed by a Tranca act by Mr Coty, in which he lies on his back, balances a pole 12 ft long on his feet, and makes it dance a fandango and turn round like a whirligig while it spurts fireworks from each end. This, incidentally, is twenty years before the earliest reference to a similar act in England.

Miss Payne now joins Mr Coty in a double riding act in which the horses are put through the motions of a dance, and she then performs "the much applauded feat of the Mermaid". This (I imagine) involves her in inserting her legs into something like a mermaid's tail and balancing herself and even skipping on a horse's back while thus handicapped. The difficulty of this feat can hardly have counterbalanced the ungainliness of its execution, and it is no surprise that other equestriennes failed to imitate her.

Another riding act follows, with Mr Garcia vaulting the horse from side to side, and when the horse jumps a hurdle he vaults horse and hurdle at the same time.

A horse named Favorite is now brought in, and it lies down, gets up at the word of command, and then sits up at table to take a collation with its master. This is four years before John Ducrow trained a couple of ponies to perform this trick at Astley's, but horses had been eating at table in America since 1810. And then Mr Coty completes this part of the performance with the comic scene of the Drunken Soldier, which we might have seen in Ricketts' Amphitheatre some twenty-five years earlier, with a great deal of tumbling off, or nearly off, the horse, sitting backwards in the saddle, clutching its tail, and hanging round its neck.

It is now the turn of Mr Ignace, a tight rope performer, who shows some surprising feats and concludes his act by seating himself in a chair balanced on the rope, which he calls the Grand Throne of Pluto, while fireworks attached to the throne explode in dazzling splendour all round him. This is an evening performance, with the arena lit only by candles, and the fireworks look especially brilliant in the dim flickering light of the candelabras.

Miss Payne now returns on horseback, riding without reins, and concludes by riding round the ring waving the Star Spangled Banner to warm and patriotic applause. Master Galrain puts on an exciting riding display, leaping over garters, balancing on his head, and concluding with a "lofty" somersault from the horse to the ground.

The whole company of male performers now fills the ring with a display of vaulting. Master Galrain returns with two little ponies. Mr Pepin introduces his trained horse, Conqueror, which fetches a hat, a handkerchief, a basket, and all the accoutrements of a huntsman's wardrobe at his master's command, and concludes by rearing up on its hind legs and fetching down a flag in its teeth from 12 ft above the ground.

Fourteen men on three horses at a circus starring Cayetano, which played at Boston in 1811.

To end the performance the whole company took part in a comic entrée described as The Miller's Frolic or the Arrival of my Grandmother. This was the famous act usually known in England as The Frolics of my Granny. The earliest reference to an English circus is only one year earlier, and the miller does not seem to have entered the act in England until six years later. The common origin must be in France, where the act had, in fact, appeared at the Cirque Franconi by 1816.[2] It became a very popular number in American circuses, and should be well worth reviving.[3]

This programme lacked a specific clown, but otherwise, with its mixture of horsemanship, horse training, acrobatics, rope dancing, and comedy it was typical of the entertainment offered in American circuses in the first quarter of the nineteenth century. The acts would become more skilled and the presentation more sophisticated, great developments lay ahead, but this was the type of entertainment that first won the hearts of the people of America, as it was already winning the hearts of the people of England and of Europe.

22
Mud Shows

UP TO THE MID-1820s most circuses in America had been presented in buildings specially constructed for them, even if some of these were no more than quickly thrown-up open-air arenas surrounded by a wooden pallisade. They were permanent structures in the sense that they were not portable, even if some of them had a very short life.

Some of the menageries, however, were using portable canvas side-walls to preserve their exhibits from the eyes of the non-paying public. Christopher Brown was showing an elephant in this way in 1820. This was a method much used by English circus proprietors at this time, and American showmen used it on occasion as well.

A proper tent, described as a "complete Pavilion Theatre" had been erected in Chatham Garden, a pleasure garden in New York, in 1823,[1] and it was not long before tents began to be used for travelling circuses as well. Several claims have been made, without much evidence, for the first tented circus in America, but Stuart Thayer, the most erudite historian of the early American Circus, has established that, as far as our knowledge goes at present, this honour must go to a quite inconspicuous outfit, directed by J. Purdy Brown, playing in Wilmington, Delaware, in 1825.[2]

Whoever was the first to use it, the introduction of the tent revolutionized the Circus in America. Hitherto shows had perforce to limit their visits to large towns, where permanent amphitheatres existed, or at least to largish communities with sufficient population to justify the labour of erecting some kind of an arena; this must have involved a stay of a week or so at least. Now the whole enterprise could move overnight to a new locality after a one-night stand. The day of the circus visit to far-flung communities became an occasion for a communal celebration that was eagerly anticipated and long remembered. The Circus found a secure place in the American folk experience.

The tents themselves were, at first, small enough. In the late 1820s Quick and Mead are said to have used a tent only 50 ft across; if this is true the ring must have been very small. In about 1830 Buckley and Weeks had a tent 75 ft in diameter, capable of holding 800 people.[3] In 1859 the Antonio Brothers had a tent 95 ft across, with a 40 ft tent as a dressing room.[4]

These were all one-pole, round tents, with side poles propping the edges up. In an attempt to enlarge the tent area oval tents were introduced in about 1840. The Philadelphia Circus in that year used one of these, that was said to be constructed on an improved plan. The principle consisted in having a circular canvas that could be erected in the form of two semicircular tent pieces, with one or more straight middle pieces that could be inserted between them. Quarter poles helped to hold the sides out, and two or more central poles went down the middle. This plan was to be extensively used in later years.

The growing popularity of the Circus in America is illustrated by this cut-out toy, published c. 1858.

These tents had to be transported on horse-drawn wagons. Quick and Mead's little tent, with most of its equipment, could be packed on a single two-horse wagon, but most circuses needed quite a cavalcade of sturdy carts for the straining baggage horses to pull along the rutted and often muddy roads of the expanding territory of the United States. By 1828 Buckley and Weeks were touring with eight wagons, forty horses and thirty-five people; in a few years that would seem a very modest little outfit.

Specifications for some of these wagons tell us that they measured 13 ft long by 3 ft 4 ins wide, and were made as light as possible and with high wheels so as to clear the mud. To save weight they were often constructed in skeletal form. The custom developed of building circus wagons with exceptionally large "boxings" to the wheels, and of using unusually long "rigging chain" to the horses' harness. The distinctive rumbling of the wagons and clanking of the rigging created a sound that signified a circus was on the road. Men and boys all over America would dart from their homes to follow it.[5]

As in England, the performers usually slept in hotels, but by the 1870s a few circuses were beginning to make use of wagon dormitories to enable the entire show to move overnight. French's was the first to introduce this arrangement, and Van Amburgh constructed two large carriages 18 ft long with swinging sides to serve as a portable hotel for fifty men.[6]

Where possible the circuses made use of water transport, loading their equipment on boats that sailed the rivers and canals. At first the shows were unloaded at suitable spots and tents were set up near the banks in the usual way. It was such a riverside circus that Mark Twain, drawing on his memories of life on the Mississippi in the 1840s, recalled in *Huckleberry Finn,* with the twenty riders circling round the ring, "the men just in their drawers and undershirts, and no shoes nor stirrups, and resting their hands on their thighs, easy and comfortable . . . and every lady with a lovely complexion, and perfectly beautiful, and looking just like a gang of real sure-enough queens, and dressed in clothes that cost million of dollars, and just littered with diamonds". And then they rode standing, "the men looking ever so tall and airy and straight, with their heads bobbing and skimming along, away up there under the tent-roof, and every lady's rose-leafy dress flapping soft and silky around her hips. . . . And then faster and faster they went, all of them dancing, first one foot stuck out in the air and then the other, the horses leaning more and more, and the ring-master going round and round the center-pole, cracking his whip and shouting 'hi! – hi!' and the clown cracking jokes behind him." And then an apparently drunk spectator climbing on horseback, shedding seventeen suits in all to appear finally "slim and handsome, and dressed the gaudiest and prettiest you ever saw . . . and the ring-master he see how he had been fooled."

By the middle of the century one of the most interesting developments in the American Circus led to the creation of complete water-borne circuses. The most famous of these was the Floating Circus Palace, built in 1851 for Spalding and Rogers. It was a barge-like structure, 250 ft long by 60 ft wide, and was fitted with a standard 42 ft ring; there were comfortable seats for an audience of 3,400 people. The contraption was apparently intended to be pushed rather than pulled by a steam stern-paddle boat, which had accommodation for its own minstrel show. The red and gold stern-wheeler and the white and gold barge, with flags flying and gas lights blazing, must have presented a brave sight as they came down the river. Their arrival was announced by the playing of a calliope. This instrument had been invented in 1856, and consisted of a series of graduated whistles through which steam from the boilers could be passed, and which could be brought into play by means of a keyboard. The sound

was discordant and harsh, but tunes were recognizable and the noise could be heard for miles. The Floating Palace carried an excellent circus up and down the Mississippi and Ohio rivers until the Civil War put an end to its career in 1862.[7]

Even more than in England the parade was an essential feature of circus publicity. This originated in the band driving round the town in a special carriage to advertise the performance, and there are references to this from the 1830s. Soon special decorated wagons were being made to house the band on these parades. When Richard Sands returned from his tour of England he put into his parade a Sacred Dragon Chariot pulled by camels and an East Indian Car pulled by three elephants. These magnificent decorated carriages had probably been bought from Hughes, who had been parading similar vehicles in England up to 1847. The style was copied widely. In 1848 Howes paraded with a Dragon Chariot, and Welch, Delavan and Nathan had an Imperial Persian Chariot, made after the style of the Imperial Chariots of Cyrus the Great, and decorated with eagles and horses in gold and silver and hung with purple velvet cloth fringed in silver.[8]

The circus parade wagon developed into a superb example of American popular art, but the seeds of the tradition came from England and were inspired by the triumphal cars of renaissance royal processions. Hughes's parade carriages bear some resemblance to

Spalding and Rogers' Floating Circus Palace on the Mississippi.

the triumphal chariots made for the Emperor Maximilian I and recorded by Durer. Although there were excellent American carvers of parade carriages, like John Stephenson, the English influence continued: Seth B. Howes brought four parade wagons back after the Howes and Cushing tour of England in the early 'sixties, and larger ones again in 1870; and Barnum had some "telescopic golden chariots" made in London in 1872.[9]

There might be at least three different band wagons in a big parade to ensure a musical accompaniment all down its length. One would carry the proper circus band, one the side show or Negro band, and one the clown band in which every clown on the show had an instrument put in his hand and was coached in the rendering of at least one elementary tune. But the great musical sensation of this period was an Apollonicon, or portable organ; this contraption was constructed for Spalding and Rogers by an eminent organ builder in 1849 and continued as a parade and show feature until at least 1873. It was shaped like a huge box-like wagon, 20 ft long by 10 ft high by 6 ft wide, and housed two octaves of pedals and eight stops. Air pressure was provided by a bellows manually operated by a boy on the contraption, and the music was played at a keyboard by an organist.[10] I am not sure whether it was this instrument or a duplicate version that was such a feature of the Howes and Cushing parade in England in 1857 and later.

Soon after this, calliopes, which had first been used on the Floating Palace, began to appear on wheels in circus parades. Nixon and Kemp had one as early as 1857, and they were adopted by most circuses in later years. They were sometimes fitted with a coal-fired boiler to provide the steam pressure, but air pressure was sometimes produced through a bellows as with the Apollonicon. However it was produced, the piercing shrieking of this extraordinary instrument signified Circus to generations of Americans, and drew them like the Pied Piper's pipe to follow it as the parade wound its way back to the circus lot (the tober in English circus terminology).

Great wagons like the apollonicon and the calliopes needed several horses to pull them, and this necessity was made into a feature of the parade by harnessing huge teams of horses to the heaviest wagons. In 1848 the Welch Circus had used a thirty-horse hitch, but in the same year Spalding and Rogers increased the hitch to forty horses driven in hand. This became a feature of major circuses for years to come, and in a horse-conscious society the sight of these long strings of horses moving down the street must have been an impressive spectacle. Driving such a team was no mean feat, for the twenty lines of leather in each hand

weighed 70 lbs. In 1857 L. B. Lent actually succeeded in harnessing a fifty-horse hitch, but this proved unmanageable and was soon discontinued.

The immediate object of the parade was to draw an inquisitive crowd after it to the site of the circus itself. Here there might be some further free attraction; in 1856 both Spalding and Rogers and the Sands Circus provided female funambulists walking on a wire from the ground to the top of the tent, and this idea was widely copied.

For some weeks before the show arrived the area would be placarded with posters advertising the circus. At first these were simply printed like theatre playbills in black and white and tacked up; later – by the 1840s – printing in two colours from wood blocks or type was introduced, and by 1870 Russell Morgan & Co of Cincinnati and Edward Purcell of New York were producing stock circus posters from wood blocks in as many as six colours. The invention of lithography

An example of early circus poster art, printed in colour from wood blocks by Farwell, Purcell and Co. Levi North was one of America's leading equestrians.

transformed the style of posters everywhere and gave an impetus to a fine flowering of poster art.[11]

As the number of circuses grew and competition became intense there was great rivalry along the routes and one circus would often paste its posters on top of those of its rival. Pitched battles were fought by gangs of advance men guarding their paper to prevent another show covering it up. "Rat sheets" were distributed decrying rival circuses, and towns were placarded with notices saying "Don't waste your money on Smith's show – Wait for Brown's". A famous war was fought up and down the Mississippi between Spalding and Rogers and a circus run by an egotistical clown called Dan Rice. Rice was something of a folk hero to the Americans, and he once teamed up with the English Shakespearean Jester, Wallett, but his attacks on Spalding and Rogers finally ended with him going to prison for slander.

The "mud shows" may be bathed in a warm aura of romance for us today, but it was a hard life. Here is the considered verdict of one who worked in them. "Looking back now at its trials and tribulations, I must say it was a dog's life. You pulled out at all hours from midnight to 4 in the morning, and tried to rest and sleep while being hauled in a jolting wagon over all kinds of roads and in all kinds of weather. You arrived at the next town between 6 and 8 o'clock, ate breakfast, then hurried down to the dressing room to overhaul your wardrobe, do a little mending, and wash out a suit of tights, and got ready for the parade. After the parade, you rushed through dinner and got ready for the afternoon show. It took all the energy and force you could muster to do your work in the ring. As soon as the afternoon show was over, you hurried through supper and back to the tent for the night performance. After the night show you packed, took you berth in the hack, and hung on like grim death to keep from being thrown out in another five-hour-long drive to the next stand. Still no sleep or rest. You kept this up for six months and wondered how you stayed in condition to do such artistic work. You went into the ring with that artificial smile and those bewitching gestures and poses, and heard such remarks as 'Oh, ain't he nice. How good he must feel. What a fine life actors must have. Golly, wish I was an actor too.' I often thought, *one peep behind scenes would sure change their notion!*"[12]

23
Menageries and Animal Acts

MENAGERIES grew up side by side with the Circus. They had introduced canvas side walls before they were used by circuses, and they developed the use of tents larger than anything the early circuses could afford. The Grand Zoological Exhibition toured with a tent 150 ft in diameter which could hold 5,000 persons. In 1834 the Zoological Institute was transported on forty-seven carriages and wagons and was "exhibited under three spacious pavilions of sufficient capacity to contain 10,000 persons". Menageries, too, announced their arrival with a parade: bands played in splendid wagons; in 1846 Van Amburgh paraded with Tuba Rhoda, a Grecian State Carriage, the subject of a Currier and Ives print and apparently copied from the Burmese Imperial Carriage and Throne that had been pulled by elephants in Hughes's parades in England the year before. The next year Raymond and Waring countered with the Chrysarma, "a great Colossean chariot". The great tradition of carved and gilded American parade carriages sprang from these vehicles.

During the summer menageries moved round the countryside, often exhibiting at inns and wherever people might gather together. In the winter they settled in buildings in the cities. Until circuses learned to travel with tents, menageries reached further into the countryside than circuses and were, perhaps, a more familiar spectacle for the bulk of Americans.

By the 1820s some kind of performance was being given in many menageries. In 1822 an elephant was

RAYMOND & WARING'S CHRYSARMA OR GOLDEN CHARIOT.

Raymond and Waring's Chrysarma or Golden Chariot in 1848.

exhibited on Rhode Island which, the handbill informs us, "will kneel to the company, balance her body alternately on each pair of legs, present her right foot to enable the keeper or any other person to mount her trunk, carry them about the room and safely replace them, draw a cork from a filled bottle and drink the contents, and then present the empty bottle and cork to her keeper". These are all standard and fairly elementary tricks. In 1825 a pony-riding monkey called Dandy Jack was widely exhibited – all monkey jockeys were called Dandy Jack, after Major Jack Downing, a famous trainer of trick horses. With the American National Caravan in 1831 Dandy Jack and his companion, dressed in uniform, raced each other round a small ring, standing erect on the back of a pair of Shetland ponies and waving American flags.[1]

In the 1830s trainers began to enter the lions' cages. In 1833 Raymond and Ogden's New and Rare Collection of Living Animals featured a Mr Gray, of whom no more is heard; the National Menagerie of June, Titus and Angevine featured a Mr Roberts from London. I have not found Roberts's name in any English source, but as we have seen, Winney had been entering the lion cage of Atkins' Menagerie at least eight years earlier. Roberts was mauled by a tiger in

Connecticut in the Fall of 1833, and it was then that Isaac Van Amburgh got the chance to show how he could cope with the wild cats. He was to become the most famous trainer in circus history.[2]

Van Amburgh's grandfather had been an American Indian, and he seems to have been a cage boy with the show since he was ten; he was now twenty-two years old. What happened next is history. He demonstrated his remarkable *rapport* with wild animals in public at the Richmond Hill Theatre in New York before the end of 1833 and caused an immediate sensation, though there was, at that date, nothing very sensational about his performance. What amazed the spectators was the way in which an unarmed man ventured into a cage of savage lions, "playing and frolicking with them, and all enjoying their wild pranks with as much seeming delight and innocence as children do their holiday gambols". Van Amburgh put a lion, a leopard and a panther into a cage together, and the contemporary handbill goes on to tell how he "plays and fondles with the inmates alternately, and demonstrates the perfect subjugation of the whole group to his unparalleled and apparently magic powers". All this was very different to the whip cracking and pistol shooting that came to accompany big cat acts later, and which brought a spurious sensationalism to their presentation.

Van Amburgh was featured as the star of various animal dramas in the theatres. There is a story that his success went to his head and the ex-cage boy began to acquire ideas above his station by courting his boss's daughter. To get him out of the way, Titus sent him to London in 1838. We have already seen the sensation he made there. He toured his own menagerie when he returned to the States, and the name continued in use for long after his death.

Van Amburgh was followed by many other wild-animal trainers, of whom the most notable was Jacob Driesbach. It was probably Driesbach who developed the type of act called *en ferocité*, feeling that this fondling and playing was all very well, but that what the public wanted was to see some signs of savage ferocity. In his performance a leopard was trained to spring at him while he was working the lion, and the

two animals were supposed to attack him from either side. It was only play acting; but the audiences were greatly impressed, people fainted at every performance, and this type of wild cat act became the regular thing. Driesbach had his own show by the early 'fifties.[3]

From the mid 'twenties menageries and circuses began to combine forces. One of the first was the Wright and Brown Menagerie and Circus in 1828, which showed a zebra, camels, and monkeys on ponies as well as horsemanship, vaulting and clowns. In 1834 the Crane and Eldred Menagerie and Circus United was presenting a similar programme. In the mid-1850s the Mabie Bros Grand Olympic Arena and United States Circus still distinguished between the equestrian and gymnastic performances "in the Circle" and the cages of the menagerie which were arranged "around one side of the Pavilion" and were on view before and after the equestrian performance;

COLE'S SOUTHERN CIRCUS AND MENAGERIE.

PORT BARRE, THURSDAY, FEB. 9

THURSDAY. FEB. 9

COLE'S NEW GREAT SOUTHERN CIRCUS, MENAGERIE, MUSEUM AND TRIPLE MUSICAL BRIGADE.

A female lion trainer with Cole's Southern Circus. A poster for 1882.

127

the "intrepid lion tamer", Mr Beasley, gave his performance in the lion and tigers' den "at the close of the entertainment".

Gradually the performing acts from the menagerie were absorbed into the circus programme and took place in the ring. The stages in this development would repay study by circus historians. As late as 1892 there were no animal acts in the ring of the Ringling Circus, apart from horses and ponies, though there were plenty of elephants in their menagerie. From about this date, however, circuses began to erect temporary steel cages round their rings, within which the big cat acts were performed. The first ring cage in America is thought to be that erected by Hagenbeck in 1893.[4]

Elephants, in particular, became as essential to a circus as horses and clowns. Indeed, Americans tended to judge a circus by the number of "bulls" it owned – all elephants are "bulls" regardless of sex, although performing elephants are almost always females as the males are potentially dangerous at certain seasons. Shortly after the middle of the century a *protegé* of Van Amburgh, called Stuart Craven, developed the training of elephants with the Mabie Bros to a much higher standard than anything seen before; and in about 1860 a trainer called Charles W. Noyce with the Dan Rice Circus is said to have trained an elephant to walk a tight rope – the feat that had been achieved at Astley's in 1846 – though whether this was a real double tight rope or just a narrow plank I don't know. But it was not really the tricks that were important; it was just the sight of these strangely impressive beasts, lumbering along in the parade or filling the ring with their huge bodies, that most effectively conveyed the magic of Circus to whole generations of Americans.

24
Competition and Combinations

AS THE AMERICAN FRONTIER RECEDED, so the American circuses followed. They had reached Chillicothe from the Ohio River by 1815; New Orleans in the south by 1816; St Louis in the west by 1823; through the Great Lakes to Detroit by 1830 and Chicago by 1836; to Mobile, Alabama, by 1831; to Tallahassee, Florida, by 1834; to the West Coast at San Francisco by 1849; to British Columbia by 1860.[1]

As the circuses multiplied, so more and more proprietors ventured their skills and their money into this fascinating but hazardous form of entertainment. The history of the American Circus is a bewildering jungle of continually changing names and ownerships. It is further confused by the large number of different people all called Bailey. I cannot attempt to chart a course through all this here. But two tendencies are apparent very early in the history of the Circus in America, and have remained a feature of it ever since. One was the cut-throat competition between rival shows. The other was the attempt to buy up or shut out competition by forming partnerships and combinations, giving rise to the enormously long double or triple-barrelled titles that American circuses often adopted.

This is well illustrated in the story of a group of respectable businessmen, not themselves performers, in North Salem. They started by acquiring a menagerie, the Zoological Institute, in the late 1820s; fearing competition from Welch and Bartlett's Circus they formed a partnership until Welch broke free; but they succeeded better with Buckley and Weeks. At this point a rival circus, Raymond and Waring, announced its intention of making a tenting tour in New York State; the North Salemites regarded this area as their own territory and warned any other concern to keep out; this is our territory, they announced, and we intend to keep it so, "we put our foot down flat". From that time on they became known as the Flatfoots.

The Flatfoots went on, acquiring new circuses and menageries by purchase or partnership, until as late as the 1880s. Some of the greatest names in American circus history joined the combine: Lewis B. Lent, G. R. Spalding, Richard Sands, George F. Bailey, concluding with a right, for a few years, to the Barnum

WES & CUSHIN

Howes and Cushing's parade organ pulled by forty horses driven in hand, 1857.

title. They sent safaris to Africa to capture live animals, and traded as animal dealers. They were the first great circus syndicate.

Some proprietors stood out against them. There was Seth B. Howes, who took the Howes and Cushing Circus to England, and after his return in 1871 traded under the title of the Great London Circus, though this was an entirely American show; there was Aron Turner, an English immigrant, who gave Barnum his first job as a ticket seller in 1836; there was John Robinson, who toured the southern states with the motto "Southern Men, Southern Horses, Southern Enterprise against the World".

An English performer who briefly formed his own circus was John Holland, who had been a noted rider and leaper in his teens and who came to America in 1839, aged twenty-two. He played with good shows, like Mabie Bros and Buckley and Babcock's North American Circus, and twice tried to run a show of his own, in 1858 and 1860–1, but it failed on each occasion like so many other hopeful ventures. He went back to performing, and in time his son made a useful contribution to the American Circus with his own show.[2]

A notorious but successful combine was that headed by John V. (Pogey) O'Brien. O'Brien's shows were the worst "grifters" in the whole American circus business – and that is saying something. Patrons were robbed by crooked games of chance in the side show, and they were short-changed when they bought their tickets. Men whose job it was to give small change to the customers *paid* the proprietor for the privilege! All

this soured relationships between the circus people and the citizens in many districts. Sometimes fights, or "clems", broke out as local gangs tried to break the circus up. Good shows suffered from association with the bad. Tent ropes were cut; wagons set on fire; and, of course, the circus people fought back. Many a black eye was given and received. Sometimes the injuries were worse and even deaths were not unknown.

An incredible story is told of a clem involving the Thayer and Van Amburgh Circus in Landisburg at the foot of the Cumberland Hills in Pennsylvania in the late 'fifties. When the mountain folk came down into the town to see the circus they were annoyed to find that all the stabling had been taken up by the circus animals. After feeding their displeasure with whisky some of them found it amusing to vent their annoyance on the circus ponies by sticking pins into them to see them jump and kick. The circus hostler tried to stop them; they turned on him and beat him up so badly that he died.

Trouble was now surging. The circus men and the hill men met in a pitched battle in the main street. The hill men tried to raid a gun store, but the circus men barred the way and then raided it themselves. The Law was powerless; in the confusion the deputy sheriff was shot dead.

Word had now gone out, and the hill men were gathering from all sides. The circus had to get out. They travelled in close formation, with skirmishers going ahead, sniped at all the way. As night fell the road led up into the hills. The hill men set up an ambush in the darkness. The sound of their wagons gave away the presence of the circus. The circus men had guns but they couldn't see their targets. Then someone had an inspiration. The programme always opened with a Grand Mounted Entry illuminated with flares. Now they fitted the flares into their guns and fired them at the ambush. Their spluttering, blazing light lit up the hillside like starshells, exposing

the hill men as they crouched by the roadside. The circus marksmen picked them off with their rifles, and the wagons got through.

In that epic engagement ten of the circus company were killed. No-one knows the casualties of the men of the hills.[3]

Men had to take the law into their own hands in those formative years of American history.

25

Permanent Circus Buildings

ALTHOUGH the American Circus found its true home in a tent, there were continued attempts to create permanent circus buildings. Ricketts constructed three amphitheatres in New York. Pepin built the Olympic Circus – one of several so named by him in various towns – on Broadway in 1810. West built the New Circus, by Canal Street, in 1817. But these were mere makeshift wooden structures.[1]

The first attempt to construct a really permanent circus building in New York was the Lafayette Amphitheatre, opened in Laurens Street, by Canal Street, in 1825. The builder was Charles W. Sandford, a colourful military figure in New York society, who was busy developing this area of what was then up-town New York into a desirable residential district. The theatre comprised a ring and stage, on the plan of Astley's in London, and was designed for equestrian spectacles. It did not last long in this form, however, and in the next year the ring was replaced by a seated pit and the place became an orthodox theatre.[2] Sandford, however, persevered as a circus promoter and constructed the Mount Pitt Circus, in Broome Street; this was a wooden structure with a brick façade, seating 3,500 people; its short life ended when it was burnt down in 1829.

The proprietors of The Zoological Institute converted their permanent menagerie into a circus in 1838 under the title of the Bowery Amphitheatre. As opposed to the many theatres in which occasional circuses were presented this boasted a proper central ring surrounded by spectators. Many of the leading circus companies of the time presented shows here

during a period of some sixteen years; we find the names of Howes, Sands and Lent, Levi North, Tourniaire, Nathan, and Chiarini among the lessees.

An even more important permanent circus was a building called the Hippotheatron, opened on 14th Street in 1864; the first manager was James Cooke, of the English circus family, but it was subsequently run for several years by Lewis B. Lent. It was an ambitious circular structure, built of corrugated iron, 110 ft in diameter, with a dome and cupola 75 ft high. The ring, measuring 43 ft 6 ins, was surrounded by 600 "arm sofa" orchestra stalls, 500 dress circle seats, and a pit. A gallery was added in 1866, and further enlargements in 1872 brought the seating capacity up to 2,800. Comfort in the winter was secured by steam heating. This was the nearest New York, or America, ever got to a permanent circus building of intimate size, on the European model; familiarly known as Lent's Iron Building, some of the greatest American circus artistes appeared here: Eaton Stone, Madame Macarte, Ed. Croueste the clown, John Robinson, Robert Stickney, Frank Conrad, James Madigan, Professor Risley, and many others. Although the building was believed to be fireproof it was burnt down in 1872 after only eight years' use.

As in London, circuses performed in the pleasure gardens. The earliest of these was Niblo's Garden, where a theatre was later built on the site. Here the Raymond and Waring Menagerie, the Cirque Franconi, Dan Rice and James Nixon put on shows; Blondin appeared here in 1835 and the Hanlon Brothers in 1858.

Circuses sometimes displaced the legitimate drama, as at Covent Garden and Drury Lane in London, from even the most prestigious playhouses. Horses performed upon the boards of the Park and the National. In 1868 Léotard flew from his trapeze in the Academy of Music, which had been designed as an opera house. Innumerable small theatres turned briefly to circuses in a desperate effort to fill their benches.

The flamboyant figure of P. T. Barnum dominated New York entertainment during the second half of the nineteenth century. We are not concerned here with the famous Museum in which he displayed curiosities of all kinds between 1842 and 1868, but with his circus activities. There had been a foretaste of these in 1851 when his Asiatic Caravan, Museum and Menagerie was housed in a tent at Astor Place, a popular pitch for tenting shows, but his major entrance upon the scene did not occur until 1871 when he entered into partnership with Coup. That winter he mounted his circus in the Empire Skating Rink; the next year he bought the Hippotheatron and was

presenting his circus there on Christmas Eve when it was burnt down, with the loss of the entire properties, costumes, and almost all the animals. By 1873, however, he was back in business at the Skating Rink, and the next year he erected the Roman Hippodrome in Madison Avenue, seating 10,000 people, where he staged chariot races and every kind of spectacular display. His circus, however, only played here for two years. In 1876, and for the two following years, he presented what he was now calling the Greatest Show on Earth at Gilmore's Garden, presumably under canvas. In 1879 and 1880 he was back at the Skating Rink. At last, in 1881, the show took possession of the refurbished Hippodrome, now entitled the Madison Square Garden. Here, in the greatly enlarged Garden of 1890, and at the later Madison Square Garden on Eighth Avenue, a great circus has been presented every spring (wartime excepted) up to the present day. This is not primarily a circus building, but rather a vast sporting and exhibition complex in which circuses can take place.[3]

In other towns the story of short-lived circus build-

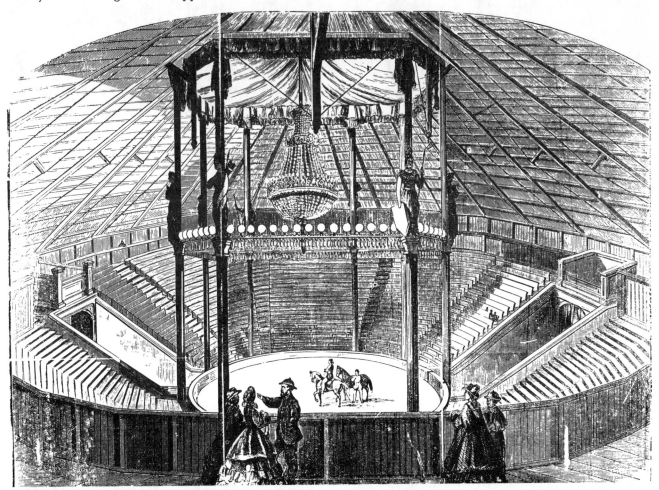

The Hippotheatron, or Lent's Iron Building, on Broadway in New York.

Chariot racing in Barnum's Roman Hippodrome.

ings was similar. In Baltimore the Circus on Philpot's Hill was adapted from an earlier theatre in 1793, changed its name to the Olympic Theatre (as popular a title in America as in England) in 1811, and was demolished in 1827. The Front Street Theatre was opened on the same site in 1829; it could seat 4,000 people and was provided with a stage and a 47 ft ring; the stage was large enough for an ornamental carriage, drawn by six horses three abreast, to turn a figure of eight upon it. This theatre was burnt down in 1838. A few years later, in 1846, the Roman Amphitheatre was opened by Sands and Lent; this was a circular brick building, 100 ft in diameter, seating 5,000 people in boxes, and with stalls for 80 horses. But it was burnt down the next year and never rebuilt.[4]

The story of Cooke's tour of America is closely bound up with permanent circus buildings.[5] In 1836 Thomas Taplin Cooke chartered a 3,000-ton ship at Greenock in Scotland to convey his company of 130 artistes, 42 horses, 14 ponies, and a complement of grooms, musicians and other staff to America. On arrival in New York he erected a stone and brick amphitheatre, seating 2,000 persons, in Vauxhall Gar-

dens, where he played for six months. He was then much in demand for supplying horses for equestrian melodramas at the American Theatre in the Bowery and at the National, but when the former was burnt down in 1838 he lost all his wardrobe and properties, though the stud of horses was fortunately stabled elsewhere. Cooke then equipped his company with fresh costumes, and three weeks later opened at the Walnut Street Theatre in Philadelphia, where they played for eight weeks. He then moved to Baltimore, where his entire stud and all his equipment perished in the disastrous fire at the Front Street Theatre. Despite this crippling loss, he gathered together a small troupe of sixteen horses and ponies and played for sixteen weeks at the Lion Theatre in Boston.

No English circus has ventured across the Atlantic since. English influences did, however, continue. Lavater Lee and a troupe of English acrobats were at the Alhambra in 1848; William Cooke's equestrian troupe was at Niblo's Garden in 1860; many English artistes appeared with American circuses. The Franconi Hippodrome, which was largely a tented structure, not a permanent building, opened in New York in 1853 with a good deal of French *réclame*, but A. H. Saxon has demonstrated that this substantially comprised the company Batty had assembled for his Hippodrome in Kensington in 1851.[6] Sanger's English Menagerie of Trained Animals was combined with Cooper and Bailey's Great London Circus in 1879, though this was not a tour by the Sanger company but, apparently, merely the purchase of some animals with a right to the use of the name. Sanger also sold the entire production of his 1866 spectacle at the Agricultural Hall, *The Congress of the Monarchs*, to Barnum for the opening of his Roman Hippodrome. At the end of the century Bostock's Menagerie toured the United States under canvas; the manner in which the elephants assisted in the erection of the tent aroused great interest.[7]

The circus buildings in America all perished within a few years by fire or at the hands of property developers. They must have provided welcome winter engagements for many circus performers, but they did not at this time play any really important part in the history of the American Circus. Small, intimate arenas were unsuited to the American style of entertainment and to the shape of the developing American Circus. The American genius lay elsewhere.

26
Railroad Shows

THE FIRST RAILROAD in the United States, starting from Baltimore, opened for traffic in 1830. By 1852 it had reached the Ohio River. By 1860 there were 30,000 route miles of track in the country. A transcontinental railroad was completed in 1869.

It was not long before circuses began to take advantage of this convenient method of transportation. In 1853 the Railroad Circus and Chrystal Amphitheatre made a tour across northern Ohio, travelling by rail. Other shows copied its example; Spalding and Rogers New Railroad Circus had 24 cars in 1857. Its advertisement proclaimed: "No more skeleton team horses! Rickety wagons! Tarnished trappings! Worn out ring horses! Tired performers as with the old fogy wagon shows, traveling all night over rough roads, but Fast Men! Fast Women! Fast children! and performers well rested! Ring horses of spirit! and Trapping lustrous!"[1]

Despite this claim, Spalding and Rogers railroad show didn't last for very long; the first proprietor to establish a successful railroad circus, running entirely on rails for several seasons, was Lewis B. Lent with his New York Circus, from the Hippotheatron, in 1866.[2] In 1868 Dan Castello made the first coast-to-coast circus tour, much of it by train. By 1872 eight circuses were travelling by rail. The great era of railroad circuses had begun.

A remarkably efficient system of loading and transporting circuses on railroads was developed. There were three types of cars: sleeping cars, with staterooms for senior staff and performers, and three-high bunk cars, often infested with bugs, for the rest; stock cars for the horses, elephants, and other lead animals, which were packed tight to prevent injury from falling during the journey; and flat cars, on which wagons carrying the tent, poles, seats, parade carriages, and caged animals were loaded. Baggage horses were still required to pull the wagons from the railroad station to the circus lot; the elephants and most of the staff walked.

When loading, the wagons were pulled by the "long team" from the circus lot to the foot of steel runs leading up to a row of flat cars, and then unhitched; a new "pull-up" team of horses pulled the wagons up the inclined runs on to the first car, guided by a "run poler", the man in charge of that part of the operation; then a new two-horse "hook team" pulled the wagons along the flats, over bridges linking each flat car with the next, guided by a "deck poler", till each one reached the end of the line; then it was unhitched, the pole pulled out and dropped to the deck of the car, and the wagon guided for its last few yards by "chalkers", who fitted chocks against the wheels to hold it steady.[3]

The staff who loaded and unloaded the trains were

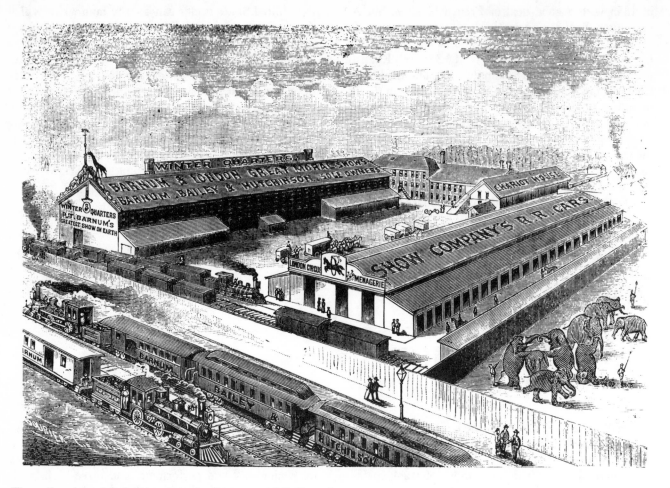

The railroad track led right up to the Barnum and Bailey winter quarters.

specialist workmen, called "razorbacks". (The name probably comes from the cry "raise her back", used when lifting a short animal cage to a cross-wise position on a flat car.) It was a dangerous job. A deck poler might be thrown fifty feet across adjoining tracks if the steel-tyred front wheel of a wagon struck an obstruction while it was being pulled into place, causing the pole to swerve. Many circus hands were injured in this way. By the 1930s the baggage horses were mostly replaced by tractors, and wagons were being fitted with pneumatic tyres, but the basic principles of loading remained the same as long as circuses travelled by rail.

The size of a circus could be gauged by the number of cars it travelled. In 1872 the Coup and Barnum show used 61; by 1903 Barnum and Bailey had increased to 92; at the height of its operations in 1947 the Ringling Barnum show used 109 cars. At the other end of the scale some little circuses travelled on only two or three cars; an average show travelled with about 30 to 40. In the 'seventies these flat cars were 60 ft long, but later this was increased to 70 ft. Not

an inch of space was wasted; the wagons were built to fit exactly on to the car lengths. The cars were owned by the circus company, and often built in their workshops; the railroad company provided the locomotive.

Not more than 20 to 25 cars made up one train, and circuses often travelled in two or more trains; this was linked with the order of dismantling the show, so that the menagerie animals and tent, for instance, might be loaded on a train while the final night performance was still taking place in the big top. By 1950 Ringling Barnum were moving 1,400 people with all their animals and equipment on one-day stands with five trains: the first train took the cook-house and menagerie; the second train took the tent, the floats or wheeled carts used in the spectacles in the ring, and other props; the third train took the horses, the performing animals, and the seat wagons; the fourth train took all the rest.[4]

All this was not achieved without trouble, and there were many accidents in the early years. The Forepaugh show suffered six train smashes in 1885; most of these were caused by couplings between cars breaking, and a group of cars running back on to an oncoming train. Better couplings and automatic brakes cured this. In 1892 the Ringling Brothers train was wrecked through flood water undermining the track; two men were killed, half a dozen badly injured, and fifty baggage horses died outright or had to be shot. In 1903 twenty-three people were killed when the second section of the Great Wallace Show rammed the

first. The worst train disaster in American circus history was in 1918, when an empty troop train, driven with criminal negligence, ploughed through the rear of the Hagenbeck Wallace train, killing eighty-six people and injuring many more.[5]

But the accidents are forgotten and the glory is remembered. No circus ever abandoned its tour after a crash. A few dates were lost, but the show always went on.

27

Leapers and Others

THE PROGRAMMES of the railroad age reflect the changing pattern of the Circus, compared with those of the early mud shows. In 1879 W. W. Cole's New York and New Orleans Menagerie and Circus was placing its emphasis upon animals, with performing elephants, lions, camels, tigers, stags, monkeys, dogs, goats and mules; the bill, unfortunately, does not precisely specify whether these performed in the ring, but there was "a wild horned horse, which hitherto considered untamable will actually be introduced in the ring and caused to go through a number of tricks". There were also six performing stallions and a stud of thoroughbred Arabian horses and ponies. There were, of course, equestrians – posing, somersaulting, and a lady in tandem menage. Other acts included Sig. Peluzio Cardozo, the Man of Fire, who entered a fiery furnace and stayed there for ten minutes, "clothed only in a garment of slight texture, his own invention"; Mon. De Ruth, who caught a shot discharged from a cannon (this was eight years after Holtum had achieved this feat in London); the comical Pico, "Prince of the Motleys"; and tumblers, acrobats, gymnasts, trapezists, and leapers.[1]

The leapers were as popular a feature of these circuses as they were in England, and there was as keen a competition among them to excel. There are many contradictory claims as to who first threw a double or a treble somersault, but here is the story of Edward Jonathan Hoyt, known as Buckskin Joe, hunter, trapper, scout and frontiersman, friend of the Indians, who joined the Great Western Circus, with

his brother, Warren, as a strong man act in 1868.[2]

Later in that year the Hoyt brothers transferred to Johnson's United Circus, where – as was the usual custom – all the members of the company were expected to take part in the leaps from the trampling board over rows of horses or other obstacles. Joe developed great proficiency in this exercise, and on September 17, at Bemont, he turned for a wager what he claimed to be the first double somersault on record. He was heavily advertised after that as "the only man in the world who ever turned twice in the air before landing after leaving the leaping board".

In 1869 Joe and his brother joined the George W. DeHaven Circus, a railroad and steamboat show. The programme here was always wound up with the leaps, Joe doing a double somersault over the backs of running horses, and Warren doing "the leap for life". One day a new running board was being used for the first time, and the leapers were not accustomed to it. They had reached twelve horses abreast and it was Warren's turn to leap; he cleared the horses, completed one somersault, "but overthrowed on the second turn and landed on his chest on the bank of the clay ring".

He managed to walk out, but the blow set up complications that killed him. Joe went to the cemetery after the funeral and turned a backward somersault over Warren's grave. "This was the custom of all acrobats of the time."

Joe thought of giving the circus up after this, but he was under contract to the show. Moreover some other leapers in the company, Kelly and Rhinehart,

135

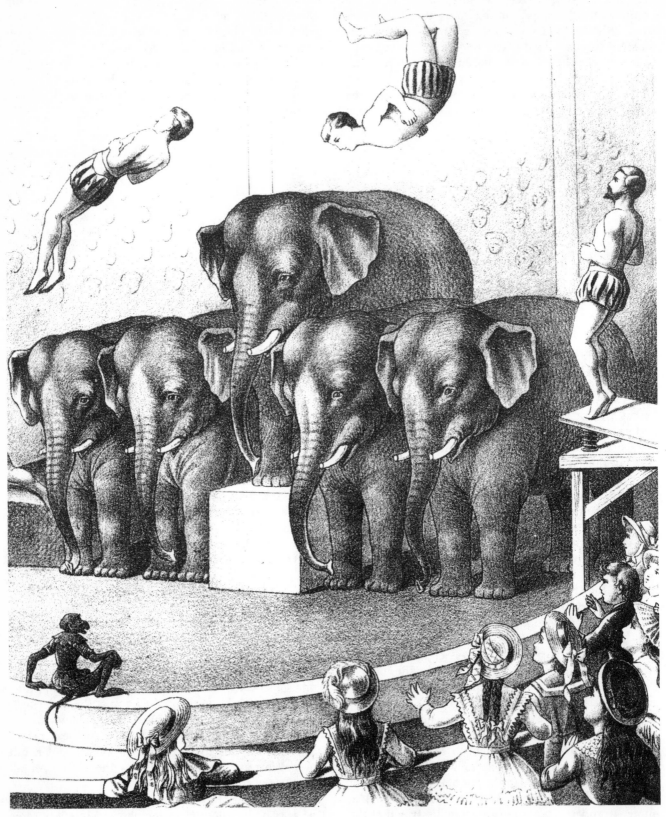

Leaping from a springboard over horses or elephants was as popular in America as in England.

were now throwing doubles too. There was a keen rivalry between them. "But I out-did them by doing a perfect thribble", Joe wrote; "I turned over three times and landed straight on my feet after leaving the board. It was my science to always alight standing, which Kelly and Rhinehart could never do. They would hold to their trick [doubled up for the somersaults] until landing, then bob up – what I called a 'prat-double'. I had perfected the art, and they acknowledged that they could not beat me."

It does not really matter whether it was Buckskin Joe in 1869, or Billy Dutton in 1860, or Bob Stickney in 1870, or John Worland in 1874 who first achieved a treble from a battoute springboard.[3] What does matter is the urge for excellence, the passion to com-pete, the overwhelming force that drove these, and hundreds of other acrobats and leapers and trapezists on, and still drives them on today to greater and still greater achievements. Not one in a thousand of the audiences in DeHaven's Circus at Cresco, Iowa, or any other town in any other state of the Union, knew whether a double or a treble somersault was a unique achievement. These performers played not to please their audiences but to justify themselves, and to set their mark upon the history of their ancient art.

The deserve whatever tribute and recognition may be granted them from the efforts of us, historians, as we grub through the records to try to establish these "firsts" in circus history.

28
Three-ring Circuses

RAILROAD TRANSPORT made it possible to carry far heavier loads than had ever been dreamed of with horse-drawn wagons, and circus proprietors, who were in the business to make money, naturally looked for ways of increasing the size of their tents and so of their audiences. The problem was that a circus ring had been standardized at 42 ft or thereabouts, and it was impossible for horses trained in rings of that size to adapt suddenly to anything larger. The solution, to which the structure of American circus tents readily lent themselves, was to put several rings side by side in one long tent.

In 1873 Andrew Haight's Great Eastern Circus and Menagerie announced that it would present its show in two rings.[1] In the same year Coup and Barnum's Great Traveling Museum, Menagerie, Hippodrome and World's Fair had two rings with a hippodrome track running round them, and announced this as a "three ring circus".[2] In 1881 they really did have three rings, and by 1885 when Barnum was briefly in combination with Forepaugh the show had four rings plus two stages placed between them for acrobats. So the race for size went on. By the 1890s three rings was standard practice with all the major American circuses. In 1926 Sells Floto put five rings in the Chicago Coliseum. In the 1930s Ringling Barnum regularly put three rings and four stages in their tenting show.

The pattern was for performances – usually of similar-type acts – to take place simultaneously in all the rings, and for big spectacles – "the spec" in circus jargon – to go round the track encircling them. Patrons in the huge tent could watch whatever was going on nearest to their seats.

And the tents *were* huge. In the 1840s Mabie's one-ring tent had measured only 85 ft in diameter; in 1878, with the beginning of the multi-ringed circus, Cooper and Bailey used a tent of 150 ft with two 50 ft middle pieces; in 1882 Barnum and Bailey had a 216 ft round with three 54 ft middles; by 1890 they were using six 60 ft middles, supported on eight poles, which must have produced a tent about 460 ft long – equivalent to about one and half football pitches in length. In 1880, when Forepaugh's tent measured 180 ft across by 360 ft long, he installed a band at each end.

In 1872 the Coup Barnum tent could seat 5,000 people at a squeeze; by 1898 the Barnum and Bailey tent could take 14,000; in 1924 they set up a record at Concordia, Kansas, by cramming 16,728 paying patrons into one performance. This could only be

Sells's Circus tent in the 1880s housed two rings, a central stage, and a hippodrome track.

achieved by seating a lot of people on straw bales round the hippodrome track – what was called "a straw house".

As well as the big top itself there were a host of subsidiary tents to be erected: the menagerie tent, which might be almost as big as the circus tent; the "connection", which linked the two together; the "pad room", an elongated tent, with men's dressing room at one end, women's at the other, and ring horses in between; the side show tents, refreshment tents, circus cookhouse, baggage horse stable tents, and so on.

The whole operation of erecting and dismantling these colossal structures developed into a masterpiece of logistics and organization. American circuses played one-night stands almost everywhere. Only in the very largest towns did they stay longer. Night after night, for months on end, with only Sunday as a rest day, the vast tented city was taken down, loaded on a train, transported perhaps a hundred miles or more, unloaded, and erected in time for a mid-day parade

and an afternoon performance. As soon as the evening performance had begun the process of dismantling started afresh.

The Barnum and Bailey tent could be taken down, loaded on wagons, and off the ground in less than one hour after the end of the show. When this circus toured Europe at the beginning of this century the German army was greatly impressed by the efficiency of the whole operation, and is said to have sent German soldiers to America to get jobs with the show to observe how it was done.

A great deal depended upon the department heads, or bosses as they were called. There would be a boss canvasman in charge of the tent, a boss hostler in charge of the baggage horses, a boss carpenter, a boss blacksmith, a boss electrician, a boss ticket seller, a boss porter on the train, a boss candy butcher in charge of the concession salesmen, and of course bosses in charge of the elephants and the cage animals. It was these seasoned professionals who controlled the gangs of often shiftless roustabouts who provided the muscle and brawn in heaving on the ropes to bring the big top up.

Mechanization was introduced here and there to assist the operation. From 1911 the ingenious William Curtis on the Sells Floto show had invented a canvas spool wagon which rolled the tent canvases mechanically on and off a wagon. From 1903 mechanical stake drivers began to replace the gangs of eight roustabouts swinging their heavy sledge hammers in sequence as they drove the vital stakes in around the perimeter of the big top.

Unionization came slowly. In the old hard days any workman causing that kind of trouble was likely to find himself "red lighted" – that is thrown off the moving train. But in 1938 a strike of the workmen closed the Ringling Barnum show. The days of cheap labour were over.

The parades for these shows became grander and grander. Coup and Barnum in 1872 had a revolving Temple of Juno pulled by twenty camels, and many of the floats could be telescoped to make them higher; the Car of Neptune, resplendent with mirrors and wood carvings, towered over 28 ft high; on one float a huge rose blossom slowly opened and closed its petals. A comic touch, popular in rural districts, was the hay wagon, on which bales of hay disguised a trampoline from which clowns bounced to enormous heights, giving the impression that they were leaping from a load of hay. And the steam calliopes still wound the procession up.[3]

In the 1880s Forepaugh's parade took five hours to wind its way through the streets of New York. Circus parades had become the finest free entertainment ever offered to the public since the days of imperial Rome. But when Barnum and Bailey toured Europe they found that the Germans were so impressed by the free parade that they couldn't believe there was anything more worth seeing, and didn't buy tickets for the show. By the beginning of the twentieth century parades were becoming unmanageable and some shows began to drop them. One of the last to negotiate the increasingly traffic-congested streets was Hagenbeck Wallace in 1934, when the Five Graces bandwagon, the 24 decorated animal dens, the Harp and Jester steam calliope, 320 plumed and bedecked horses, and 29 elephants made a brave show of recapturing the splendours of the past.

Posters, now always lithographed in colour, many from the firm of Strobridge in Cincinnati, played an increasingly important part in publicizing circuses, and became bigger and bigger. In 1887 Forepaugh had over a hundred different styles and designs, including a monster 128 sheet depicting his son's riding act

(1 sheet is about 28 by 42 ins); his bill posters entirely covered a 12-storey building without once repeating a subject. In 1892 Ringling were employing seventy advance bill posters, and in 1915 it was estimated that they were pasting up 10,000 lithos a day.[4]

In addition to the posters, most circuses distributed heralds, or handbills measuring about 28 by 10 ins, packed with small type on both sides in an efflorescence of superlatives, and couriers, or small newspapers, usually of four pages and often printed in colour. As well as this, lavish advertising space was taken in the local press, running sometimes to several columns of close print and illustrations. The total impact of the Circus upon American society by the end of the nineteenth century represented a remarkable exercise in advertising and public relations.

Despite attempts to call a truce, paper wars broke out again and again, with the profits from performances being spent on buying mountains of posters to cover up the bills of rival circuses, only to be covered up themselves a few days later. Sometimes the weight of posters, pasted half an inch thick on top of one another, was too great and the whole lot fell off the walls. The publication of a Code of Ethics in 1911 by the short-lived Showman's Association had little effect in controlling this wasteful competition.

And so, the shows went on, bigger than ever before and despite every obstacle of man and nature. There were quarantine regulations that might shut up a show within a state boundary; poor harvests or mill closures or strikes that left the locals with no money for circus tickets; bankruptcies, with many a small show going broke on the road, stranding the performers with salaries unpaid. There was mud: in 1929 five heavy baggage horses died in their traces trying to pull Robinson's wagons out of a lot with mud up to the axles. There were blow-downs: in 1889 a storm hit Barnum and Bailey's big tent during a performance with such violence that the wildly flapping canvas lifted the quarter poles into the air, tossing them dangerously about above the spectators' heads while tentmen desperately hung on to the madly bucking spars to ride them back to earth; in 1905 the Ringling tent was hit by a cyclone, with many spectators injured; in 1914 the rain-soaked Hagenbeck Wallace tent collapsed on a seated audience, killing one and injuring over twenty. There were floods: in 1913 the winter quarters of Hagenbeck Wallace at Peru, Indiana, were flooded; twelve elephants and over 300 horses swam aimlessly in the rising water till they sank exhausted and were drowned; the big cats were all drowned in their cages. Elephants stampeded, wrecking shop fronts as they went and leaving a trail of destruction behind them; in 1926 the Sells Floto herd broke loose in British Columbia, and were never all recovered. There were epidemics and disease: in 1941 eleven of Ringling Barnum's forty-seven elephants died from eating grass that had been sprayed with an arsenic weed killer. There were fires: many winter quarters were burnt to the ground; Barnum and Bailey's tent caught fire during a performance in 1910, but all 15,000 spectators were evacuated safely; in 1942 the Ringling Barnum menagerie tent caught fire, with the loss of forty animals; 1944 saw the worst disaster that ever struck the American Circus, when the Ringling Barnum tent caught fire during a performance at Hartford; 168 people lost their lives and nearly 500 were injured.

The American Circus survived this apalling tragedy, as it had other fires, and Puritan denunciations, and disasters of every kind in the past, and as it will survive whatever the future holds in store. But the Hartford fire came at the end of an epoch. Parades had disappeared; railroad circuses would soon disappear; American circuses would shortly find a new

formula. But one achievement remained, and still remains – the three-ring circus.

As we have seen, George Sanger had experimented with three rings in England in 1860, over ten years before any American circus adopted the idea; but he dropped the practice; English audiences and English circus performers did not care for it. Three-ring circuses have been tried from time to time in Europe: Sarrasani, for instance, had a three-ring tent in 1908; Krone in 1924; Court's Zoo-Circus in 1928; Bostock at Earls Court in London in the same year; and Franz Althoff in 1959.[5] But they never really caught on.

The general English and European feeling is that a three-ring circus, with simultaneous acts, destroys the concentration of an audience wrapped around one ring that should be the essence of Circus. The intimacy of "the theatre in the round", the almost physically sensed bond of absorption linking audience and performer, is completely lost. How can one follow a performance that is going on at three different places at the same time? Artistry and subtlety must be

A forty-horse hitch pulls Barnum and Bailey's band-wagon on a parade in 1903.

abandoned in favour of coarse mass effects. This cannot be a presentation for discriminating patrons, but for an ignorant audience, dazzled by show, incapable of appreciating the fine points of the art. Patrons in the cheaper seats by the end rings must be fobbed off with inferior acts. Three-ring circuses may be a good way of filling vast tents on one-day stands; they may be a good way of making money for circus proprietors; but polished performances are difficult to achieve in the conditions of one-day stands; and the multi-ring circus destroys everything that the Circus ought to stand for.

Well, that is all very well, and as an Englishman, brought up in the tradition of European circuses, I must confess it is what I feel myself. When I have attended a Ringling Barnum performance in America, however excellent the acts and the production may be, I have found my attention divided, the band too loud, and the audience too restless. But, in all fairness, there is another side to the picture. Spectacle *is* part of Circus, and always has been; and the spectacles that can be mounted in the track round a three-ring circus can be breathtaking in their magnificence, especially now that the street parade is a thing of the past. And the sight of three rings full of circling horses, or

mounting elephants, or leaping acrobats, can be an exciting sight too, even if one can only follow the action of one ring in any detail.

Moreover, it is simply not true that three-ring circuses produce inferior and less artistic acts. During the years between the wars and immediately after the Second World War, which are still fresh in the memory of many circus-goers, many of the world's greatest circus acts originated or found a regular place in American three-ring circuses: the Codonas, the Concellos, the Clarkonians on the flying trapeze; the Wallendas on the high wire; Con Colleano on the low wire; the Hannefords on horseback; Lilian Leitzel on the Roman rings; Clyde Beatty with the big cats; Emmett Kelly as the hobo clown. The same standard is maintained today. The acts in the outer rings of a Ringling Barnum circus are as good as, or better than, anything you will see in the single ring of most English or European circuses.

Whatever one's feelings – and in this matter American and European audiences have come to different decisions – one must recognize that the three-ring circus is an authentic expression of the art of the Circus, and America's major contribution to that art.

29

The Greatest Show on Earth

THE NAMES of most of the major circus proprietors of the railroad age have been mentioned incidentally already in this narrative. But to sort them out in their rises and falls, their partnerships and their combinations, is a mammoth undertaking. I must confine myself to sketching the development of just a dozen or so shows, and demonstrating how they have almost all ended up in one great circus syndicate.[1]

John Robinson is the oldest name to have survived in the American Circus. He had been a great favourite south of the Mason Dixon line in the 'forties, and his name passed on through various ownerships for many years.

Yankee Robinson, no relation, was a Shakespearean actor and lion tamer who had established a popular

circus in the Middle West by the 'fifties. He had plenty of panache, but wasn't much of a businessman.

Adam Forepaugh, who often advertised his show as 4 Paw, was a butcher in Philadelphia who sold horse meat to a passing circus, and – seeing the size of the order – thought there must be something in that line of business. He had a show by 1865, and at one time challenged Barnum in a ridiculous competition to exhibit a sacred white elephant. After his death in 1890 the show was controlled by James Bailey, and after a merger in 1896 it became the Forepaugh Sells show.

The four Sells brothers had been associated with a livery stable in Ohio; they put a show on the road in 1872, and in the early 'eighties were boasting that with eight elephants they had more than all the other circuses put together (it wasn't true). In various combinations, involving other members of the family, their name became one of the best known in the circus world.

Harry Tammen and Fred Bonfils were newspaper proprietors in Denver, Colorado, who had started a little dog and pony show as a hobby in 1902, and named it after their sports editor, Floto. It only lasted three or four years, but when they combined with Sells, the Sells Floto became one of the best circuses of the early twentieth century.

Carl Hagenbeck, the famous German wild animal trainer and dealer, entered the American circus business in 1904, but the competition proved too great and he was obliged to sell out two years later. Somewhat to his disgust, the purchaser was Ben Wallace, an old-time circus man who had founded his show in 1884 and made a fortune by taking as much as he could from every "grift" in the game. As the Hagenbeck Wallace show it acquired a good reputation after it

had been acquired in 1919 by an Irish American, Jerry Mugivan, and his partners, Ballard and Bowers.

The Al G. Barnes show had been started by Al G. Barnes Stonehouse in 1909 as a small animal act on fairgrounds and carnivals. Stonehouse was one of the greatest wild animal trainers of his day, and it was said that there was no animal that he could not train. A huge elephant called Tusko had to be kept permanently shackled with heavy chains after Stonehouse's death, as no-one else could handle it.

Clyde Beatty was a young polar bear trainer with Hagenbeck Wallace in 1925 when the regular lion and tiger trainer was injured. Beatty took the act over and showed it very successfully. He never trained any animals himself, but he put on a very exciting performance with a great deal of whip cracking and pistol shooting, fights between the animals and attacks on himself. People working in the circus maintained that these were not all rehearsed, and that no-one quite knew what would happen next in his act. At one time

A poster for Forepaugh's Circus in 1894.

he worked as many as forty lions, tigers and leopards in the big cage at a time. Beatty's became the star wild animal act in the American Circus for nearly forty years; working at first with Hagenbeck Wallace, from 1935 he had a show under his own name in association with Cole Bros. (The American Circus has always been fond of partnerships of brothers – Campbell, Christy, Gentry, Gollmar, King, Miller, Orton, Ringling, Robbins, Sells, and many others.)

The John H. Sparks show had been started in about 1893 with a few dogs and horses. It was always one of the smaller shows, but was run economically and had a good reputation.

By 1923 the owners of Hagenbeck Wallace – Mugivan, Ballard and Bowers – had brought most of these shows into one combine (the exceptions were Yankee Robinson and Forepaugh), under the name of the American Circus Corporation, based at Peru, Indiana. It was a big, and, on the whole, a well-run syndicate. The routes were mapped out so that the shows didn't fight each other; performers and equipment could be shifted as required to support any weak areas; but each show was run independently, with its own special traditions and loyalties.

But there was competition, and big competition at that. And to tell that story we must bring in three more names.

Phineas T. Barnum is the best-known name in the history of the American Circus. It is typical of the man that this is the result of publicity rather than of achievement; he had dabbled with circuses at an early stage in his career, but he was a man with too much contempt for the public to devote his life to putting on a show of real skill and merit; his genius lay in the publicity he got for everything he touched. His return to the Circus, at the age of 60, was due to the astute mind of William C. Coup. Coup had a vision of a really big show, but he realized that he needed something like Barnum's name and personality to put it over. The Coup and Barnum show – it was called the P. T. Barnum Museum, Menagerie and Circus, International Zoological Garden, Polytechnic Institute and Hippodrome – was launched in 1871; the next year it went by rail; the year after that with two rings; it was a pioneer in both these revolutionary developments. But Barnum was a difficult man to work with, and the partnership broke up. The Barnum name and good will was then hired out to the Flatfoots, who were still in the business of owning circus property.

The figure of James A. Bailey now comes on the scene. He was a small man in size but a big man in ability. He had owned a circus, in partnership with Cooper, which had toured Australia, New Zealand and South America in 1876–7; now he fancied latching

An early poster for Barnum and Bailey's Greatest Show on Earth in 1881.

on to the magic of the Barnum name. He got it away from the Flatfoots, who now fade out of history, and in 1881 the Barnum and Bailey Circus was born.

Barnum died in 1891, but the show that he had christened "The Greatest Show on Earth" went on to deserve that title. The number of references in these pages indicates its importance. After Bailey's death in 1906 the business faltered, for there was no obvious successor and a new rival had appeared on the scene.

Back in 1882 the five sons of a harness maker of German extraction in Baraboo, Wisconsin, called Al Rüngeling, were circus-mad. With absolutely no

The "five moustaches" who founded the Ringling Circus. A poster of 1905.

money or resources they had formed the Ringling Bros Classic and Comic Concert Company. It wasn't a circus, but the boys were keen and hard working, and they caught the eye of old Yankee Robinson, who fancied the idea of sponsoring them. In 1884 they acquired a little 45 by 90 ft tent seating 600 people, with nine farm wagons, and the first tour opened of Yankee Robinson's Great Show, Ringling Brothers Carnival of Novelties and DeNar's Museum of Living Wonders – American circuses delighted in these omnibus titles.

Yankee Robinson died within the year, but the brothers went on. We can't follow their progress here in detail. The show got steadily better and bigger; it left a good reputation behind, for "grifting" was forbidden; the show was always, as circus people call it, strictly Sunday School. It took a good many years before all other American circuses followed their example. By 1889, their last season as a mud show, they had 110 horses. In 1890 they had expanded to two rings and a stage, and put the show on their own rail cars. In 1891 they owned 22 cars; the next year it had grown to 32. By 1907 they were strong enough to buy Barnum and Bailey after James Bailey's death.

Ringlings were now in a powerful position in the circus world. For some years they ran the Ringling and the Barnum and Bailey shows as separate units, but after the Great War there wasn't room for two such large companies in the whole of the United States. In 1919 they combined them as the Ringling Brothers Barnum and Bailey Circus. In 1927 the Greatest Show on Earth moved its permanent quarters from Bridgeport in Connecticut to the warmer winter climate of Sarasota in Florida.

It was "the Greatest" perhaps, but only just; for the American Circus Corporation, with its five excellent associated shows, gave it keen competition. As the post-war boom faded and the first signs of the approaching Depression showed themselves in falling attendances, it became clear that the market wasn't

A Barnum and Bailey poster from the Strobridge Litho Company in 1916.

big enough for two giant circus corporations to cut each other's throats in. Hesitant agreements not to fight each other broke down. A dispute about the 1930 lease of the Madison Square Garden booking brought matters to a head.

Jerry Mugivan of the American Circus Corporation was ready to buy Ringling Barnum up, but John Ringling, now in sole charge of his syndicate, refused to sell. Mugivan's partners indicated that they might be willing to sell out if Ringling could raise the money. He borrowed what he needed from the bank, and became the owner of all five major Corporation shows as well as the great but unwieldy outfit he owned already. In one swoop, eleven different circuses now came under one control.

The next year the Depression really struck. One after another the circuses whose names had filled a quarter of a century of American circus history were taken off the rails: John Robinson in 1930, Sparks in 1931, Sells Floto in 1932, Hagenbeck Wallace in 1935, Al G. Barnes in 1938. Meanwhile John Ringling found himself unable to repay the money he had borrowed, and in 1932 lost control of the syndicate to an amusement caterer called Sam Gumpertz.

In 1938 the Ringling family managed to regain control of the syndicate, with John Ringling's nephew, John Ringling North, in command. North had to manage the show through the labour disputes and strikes of 1938, through the labour and material shortages of the war years, through the consequences of the terrible fire of 1944, and up to the insoluble problems of keeping a railroad show on the move in the 1950s. It was some achievement that the show survived all this, as well as the family bickerings and law suits that followed John Ringling's death. But it was no surprise that after nearly thirty years some of the steam had gone out of the enterprise. The genuine circus atmosphere was becoming increasingly swamped by Broadway-type spectaculars.

In 1956 what seemed to be the end came. The show was moving too slowly, dates were being missed, labour troubles loomed afresh. In Pittsburgh on June 16 the Greatest Show on Earth gave its last performance under canvas; the big top was taken down for the last time, and the tour was abandoned.

But it wasn't the end. For very many years, ever since Barnum's day in 1881, the show had played in the Madison Square Garden building in New York. Now every major town in the United States had acquired a big air-conditioned exhibition hall of the same type. The Ringling Barnum Circus changed to playing exclusively in permanent arenas. It was, after all, only a return to the conditions of America's first circus, though the scale was very different. Of course

many people missed the atmosphere of the big top, but the staff needed to mount the show was reduced from 1,000 (some say 3,000) to less than 300, the daily expenses from $26,000 to $7,500. And the show went on.

The switch of policy was successful, but John Ringling North was getting old, and living for most of the year in Europe. New blood was needed. And in 1967 Irvin and Israel Feld, promoters of jazz and rock and roll concerts, made an offer to buy. North made only one condition: the name must stay the same. With a flair for publicity that Barnum would have approved, the document of purchase was signed in a public ceremony in the Coliseum of Rome. Some circus lovers feared the worst. But they need not have worried. The show goes on, some people think better than ever before.

Many people regret the disappearance of the splendid circuses that have been swallowed up in the Ringling Barnum maw. Many people regret the mania for hugeness that has possessed the American Circus, and the Greatest Show on Earth most of all. Many people like the atmosphere of tented circuses and the programmes of small circuses. But there are still many tented, and small and medium-sized circuses in the United States. That tradition has not been lost. And the Greatest Show on Earth is an American institution.

Ringling's and Barnum and Bailey united in the biggest combination in circus history. A poster of 1935.

30
Truck Shows

THERE WERE certain major disadvantages to railroad circuses. They could only play towns on the railroad track. Their routes were circumscribed by the layout of the rail networks. And the high rates charged were a heavy load on the expenses.

Many small mud shows continued to tour the continent with horse-drawn transport; the Mighty Haag, "a Southern show for Southern people", was still using some baggage horses up to 1928; but the invention of the automobile opened up an entirely new chapter for overland circuses. As early as 1918 the fairly large Coope and Lent Circus tried out a fully motorized circus on the roads, but there were too many mechanical breakdowns and the attempt was abandoned. Other ventures followed: in 1920 the Yankee American and Lindemann Bros started out with four Model T Ford trucks and an 800-seater tent; by the early 1930s they had a fleet of fifty trucks and a four-ring tent and called themselves the Seils-Sterling Circus (it had been the Sells-Sterling until Ringling pointed out that they owned the Sells title; the Lindemanns found it cheaper to rub out the bottom stroke of the L than to repaint all their trucks!). They were a big, splendid circus till economic recession forced a closure in 1938.[1]

The first large, successful, fully motorized circus went on the road in 1926. It was the Downie Bros Circus, launched by Andrew Downie, who had sold his Walter L. Main railroad circus two years before, but who itched to get back into the business.[2]

In its first season the Downie Bros travelled with 38 trucks, 5 trailers, 3 tractors, and 3 advance trucks. The tent consisted of an 80 ft diameter top with three 30 ft middle pieces; it contained one ring, a platform, and a steel arena for the cage acts.

By the next year they had a bigger tent with three rings, and the whole motorized caravan consisted of about 75 vehicles. Of these about 50 belonged to the show, and 25 to individual performers and staff; some of these still stayed in hotels or rooming houses overnight – this had been the regular American practice hitherto – but a number of them were beginning to sleep in their own living cars or caravans.

By 1930 Downie was boasting that it was "the largest motor circus in the world", with a tent seating 5,800 people. By 1934 it was travelling with 110 vehicles. This was the most it ever mustered, as the larger trucks now being manufactured tended to reduce the number required.

Other circuses followed Downie's example. In 1931 only six circuses – the really big ones – still travelled by rail. Seventeen good-sized circuses were recorded as truck shows that year. The last tented circus to go by rail was Clyde Beatty's in 1956.

In the late 'thirties straight bed trucks began to give place to tractors with semi-trailers, and a whole fleet of vehicles was adapted to the varying needs of a travelling circus – mechanized canvas spool trucks, retractable seat trucks, elephant vans, and so on. Parades were still held, though they must have lost something of their appeal from the absence of the baggage horses.

Considerable numbers of animals were carried on some truck shows. In the early 1950s the Al G. Kelly and Miller Bros Circus toured with fourteen elephants, a giraffe, a rhinoceros, a hippopotamus, a tapir, and about sixty horses and ponies. This show comprised about sixty trucks and private cars, but it kept the spirit of mud shows alive by sending a wagon drawn by six fine percheron draught horses round the streets of each town visited.

The programme of a truck show was a little smaller in size and quantity than that of a big railroad circus, but it did not differ in essence, nor necessarily in

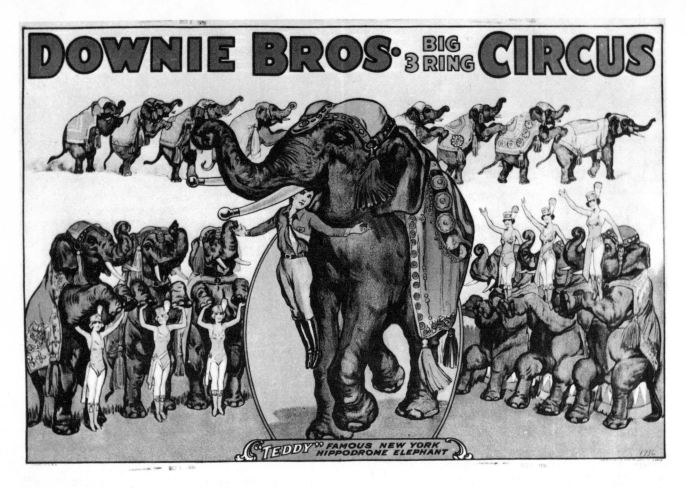

Elephants in a large motorized circus in 1936.

quality. In 1934 the Downie programme was as follows. It opened with the spec, a march round the track with elephants and dancing girls; then the leaps, which were being revived for a few seasons, concluding with a double somersault over five elephants; then dogs and monkeys riding on ponies; a clown boxing act; a head-slide on a sloping wire; a riding act, with a different rider in each ring; the swinging ladders, an aerial act with twelve girls; elephants; comedy acrobats; trained pigs in one ring, dogs in another; flying trapeze; and "iron-jaw" act; clown walk-round on stilts; liberty horses in the centre ring, dancing horses and ponies in side rings; comic motor car; high wire act, with Russian dance steps; "wire-walking" elephant (actually on a narrow plank); girls on trapeze;

riding act with men and ladies in evening dress (the Hannefords); high school riding with twelve riders, including side-saddle fallback, rhumba dance, and high jumping; perch act, and heel catch on a swinging trapeze; closing spec in the form of an Indian fantasy, with whooping Indians, fire-lit tepees in each ring, and concluding with the unfolding of enormous American flags from the top of the tent.

The show travelled lions and tigers, but the big cats were, at this time, reserved for the menagerie and did not appear in the ring.

Forty years later the pattern has not changed. That programme is one that we would enjoy today, and one that we can, with very little alteration, enjoy today in many American circuses.

31
Features of the American Circus

THE AMERICAN CIRCUS is very much a part of the international art of the Circus, but the Circus in America developed certain distinct features that are not found, or hardly found, in English or European circuses. The most important of these was, of course, the multi-ring circus, which has already been described. It may be convenient to group some of the others here for separate consideration.[1]

The approach to all except the smallest circuses was through the midway, a kind of fairground alley with games of chance to lose your money at, which were a popular field of activity for the grifters, and exhibitions of novelties and freaks. There might be fat women and living skeletons, midgets and giants, tattooed men, snake charmers, fire eaters, sword swallowers, marionette shows, Punch and Judy, conjurers, and a whole range of acts that were on too small a scale for the big tent. The midway was lined with banners, and one usually paid a single admission fee to see the lot; a man might gather a crowd from the bally platform and then, as the so-called lecturer, walk round the show describing the exhibits. The concessionaire paid a good sum to the circus proprietor to run these sideshows; they were called "the kid show", though some of the dancing girl acts were for adults only. The circus proprietor, unless his show was Sunday School, used to give a donation to the local police on the hopeful understanding that they wouldn't interfere with the illegal games being played.

Patrons usually entered the circus through the menagerie tent. Almost all circuses took a menagerie with them, and these menageries were often quite considerable and their tents almost as large as the big top itself. The Hagenbeck Wallace menagerie was on nine poles. It was customary for the "candy butchers" – the concession salesmen of drinks and other refreshments or novelties – to have to erect the menagerie tent as part of their duties. One ticket normally admitted patrons to both menagerie and circus, and they passed through the menagerie on the way to the big top.

European circuses usually speak of a one-pole tent with the pole in the centre of the ring, of a two-pole tent with a ridge above the ring, or a four-pole tent with the poles – often lattice masts nowadays – equally spaced round the ring. American circuses, with their long, oval-ended tents, have their poles spaced down the central spine of the arena, between the rings, and speak of four-, six- or eight-pole tents.

Inside the tent the seating was (and is) divided into "the blues" or bleachers, the unreserved benches at either end of the big top, and "the starbacks" or reserved seats, the best seats near the central ring. Prices in those pre-inflationary days actually fell during the nineteenth and early twentieth centuries: in the first quarter of the nineteenth century, circuses commonly charged a dollar for a seat in a box, and 75 or 50 cents in the pit; from about 1825 the standard admission to a good circus was 50 cents, with children half price; in 1912 Sells Floto cut the price of all tickets to 25 cents, but this lasted barely three years; by the 1920s the best seats were being priced at 75 cents; by the late 'thirties they were back at a dollar. The subsequent escalation of ticket prices is too horrible to be recounted!

A speciality of the refreshment offered in American circuses, along with peanuts and candy floss, was pink lemonade. The story goes that some candy butcher, running out of iced water, darted to the back of the tent and grabbed a pail of water in which a clown had just rinsed his red tights. The "strawberry lemonade" sold like wildfire, and lemonade has been dyed pink in American circuses ever since. (Circus performers like to tell an alternative – and unprintable – version of the origin of this drink.)

Before the performance began there was often a

half-hour concert by the band while the seats were filling up. During this the candy butchers were hard at work, and a clown might try to keep the people amused. Some very good bands travelled with circuses: Cooper and Bailey, for instance, had a 36 piece band in 1880. Merle Evans was a famous bandmaster with Ringling Barnum from 1919 up to 1969.

The ring was usually spread with tanbark rather than sawdust. Tanbark is shredded bark after the tannin has been extracted from it. In the mud shows the ring fence was usually built up with earth; it was not unknown for the corpse of a towner who had been killed in a clem to be left buried in the ring bank. These rings remained for years to mark the sites of circuses, like relics of some ancient pagan rite.[2]

When the show was over it was almost always followed by a concert or after-show, for which the patrons had to pay extra. This was a useful way of coaxing a few more cents out of the spectators, but if the after-show was feeble they had been known to wreck the tent in disgust.[3] In the early days the concert was usually a minstrel show; later it was often a Wild West Show. Cowboy stars, made famous by the movies, were often featured in these after-shows: Tom Mix with Sells Floto in 1929, Jack Hoxie with Downie Bros in 1933. The champion prize fighter, Jess Willard, appeared in the Sells Floto after-show in 1916; Jack Dempsey appeared with Cole Bros.

The Wild West Show was closely linked with the Circus in America. It may be said to have originated with "Buffalo Bill" Cody in 1883. The sharp-shooting girl, Annie Oakley, joined the show in 1885. It was an enormous success for some years, and imitators soon followed. In 1887 it embarked on the first of a series of tours in England and Europe which gave Buffalo Bill an international reputation, but interest in the States was declining; in 1910 Buffalo Bill merged his show with that of Pawnee Bill Lillie, but three years later it was forced to close. An ageing and drink-sodden Buffalo Bill joined the Sells Floto Circus as a special attraction, but relations soured and after much dispute he transferred to Miller Bros 101 Ranch Wild West Show two years later. Miller Bros tried a tour of England with a second unit in 1914, but it was caught by the outbreak of war and closed early. By the time of Buffalo Bill's death in 1917 the great days of the Wild West Show were over; its spirit went on to blossom in Western movies. Some live shows have kept the name alive, and one of these came to London in 1978; but, though it made a passable entertainment, it was a pale reflection of Cody's original Rough-Riders of the World, when more than three hundred horsemen swept into the arena, riding hell for leather, to set the scene for Buffalo Bill's

"Buffalo Bill" Cody, the founder of the Wild West Show.

entrance.[4] The Wild West Show was not a circus; the show was given in a big open-air arena rather than in a ring; but it exercised a considerable influence upon the American Circus. Cowboy whip cracking, sharp shooting, knife throwing and lassoo spinning acts found a place in circuses everywhere, and are still often seen.

Many American circus proprietors – and European ones, too, for that matter – were members of the Masonic Order. It provided a structure of brotherly community that transcended any professional rivalries. It was probably from masonic connections that the

The poster for a Danish Wild West Show.

Shrine circuses originally developed. The Ancient Arabic Order of the Nobles of the Mystic Shrine is a specifically American off-shoot from the Masonic Order; it was founded in 1872 and has devoted itself to establishing a network of hospitals for crippled children. In the process the members have a lot of fun; their red fezzes make them instantly recognizable, and their street parades are fabulous. One of their chief methods of raising money is to sponsor circus performances, and these play a regular part in many circuses' annual schedules, often in the Fall when the regular tenting season has come to an end. The Shrine shows seem to a foreigner to indicate the special way in which the Circus has become a part of American life, but – welcome though these engagements are to the artistes – there are some who see a certain danger in the practice. In so far as audiences for a Shrine circus buy tickets rather to assist the charity than to patronize the show, there must be some temptation for the circus proprietors involved to be not too particular about the quality of programme they are offering. It is a situation that does not entirely make for first-class performances.

At a time when circuses were getting bigger but their number was diminishing, the Circus found a new home on the midway of the travelling Carnival. This was a fair, with all the usual fairground attractions but including also a small circus, wild animal or Wild West show. The performances would not last more than about 45 minutes, and as many as possible would be given in a day. This was hard work, but the carnivals stayed a week in each location, so that the labour of one-day stands was avoided. Admission in the early 1900s was only 10 cents, but a good living could be made here. The number of carnivals increased as the number of circuses declined: the first carnival working on this pattern set up its midway in 1899; by about 1911 there were as many carnivals as circuses on the road; by 1923 there were less than 50 circuses and over 150 carnivals travelling the country.

The pride in the achievements of American circuses that is shown by all who have worked in them is illustrated by the custom of publishing Route Books. These were issued by many shows at the end of the season, and listed the route taken, the acts and staff, and much information relating to the show. The earliest was published by the Zoological Institute in 1835, and the gathering of them provides an attractive quest for collectors.[5] The information available in these route books, together with the very full reports of circus activity published from 1894 in *The Billboard*, makes possible a much fuller and more detailed history of Circus in America during the past hundred years or so than is possible in England, where information on travelling circuses is very difficult to locate.[6]

In general, the American Circus reflected many aspects of American society. The spirit that opened up the West was identical with the spirit of the early mud shows, battling their way across difficult and sometimes hostile territory. The American genius for inventiveness was shown in the development of innumerable devices for erecting and dismantling tents and transporting them with remarkable speed from place to place. The German High Command could recognize logistical efficiency when it saw it.

The drive and thrust of American business was reflected in the competitiveness of American circuses, in their rivalries, in their wasteful poster battles, and in their restless formation of partnerships and combinations. Free competition and monopoly tugged against each other in the circus world as they did in the world of big business elsewhere.

The American pride in massive achievement, which their critics call bragging and boastfulness, was shown in the advertising of their circuses. We do not hear much about the skill of the acrobats, or the grace of the equestrians, or the wit of the clowns. We hear a great deal about the number of elephants (Ringling Barnum had over fifty in 1955), the size of the tent, and how much money the show grossed.

The American appetite – some would say weakness – for something bigger than anything else was reflected

The Wild West Show has inspired knife throwing acts in circuses all over the world.

in the huge size that the big circuses grew to. No mere economic considerations could justify the size of the Barnum and Bailey or the Ringling Barnum operations. In the American Circus, Big was Beautiful.

It was a hard, tough, man's world, in which the weak went to the wall. It was a proud, self-sufficient world, contemptuous of people who lived in houses, not above fleecing them a little, but jealous of the quality of the entertainment they were giving them.

It was a world governed by a well-defined hierarchy and subject to a strict etiquette. In the dining tents, workmen ate on one side of a canvas partition, staff and performers on the other. Even on this side divisions existed; it was often forbidden for a male on the staff even to speak to an unmarried girl performer; if he was seen doing so, he could be fined; if he persisted he would be sacked. There were romances, of course, across the "class barrier", but they had to be conducted in secret. Even among the performers, the *élite* were the riders, entitled to a position at the head of the table, long after riding acts had ceased to be the prime attraction in the ring.

If it was a hard world, it was not a loose one. Circus girls were not there for the picking. Towners who thought they could get an easy lie at the back of the tent were soon taught their mistake. Real circus families observed very strict moral standards – for the women, at least, and for the men after marriage. The old New England puritans may have preached against the Circus as a bed of vice, but the puritan standards of morality were maintained in the Circus long after they were collapsing in other areas of American society.

America today, after Vietnam and Watergate, is not quite the proud self-confident society of the late nineteenth and early twentieth centuries in which the Circus enjoyed its golden age. The American Circus may be in a process of adjustment. It seems possible that the example of the Moscow Circus, which has toured coast to coast on several occasions, will help to persuade American audiences that a one-ring circus is not necessarily an inferior show. The three-ring circuses may become limited to just a few really big companies. There may perhaps come a new emphasis on quality in smaller shows. Indeed, Ringling Barnum is putting a one-ring circus on the road in 1979, featuring star acts from the Monte Carlo Circus Festival. A fascinating question mark lies over the future of the Circus in America, but we can hardly doubt that there will be a future to be proud of.

Opposite: Adolph Friedländer printed thousands of magnificent posters for European circuses. A design of 1913.

The latest circus king in France is an actor with a passion for the Circus who set up his own show in 1969.

Circus Knie commissions some of the best artists in Switzerland to design its posters. This poster of 1972 was inspired by the act of a tiger riding on a rhinoceros.

A balancing act by the clown.

A girl shot from a cannon.

A Stafford poster showing a horseback voltige act, flanked by clowns on stilts and the ladder.

The poster for the Covent Garden Circus in 1884. Six Christmas circuses were presented at the Opera House up to 1893.

The Cirque d'Eté in Paris featured a pigeon act with a male rider, c. 1880. The bill is studded with the names of famous circus families.

A scene in an indoor circus in the 1870s. Young artistes ride on ponies, a clown holds a balloon for a dog to jump through, the ringmaster keeps the horses up, a Shakespearean clown cracks jokes, and a groom is in attendance.

A noisy pistol-shooting type of lion act, as depicted by Blamire.

A stock Stafford poster illustrating most of the acts in a late 19th-century circus: the Jockey act, the Courier of St. Petersburg, voltige and jumping on horseback, the leaps, and the trapeze.

A fearless equestrienne leaps through a blazing hoop, as depicted by J. L. Blamire in 1882.

A stock Stafford poster of an equestrienne jumping through a paper balloon, c. 1890.

V
THE GOLDEN AGE OF THE CIRCUS IN EUROPE

32
The Circus spreads across Europe

FROM THE AMPHITHEATRE and the Royal Circus in London, the Circus spread across Europe. The riders with single or double displays of trick riding were succeeded by riding troupes, in France, in Germany, in Scandinavia, in Russia, all springing from their origins in England.

In France, Philip Astley had paid several visits to Paris in the 1770s, and set up the Amphithéâtre Astley in 1783. For a man who had spent a great deal of his life fighting foreigners, especially Frenchmen, Astley displayed a commendable belief in the power of entertainment to heal the scars of war. He travelled widely, possibly as far as Vienna and Belgrade,[1] certainly to Brussels. No doubt, many of the nineteen circuses that he is said to have built were on the continent of Europe. He was in Paris when he died in 1814, as was his son John in 1821.

In the German-speaking lands, Price – presumably the man who had ridden at Dobney's – was performing in Vienna in the last quarter of the eighteenth century. He seems to have died abroad and his widow married Christoph de Bach, who had run away from home at the age of ten to join the troupe. By 1797 Christoph de Bach was presenting riding and acrobatics on the rope in Prussia with a troupe of six, including Price's widow, her daughter, and small son.[2]

In Denmark, James Price arrived with a company of riders and rope dancers in 1795. He had been born in 1761, so may have been an elder son of the man who rode at Dobney's. He came from London via St Petersburg, Vienna, Constantinople and Hamburg, so he was perhaps the most widely travelled of all these English riding masters. Anyhow, he now settled in Scandinavia, and founded the famous line of pantomime actors whose successors still perform in the Tivoli Gardens in Copenhagen.[3]

In Italy, Alessandro Guerra married the Miss Price

who had been touring with Christoph de Bach, and created a fine circus in the first half of the century.[4] In Spain, the riding master, Balp, had found himself a pretty Spanish wife by 1779;[5] later, yet another Price, Thomas, established permanent circuses in Madrid and Barcelona in the 1850s.

In Russia, Charles Hughes arrived in about 1790. At a time when he had been involved in endless friction in trying to run the Royal Circus, Hughes was approached by Count Alexis Orlov, who had been sent to Europe by the Empress Catherine the Great to obtain blood stallions and breeding mares to improve the stock of horses in Russia. Charles bought horses for Orlov at Newmarket and elsewhere, and was persuaded to accompany them on the voyage to St Petersburg. He took his own stud of performing horses with him, being unwilling to leave them behind at the Royal Circus.[6]

At St Petersburg Hughes soon found an opportunity to give displays of his skill in horse riding and of the other entertainments that had been featured at the Royal Circus. The Russians were fascinated, and the Empress Catherine most of all. Hughes was a tall, handsome man and became a favourite of Catherine; Decastro hints that he was her lover, and this is not improbable for though she was now sixty her sexual appetite was insatiable, and her fondness for tall, handsome soldiers was notorious. At last she tired of him, and by 1793 he had returned to England. But he left his ring horses and his performers behind. From that beginning there flowed the rich development of the Circus in Russia.

Wherever it was planted, the art of the Circus found an enthusiastic welcome for its mixture of horsemanship, acrobatics and clowning.[7] In Paris a new war between England and France interrupted the development of Astley's enterprise. Astley's original

The Cirque d'Eté in Paris staged splendid programmes between 1841 and 1897.

Amphithéâtre was taken over by an Italian bird trainer and equestrian, Antonio Franconi, in 1791. Here and at the various Cirques Olympiques (that name again!), the Franconi family, sometimes in association with Louis Dejean, dominated the development of Circus in France throughout the nineteenth century. They were seen in England and Germany several times during the late 'forties and early 'fifties. When the Cirque Olympique became an orthodox theatre without a ring, purely equestrian circuses replaced it: the Cirque d'Eté, the Cirque d'Hiver, the Cirque Fernando, the Nouveau Cirque, the huge Cirque Métropole and, on an even larger scale, a succession of Hippodromes.

On the road in France, Jacques Tourniaire had formed a company of riders by 1801; by the 1820s Johann Hinné was touring with a troupe of English rope dancers. Both these names were to crop up all over Europe in the years to come. By the 1840s the Paul Cuzent troupe was touring Austria, where a critic rated them superior to Ducrow and Franconi, and by 1850 they had become the toast of the Russian court at St Petersburg.

In Austria, Christoph de Bach, who became a

Master of Horse to the imperial court, had established a permanent circus on the Prater in Vienna – the Circus Gymnasticus – in 1808, and went on to direct a touring circus that was known in all the capitals of Europe. Eduard Wollschläger, the child of travelling acrobats, established a reputation as a rider in character, and directed a travelling circus that toured Germany and Belgium by mid-century. Ernst Jacob Renz, the son of a rope dancer, was apprenticed, like several other great performers, to the horse trainer Rudolph Brilloff, and went on to build permanent circuses in Hamburg, Breslau and Vienna, engaging in a famous contest with the Franconi–Dejean company for the patronage of Berlin, where he built his most luxurious circus in the Karlstrasse, later famous for its Max Reinhardt productions. In the 'seventies his chief rival in Berlin was Albert Salamonsky, descended from a long line of Jewish fairground performers, who had played with Tourniaire in the 1830s; he, too, made the journey to Russia and established a circus in Moscow.

One of Renz's riders, Gotthold Schumann, set up his own company in 1870; his son, Albert, became the greatest trainer of liberty horses in Europe, taking over the Renz building in Berlin and building circuses in Vienna and Frankfurt; his brother, Max, founded a circus in Scandinavia with a building in Copenhagen. Another member of Renz's company, Lorenz Wulff, founded a circus in Austria in the 1860s; his son, Edouard, became a star horse trainer at the Cirque Royale in Brussels, and built up a fine touring circus, erecting a portable iron circus building in Munich which he transported through Austria-Hungary as far as Budapest.

In the last quarter of the nineteenth century the Prussian officer class did not find circus ownership beneath them. Heinrich Herzog, Honorary Master of Horse to the Prince Regent of Bavaria, founded his own circus, at first in partnership with Schumann. Paul Busch, a Prussian officer too, had succeeded Renz as the first name in the German Circus by the end of the century, with a second magnificent building in Berlin; his daughter, Paula, went on to become the Grande Dame of the German circus world.

A doctor's son, Friedrich Knie, ran away from home to join a circus in Innsbruck in 1803, and founded a troupe that travelled mostly through Austria and Bavaria; during the Franco-Prussian War they sought refuge in peaceful Switzerland, where they performed tight rope acts in the open air; they acquired their first tent in 1919, enlarging their show with animal acts, and came to be recognized, unofficially, as the National Swiss Circus. Wilhelm Carré, the son of an acrobat and rider, set up on his own in 1854, built a circus in

Amsterdam, and founded the Royal Netherlands Circus; his son, Oscar, carried on the tradition.

From Italy, Alessandro Guerra, known as Il Furioso, toured his Circo Olimpico as far as Russia, where he disputed with Paul Cuzent for the favour of the Russian people. He engaged artistes like Ciniselli and Chiarini, whose names were to ring round the circuses of Europe and America for several generations. Gaëtano Ciniselli married Wilhelmine Hinné in one of those alliances of circus families that have marked its history as significantly as the marriages of royal dynasties; after touring most of Europe he, too, established a famous circus in St Petersburg. The first native Russian company was founded by the Nikitin brothers in 1873; by the time of the Revolution there were permanent circus buildings in many provincial towns, and a keen appreciation of the art both among aristocrats and peasants.

Circuses were formed and circus buildings erected in all the countries of eastern Europe. Perhaps the most famous of these was the Royal Rumanian Circus Sidoli, originally founded by an Italian, which toured widely from the second half of the nineteenth century.

By the end of the nineteenth century it was calculated that there were some two hundred large and medium-sized circus companies in Europe. Every country can tell its own story. Every country has made its own contribution to the total art. Yet, to a certain degree, every country will tell the same story, for the same artistes and, to some extent, the same circuses crossed and recrossed the frontiers of Europe. Their tents were erected and dismantled by teams of Czech labourers, some sixty to a company, who lived frugally, eating only one meal a day and saving their pay until they could buy a cottage and a little plot of land in their homeland.

To advertise these performances, a school of pictorial circus art was created, in Europe as in England and America. In France many fine designs were created by Jules Chéret and the Lévy brothers from the 1870s to the end of the century in an astounding flowering of poster art; in Germany the firm of Adolph Friedländer turned out over 9,000 designs for every type of circus and fairground attraction between 1872 and 1935.[8] In these brilliantly coloured lithographs the Circus achieved a new dimension in a naive, surrealistic vision of incredible feats by a race of superhuman performers.

From Europe, these circuses set out with their

A superb Chéret poster for a snake charmer illustrates the perfection of colour lithography.

caravanserais of wagons and animals in vast tours to every continent of the globe. Louis Soullier, who had married Christoph de Bach's widow from his second marriage, directed a circus that travelled through Russia to Siberia, China and Japan, bringing a Japanese troupe of acrobats back to Paris in 1866. Giuseppe Chiarini was in South and Central America in the 1860s, in China in the 1870s, in Australia, New Zeland and India in the 1880s, and in South America again in the 1890s. Théodore Rancy played for a year in Egypt in 1869 to celebrate the opening of the Suez Canal. Other companies followed in the first decades of the twentieth century, hiring yet bigger ships, with yet more artistes and yet more animals.

We cannot chronicle this vast story in detail here, but let us pause for a moment in Paris in the third quarter of the century, where the Circus reached a level of artistic perfection and gained a degree of critical appreciation that it has never enjoyed since. This, if at any time, was the Golden Age of the Circus.

157

33
Equestriennes

IN ENGLAND, and even more in America, the Circus had grown up, to a large extent, as a popular entertainment, in the sense of being an entertainment patronized chiefly by "the common people". In France, however, it acquired a marked aristocratic, or at least *haut bourgeois*, association. This was best exemplified in the popularity of its displays of high school riding. The greatest exponents of the art of equitation, like François Baucher in the first half of the nineteenth century and the Englishman, James Fillis, in the second half of the century – men who gave their names to whole schools of horsemanship – trained horses for the circuses of Paris and rode in their rings. The greatest public acclaim, however, was given to the women who mastered these principles of horse training and displayed them in circus performances.

The first equestrienne to achieve popularity in this way was Caroline Loyo, who appeared in the Cirque Olympique in about 1833 and drew the cream of masculine society to the ringside to applaud her. Although she was compared to ballet dancers like Taglioni and Carlotta Grisi for the grace with which she rode, it was the firmness with which she mastered the most lively mount that evoked the greatest admiration. She was known as "the *diva* of the riding whip". The critic, Jules Janin, who may perhaps have been betraying a certain masochistic pleasure from watching her, wrote as follows: "What a learned and terrible rider is this! Is she really a woman? ... She says that for her the horse is like rhyme for a poet, a slave who must obey."[1]

Some indication of the prestige enjoyed by Loyo is provided by the following reported conversation. "Did you see her last year on the bay horse she has trained?" one gentleman asked his companion. "No, I went to

Florence last year to admire the masterpieces in the Palazzo Pitti", was the answer. "Sir", replied the first, "when Caroline mounts a new horse one does not go to Florence; one does not admire the Palazzo Pitti; one stays at the Circus!"

Contemporary with Loyo was Pauline Cuzent and her sister, Antoinette Lejars, who rode side saddle in an attractive feminine version of military uniform, and who travelled with the family circus all over Europe. Throughout the gay, delirious years of the Second Empire handsome and rich young men, and older connoisseurs of the *haute école*, judged and compared and admired these *écuyères* of the Circus. They received the kind of adulation given to ballerinas and *divas* of the opera. By the 1880s three riders were preeminent.

There was Emilie Loisset, from a circus family, who had been performing on a pad horse by the age of fifteen but took up high school riding after an accident. Her beauty attracted many admirers, including a prince who wanted to marry her, but with imperious disdain she inscribed on the pommel of her riding whip, "Princesse ne daigne, Reine ne puis, Loisset suis". But in 1882, at the Cirque d'Hiver, her horse refused the leap into the ring to acknowledge the applause after her act; as she whipped it, it dashed for the stable, reared up on finding the door shut, and fell on top of her; the horn of her side saddle pierced her stomach, and she died two days later while all Paris mourned.

Elisa Petzold came from a very different background. Her grandfather was a wealthy Austrian soap manufacturer, and a good marriage was planned for her by her parents; but as a young girl she saw the Circus Renz in Dresden, and from that moment she had no other ambition than to ride high school in a circus. Her family, in despair, sent her away to a convent; but she came back with her mind unchanged. She eventually obtained a position in the Circus Renz, and astounded Paris with her riding. The Baron de Vaux, who wrote an entire book about circus riders, described her as follows: "This charming artiste was delicate, supple and elegant in the saddle, the horse naturally balanced. Every movement was obtained without appreciable effort either by the rider or the animal ... which marked time in a demi-courbette with the regularity and the rhythm of a conductor's baton." The Empress Elizabeth of Austria became her close friend, and she married into the aristocracy.

The third of these star equestriennes was Anna Fillis, the daughter of James. Baron de Vaux wrote of her that "her talent had arrived, through work and study, at such a pitch of perfection that equitation is for her no longer a science but an art. ... No man who is susceptible to those two great seductions, the woman and the horse, could have before his eyes a more adorable spectacle." That phrase sums up the magic of these *écuyères* of the Belle Epoque: it was the conjunction of feminine sexuality, beautiful but strict, with equine grace, powerful but obedient, creating a single almost centaur-like entity of woman and horse.

There is one other rider whose story is too strange and sad to leave untold. The Baronne de Rahden was the daughter of a rich bourgeois family which fell on hard times; she joined a circus as a rider, where the Baron de Rahden saw her and married her. She continued her career, touring the cities of Europe, and was in London at the Alhambra in 1900; everywhere she was accompanied by the Baron, who was insanely jealous of any other man who seemed too intimate with her, eyeing with suspicion every bouquet that was sent her. A Dane fell madly in love with her, and took a job as a groom in the circus so as to be near her. The Baron perceived the relationship and there was a violent quarrel in the course of which he shot the Dane and killed him. He was acquitted on pleading a *crime passionel*.

The Baronne continued her career alone, troubled perhaps by some hints of failing eyesight. One morning, at Nice, her maid woke her. "Why have you called me in the night?" she asked. She had turned stone blind! That evening, without saying a word to anyone else, she was escorted to the circus and mounted her horse to enter the ring. At the climax of her act she used to make her horse rear up on its hind legs while she leaned backwards in the saddle, rather then

Pauline Cuzent was, in the opinion of Baron de Vaux, "the ideal type of elegant horsewoman ... whose name has remained a legend in the annals of the Circus".

forwards in the orthodox manner. This was always a dangerous feat, disapproved of by strict horsemen. That night it was fatal. She was thrown, terribly injured, but did not die. Perhaps she had hoped to kill herself. Instead she had to eke out the next thirty years of her life in a garret, blind and penniless.[2]

Most of these equestriennes rode side saddle – and indeed this can be a most charming style, providing firm control over the horse's movements, as exemplified by Katja Schumann, who rides high school exquisitely in this way in circuses today. But a few women riders were beginning to ride astride, in men's clothes, by the 1880s. There was Mlle Chinon, who appeared as a military cadet of the Saumur riding school; Louisa Lankast, who adopted the uniform of an equerry to Louis XIV; and the Comtesse Ghyka, a Hungarian noblewoman who ran away from her husband to ride in a circus, and who travelled with a vast wardrobe of theatrical costumes, almost reminiscent of a pantomime principal boy's in style, and never appeared in the same costume twice before the same public.

In their dress and in their manner of riding, these women brought technical skill, grace, beauty and sex appeal to the Circus. But above all they brought style; and they found an audience eager to appreciate it. It was Balzac who wrote, "For me, the equestrienne in the fullness of her powers is superior to all the glories of song, of dance, and of dramatic art."

Amateur performers, probably at the Cirque Molier. A painting by Tissot at the Museum of Fine Arts, Boston.

34
Acrobats, Amateurs and Artists

SECOND ONLY to the equestrians came the acrobats in the appreciation of the French connoisseurs. The French had not, in the nineteenth century, adopted team games to any great extent, and many gentlemen took their physical exercise in gymnasiums. They were all the better qualified, therefore, to criticize and applaud the feats of professional gymnasts and acrobats.

There were some remarkable performers. The little Uessems threw a handstand, supporting himself on free-standing ladders with either hand, while holding in his mouth the rope of a trapeze, on the bar of which his partner also threw a handstand. The Marty brothers performed "the devil's ladder", in which a ladder is balanced across the bar of a trapeze; one brother stood on one end of the ladder, while the other brother hung from a small trapeze suspended at the other end. The Ancilloti troupe on bicycles – which had only recently been invented – performed head to head balances and shoulder to shoulder somersaults from one carrier to another.[1]

It was the flying trapeze and the Risley act that attracted some of the greatest acclamation. Georges Strehly, the author of a book devoted to an artistic as well as a technical appreciation of circus feats, wrote as follows: "I should say that the flying trapeze is the majestic epic skimming the clouds with its wings, while Icarianism is lyric poetry, less grandiose in inspiration but richer art, which causes the most delicate fibres of our heart to thrill.". It was when a boy somersaulted to and fro upon the feet of two or three carriers that this act reached perfection: "The rapidity of these evolutions is such that the eye is dazzled, as if by brilliant fireworks. ... One cannot understand and appreciate a true Icarian work at the first seeing. It is not a simple melody within the grasp of all but a scholarly orchestra, addressed preferably to connoisseurs who can taste all its beauties only after several performances. The repetition of the performance, far from causing satiety, only augments the admiration."

National styles were analysed and compared. The French were graceful and daring on the trapeze; the Germans were clever and methodical in the Icarian games; the Anglo Saxons were vigorous and full of endurance in carpet acrobatics and on horseback; the Spaniards were supple and light; the Italians impetuous; the Japanese hieratic in balancing; the Arabs fiery, as if the burning wind of the Sahara was animating them.

The enthusiasm for the Circus at this time is indicated by the amateur circuses that sprang up, notably that founded by M. Molier in his home in the rue Benouville in 1880, which only closed with his death in 1934. Here Parisian Society was invited to select performances – separate ones for the *haut monde* and the *demi monde* – to watch keen amateurs in the ring, who by all accounts gave a good account of themselves on horseback and in gymnastics.[2]

French men of letters followed the Circus keenly. Théophile Gautier, the critic, wrote of it with the same respect as he gave to the theatre, opera or ballet. It was Gautier who summed up the appeal of Circus as "consisting precisely in the absence, or rather the insignificance, of speech", it was "the opera of the eye"; and Barbey d'Aurevilly, a Bohemian dandy of the Paris cafés, wrote: "I have always been a great frequenter of circuses, an amateur of those physical spectacles which not only give me a pleasure of the senses, although it gives that also, but an intellectual pleasure far more deep and refined. If only we writers could write as these people move, if only we had in our style the inexhaustible resources of their vigour, their almost fluid suppleness, their undulating grace, their mathematical precision, if only we had the control of words that they have of their movements we should be great writers."[3]

Painters, too, were sensitive to the visual enchantment of the Circus. Tissot painted monocled performers on the trapeze and perfumed ladies in the boxes at the Cirque Molier; Toulouse Lautrec sat beside the ring at the Cirque Fernando, and Degas gazed up at Miss Lala in the roof; Daumier and Rouault found inspiration in the grotesqueness of clowns; Renoir in their humanity; Leger in the pattern of acrobats on the trapeze; Seurat in the dancing points of light as the rosinback circles the ring; Picasso in the sad faces of hungry saltimbanques; and most recently Chagall has devoted a volume of lithographs to the Circus, "a magic word, a thousand-year-old dance, where tears and smiles, the play of limbs and arms, take the form of a great art".[4]

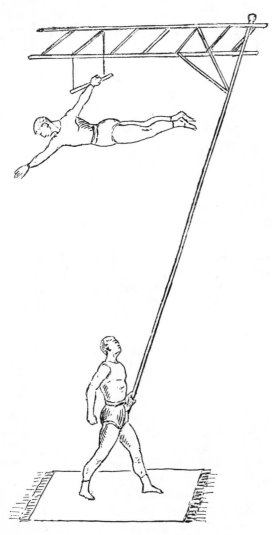

The silver ladder. A sketch by Georges Strehly of an outstanding perch act.

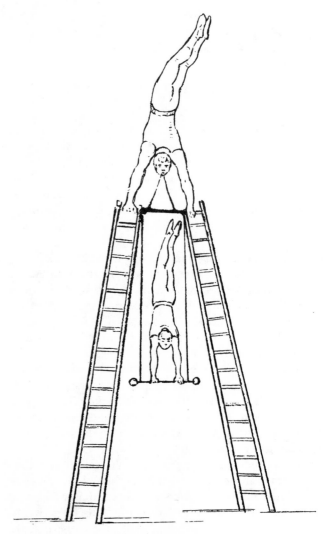

Little Uessems in an acrobatic feat. Strehly was no artist, but he was a keen judge of acrobatics.

Opposite: Gunther Gebel-Williams, the greatest circus star of the present day, with the Ringling Brothers Barnum and Bailey Circus.

VI
THE CIRCUS IN THE TWENTIETH CENTURY

35
Proprietors

Great Britain

WHEN WE LEFT the story of the Circus in England at the end of the nineteenth century, the picture was not very encouraging. The music hall was attracting all the best talent, and the permanent circuses almost everywhere were closing: in London the Holborn Amphitheatre had been converted into a theatre, after only six years, in 1873, eventually ending its life as a boxing stadium; Astley's was closed in 1893 when the building was condemned as unsafe; Hengler's closed in 1909, to be rebuilt (with the façade unchanged) as the Palladium; the Hippodrome had been opened in 1900 for spectacular circus-type entertainments, with a ring that could be flooded, but it, too, filled its ring with seats in 1909 and became an orthodox theatre.

Tenting circuses, however, remained popular in the country districts, with John Sanger and Robert Fossett still well-known names. An important newcomer was Bostock's, which toured in Europe as well as in Britain from the 1880s to 1923; Frank Bostock was a great wild-animal trainer; his brother, E. H. Bostock, was in charge of the famous Bostock and Wombwell Menagerie.[1] Also successful on quite a large scale was Chapman's Great London Circus, which toured from 1929 to the war.[2]

Circuses still made seasonal appearances in London at the Crystal Palace, the Agricultural Hall, and Olympia, and it was from one of these that the renaissance of the English Circus sprang. A carriage builder called Bertram Mills attended the 1919 Christmas circus at Olympia that had been mounted by Wilkins and Young; when pressed by the owners of the hall to give his opinion of the show, he replied, "If I couldn't do better than that I'd eat my hat."

They took him up on that, and the result is history, too well known to be repeated in detail here.

Apart from the war years, Bertram Mills, followed by his sons, Cyril and Bernard, put on Christmas circuses at Olympia from 1920 to 1966, and ran a tenting circus from 1930 to 1964. At its best it was, arguably, the finest circus in the world; Mills was a master of publicity; he searched the world for the finest performers; he imposed strict time schedules on their acts; he insisted upon the best; and circus artistes came to regard an Olympia booking as the summit of their careers. When economic conditions changed and the circus began to lose money, Cyril and Bernard decided to close the show down rather than lower their standards.[3]

The success of Mills gave an uplift to the whole circus industry in England. Very good acts from some of the best European circuses appeared between the wars at the Christmas Agricultural Hall Circus, booked by the experienced agent, Stanley Wathon. Other promoters mounted Christmas circuses at Earls Court and Harringay after the Second World War, so that at one time there were three major circuses playing in London – something that had not occurred since the 1880s. Among the tenting circuses one of the best to benefit from the "up-market image" that Circus had now acquired were the brothers Jimmy and Dick Chipperfield. The Chipperfields had been animal showmen since the seventeenth century, and had run a menagerie and small circus during the nineteenth century, but they were still very much small-timers when the two brothers put a tenting circus on the road in 1932. It was still fairly modest when the war interrupted its development, but after the war they

Three popular clowns in the Bertram Mills Circus: Coco, Percy Huxter and Little Billy.

The Chipperfield Circus has always been noted for its animal acts.

went right ahead and by the mid-fifties they claimed to be running the biggest circus in Europe, employing 250 people, and with the biggest tent in the world, seating 8,000-9,000 people (this must have been after Ringling Barnum ceased tenting). In 1955 the brothers split up, amicably, Jimmy to found safari parks all over the world, and Dick to continue with the circus. Like Mills, they found tenting unprofitable in the mid-'sixties, and in 1964 embarked on an extended tour of South Africa. They were back in England by 1968, and still tour with a tenting circus that is modest compared with earlier years but which remains particularly strong in their own animal acts. Jimmy's daughter, Mary, as well as being a first-class animal trainer, has occasionally put on a show under her own name; Dick's daughter, Sally, started her own circus in 1978; and Jimmy returned to the circus scene with his own show in 1979. So at the time of writing there are four circuses, each of which has a claim to the distinguished name of Chipperfield.[4]

A fairground operator, Billy Smart, started a circus immediately after the war, taking advantage of the post-war boom that attracted a number of very poor "rogue circuses" as well as genuine showmen. It had grown into a very big outfit by the 'fifties, but in 1972 it ceased tenting – the last of that generation of big English circuses – though it continued to stage occasional shows for television.

Today there is no really big tenting circus in Britain, but there are some sixteen to twenty shows on the road every summer, of whom half a dozen or so are medium-sized. Some, like Sir Robert Fossett's and the Robert Brothers, are run by old circus families; some, like Austen Brothers and Gerry Cottle's, by new proprietors venturing into this area of entertainment; but they all offer good, honest circus entertainment, and keep the flag flying with considerable courage in difficult conditions. While several provincial towns, notably Glasgow and Manchester, put on good Christmas circuses, London – to its disgrace – has had none since the Olympia seasons closed, unless a tenting circus braves the weather on some outlying open space. There still survive, however, two permanent circus buildings which mount excellent programmes throughout the summer. The Great Yarmouth Hippodrome, erected in 1903, admirably exemplifies the intimate atmosphere that a small circus building can create. The Blackpool Circus, built between the legs of the Tower in 1894, is a dream of late Victorian Moorish fantasy and certainly the most beautiful circus building in the world; it deserves to be much better known.[5]

Ireland

English circuses have toured in Ireland from time to time, but the chief Irish circus is Fossett's, a branch of the English Fossetts, which was established there in about 1914 when Edward Fossett joined in partnership with Dr Powell, a showman, conjurer and actor, and married his daughter. Other respected circuses are Duffy's, originally founded in 1875, and Courtney's.

France

Two names dominated the French Circus at the beginning of the twentieth century. The Cirque Rancy had been founded in 1856 by a brilliant horse trainer, Théodore Rancy, and his descendants had intermarried with every leading circus family in Europe, creating several circuses of high renown. The last in the line, Sabine, married Dany Renz, a member of the Great German circus family, who was tragically killed by a mad elephant in 1972. In recent years the Sabine Rancy Circus has fallen from its best days, and it was

cirque d'hiver
de Paris

BOUGLIONE
programme

The Cirque d'Hiver still presents authentic circus performances.

launched a complete circus in 1924. It grew into a very considerable enterprise, but as the family grew, Amar Cirques multiplied, producing the usual consequences of Gresham's Law, and the currency of the title became somewhat debased. In 1973 what remained of the great Cirque Amar was bought by Bouglione, under whose control it sometimes still appears with the original name.

The latest circus king to arise in France has sprung, not from a traditional circus or menagerie family but from the world of cabaret and television, where he is a star of the first order. Jean Richard had long dreamed of owning a zoo and circus, and his success as an entertainer, above all in the role of Maigret, made this possible. After a prior essay in partnership with the Gruss family in 1957, he launched the Cirque Jean Richard in 1969, and in 1972 he bought the Pinder Circus. He has run both these outfits as major tenting circuses, and in 1978 he added a more modest unit, the Medrano, for visiting smaller towns. Like Bertram Mills, Jean Richard has shown that it is not necessary to be born in the sawdust or in a caravan in order to run a successful circus. But success is a fickle quality in the world of entertainment, and a combination of bad weather and competition from the World Cup on television forced him to put his enterprises into liquidation in 1978. He has declared, however, that after a reorganization "the show will go on".

In addition to the big tenting circuses there are several small ones; indeed, in my experience you are unlikely to take a fortnight's holiday in Provence during the summer without running into one or other of them. Perhaps the best of these small troupes, in which the members of one family provide the bulk of the acts as well as selling the tickets and showing the patrons to their seats, is the Cirque Morallès, with its dogs and ponies and enthusiastic youngsters. In the towns the permanent circuses have almost all disappeared, but the Cirque d'Hiver in Paris, recently restored by the Bougliones to its original splendour of red, yellow and blue, still offers a winter programme; while in the last few years the tented Cirque à l'Ancienne, largely featuring members of the talented Gruss family, has played in the heart of Paris with an intimate presentation of acts that recalls the very origins of Circus.

There are now two training schools for circus artistes in Paris, one of them with a state subsidy, and despite current difficulties there seems to be a keen appreciation of Circus in France, extending to artistes, writers and the general public. Two years ago no less than eleven different circuses could have been seen playing in the Paris region at Christmas time.[6]

forced into liquidation while tenting in Italy in 1978. The other leading tenting circus was Pinder's, which had been founded in England in 1854 by two brothers, George and William. They began touring in France in 1868 and eventually settled there, specialising in one-day stands; the show was famous for the magnificent parades it mounted. In 1928 it was sold to Spessardy, who gave it a new lease of life, though at the cost of mingling a good deal of music hall entertainment in the programmes, but by the 1970s it was in low water.

Meanwhile two new names had appeared in the circus firmament. The Bougliones were gipsy menagerie proprietors who began to expand into circus, trading in the 1920s under the name of Buffalo Bill. In 1934 they took over the Cirque d'Hiver in Paris, and they now present a big tenting circus that is well known all over France and Belgium. A little earlier than their rise to prominence, an Algerian called Ahmed ben Amar, who ran a fairground belly-dancing booth, had married the sister of a French fairground menagerie owner; their children enlarged the menagerie, and under the title of the Frères Amar finally

Germany

If the European Circus was at its best in England in the first half of the nineteenth century, and in France in the second half, it was in Germany that it achieved its highest standards in the first half of the twentieth century.

One of the greatest names in Circus throughout the world is Hagenbeck. The original Hagenbeck had been a fish merchant in Hamburg who had the idea of exhibiting some live seals that had been caught up in the fishing nets; his son, Carl, developed the display of animals further, and in 1903 he created a wonderful zoo at Stellingen, where wild beasts were shown in natural surroundings and without cages. He not only initiated the whole modern approach to zoological gardens but pioneered a method of training animals that was based upon rewards, and he built up a substantial business in supplying trained animals to circuses all over the world. In this way the Hagenbeck style, particularly of big-cat acts, has had a decisive influence upon their presentation everywhere.

One of Carl's brothers had started a circus as early as 1887, and this was a big affair for many years. It is believed that the idea of a caged ring for the big cats, rather than a small cage drawn into the ring, originated here. The circus succumbed to financial difficulties in 1953; but another member of the family, Willy Hagenbeck, has revived the show, which is now growing in size and importance.

The biggest German circus between the wars was that of Sarrasani. The founder, actually named Hans Stosch, had run away from his wealthy Prussian family to join the Ciniselli Circus. In 1901, when he came into a legacy, he formed his own show which was autocratically run but surpassed all others in elegance and grandeur; he toured widely throughout the world with 250 white and green wagons, and erected a splendid circus building in Dresden. The Sarrasani Circus was revived after the war and still tours in Germany today, though on a smaller scale.

In 1903 a menagerie owner, Carl Krone, inspired by the European tour of Barnum and Bailey, created a circus menagerie that was to become the largest of its kind in Europe and the chief rival of Sarrasani. The Circus Krone today is directed by his daughter, Frieda Sembach-Krone, and is based upon an excellent new permanent circus building in Munich, the only one now in West Germany, where three entirely different programmes are mounted between December and March; during the summer the circus tours Germany, Austria and Holland with a truly impressive encampment of tents and vehicles.

Rivalling Krone in size and quality is the Circus Busch Roland, formed from a combination between

The old-established Circus Busch is now combined with Circus Roland.

the Circus Busch of Berlin and the Circus Roland that had been founded in Bremen in 1948. Like several other European circuses, this show travels its own school with a teacher for the children of the artistes, who put on their own performance on occasional Sundays.

Other major German circuses on the road today are the Barum, founded in 1878 and now owned by the superb big-cat trainer, Gert Siemoneit-Barum, who is planning a permanent circus in Hamburg; and Althoff, directed by members of a family whose representatives seem to appear presenting animal acts wherever Circus is to be found.

Austria

Vienna has a rich circus tradition, with several permanent circuses, among which the Circus Renz survived until 1944, but the only large tenting circus to evolve in Austria was that of Kludsky, which toured between 1900 and the 'thirties. A smaller, but well-liked circus, is that of Rebernigg, popularly known as the Austrian National Circus, whose history goes back to the early nineteenth century.[7] In 1976 an interesting experiment was tried of using the basic facilities and acts of the Circus Rebernigg to create the Zirkus Roncalli, described as "a poetical spectacle" in which traditional circus acts were presented with something of the approach of the contemporary art theatre – a very different concept to that of filling the ring with chorus girls. I confess that I attended a performance of this fearing the worst, but in fact it turned out much more effective than I had expected. The show had a great success on its first tour in Germany, but the artistic directors have separated in a well-publicized row and it will be interesting to see how the idea develops further.[8]

Italy

Italian circuses tend to change their names so frequently that it is difficult to keep track of them, but any outfit directed by members of the Togni, Orfei or Casartelli families is sure to be in capable hands. Italian circuses often mount very spectacular productions, sometimes in three rings, and in general the Italian Circus is closer in spirit to the American Circus than are any others in Europe. There are many smaller circuses, totalling about 180 in all.

Spain and Portugal

Tenting circuses in these countries are fairly modest affairs, often weak in animal acts. The clowns tend to talk and sing for what seems to uncomprehending foreigners an interminable time! The Circo Price, Madrid's permanent circus, was pulled down in 1971, but the huge Colisee de Recreios in Lisbon, built in 1890 and seating 7,000 spectators, still survives.

Switzerland

The Circus Knie continues to tour Switzerland with what is probably the finest circus in Europe today, presenting outstanding acts in a superbly equipped tent. Its posters, designed by some of Switzerland's leading artists, are the finest I have seen, closely matched by those from Poland. There are a number of smaller circuses in Switzerland, notably that of the Nock family.

Holland and Belgium

These countries have been too dependent upon France and Germany to create very big circuses themselves.

The Toni-Boltini Circus tours in Holland, and has acquired something of the standing of a national Dutch circus. There are some half dozen smallish circuses in Belgium, of which the oldest is Circus Jhony and the largest is Circus Piste.

The Cirque Royal in Brussels, which has been the setting for many fine shows, was reconstructed in 1954 but scheduled for demolition in 1978. But the Cirque Carré still stands proudly on the Amstel in Amsterdam. This splendid building was erected in 1887 and is the last survivor of the great circus theatres of the nineteenth century. The ring is now filled with seats, and performances take place on the stage behind it, but the stalls for horses are still *in situ* behind the scenes, and I have been assured that the building could be converted to a true circus in forty-eight hours. The sight lines, with all the seats angled towards where the ring once was, make this an ideal building for a circus, and it was, indeed, so used by the Moscow Circus in 1979.

Scandinavia

The Schumann circus building in Copenhagen, built in 1886, still stands, near the Tivoli Gardens and very dear to the Danish people. The Schumanns were obliged to relinquish it in 1969, but it was then taken over by the Benneweis Circus, founded in 1887, which presents regular summer seasons there. Members of the Schumann family are still active in the circus world, and a new tenting show was launched in 1977.

In Sweden the Circus Scott, and in Norway Arnardo and Merano are among the circuses presenting tenting shows.

Eastern Europe

After the Second World War and the imposition of communist regimes, circuses, like all other kinds of entertainment, were taken over by the State. Some circuses retain individual names, but it is not possible to write of circus proprietors. The Circus flourishes in all these countries today, with fine modern circus buildings in Budapest, Bucharest, Sofia and East Berlin, and many travelling companies. Most eastern European countries maintain state circus schools, producing many excellent artistes, some of whom appear in the circuses of the West. These often work in groups of half a dozen or so acrobats in a style not now often found in our own countries, and all the more welcome for that. Polish bands, in particular, have a high reputation.

A four-pole tenting circus in Hungary.

The Orfei Circus works in the American style with three rings.

USSR

Russia had a great circus tradition in Tsarist times, and this has been continued and greatly encouraged in the Soviet Union. There are two permanent circus buildings in Moscow, and a third is planned: the old circus in Tsvietnoi boulevard was built in 1880 by Salamonsky, and has all the intimate atmosphere of the circuses of that period; its facilities are due to be modernised in two years' time; the new circus in Vernadsky Prospect was opened in 1972 and is superbly fitted with every conceivable type of modern equipment, including four automatically interchangeable rings; I have noticed, however, a tendency for this marvellous building to present a type of mixed variety show rather than a pure circus. In Leningrad the permanent circus is Ciniselli's original building, dating from 1877, which incorporates a circus museum on the premises.

To try to tell the story of Circus inside the USSR, with its 4,000 artistes, 62 permanent circus buildings, 16 tenting circuses, a famous circus school in Moscow, and 50 million spectators annually, is, alas, a task beyond the scope of this volume.

Russian circuses have toured extensively in the West since the 1950s, presenting some fine programmes. Their performances are not only remarkable for the

171

A Russian circus poster for the Sobolyevskiye Riding Act, one of the best voltige troupes performing today.

quality of their acts but for the smoothness of their productions, with perfectly coordinated lighting effects and brilliant costumes. Acts like "Prometheus", created on the high wire by the Vladimir Volshanski troupe, and the Vladimir Rakchyev flying trapeze troupe with four platforms and eight flyers, who follow each other in a bewildering succession of leaps and passes, must count as the most visually exciting presentations that I have ever seen in any circus anywhere.

North America

The Ringling Barnum Circus is now part of the vast Mattel Inc. organization, but it continues under the direction of Irvin Feld, assisted by his son Kenneth, and has gone from strength to strength. It now puts out two quite separate shows each year – the Red and Blue units. In principle, each unit plays one year in the East and one year in the West, so that each production has, basically, a two-year run. A third presentation is near Orlando, Florida, where a Circus World amusement park has been created; and a fourth

unit has been formed to present a Thrill Circus at big fairs. A one-ring Monte Carlo Circus was launched in 1979, and an International unit to tour Australasia is planned for 1980.

There are now no tenting circuses transported by rail. That chapter is finished. But a number of tented circuses, some with three rings, still tour by road. That story is still very much alive. There is Circus Vargas, claiming the largest big top in the world; Carson and Barnes, with five rings and a big menagerie; the Clyde Beatty–Cole Bros, continuing the tradition of opening with a wild animal act in a steel arena; Hoxie Bros, with nine elephants; and many others. At the other end of the scale, a number of small, one-ring circuses are on the road, like Hanneford, the Stebbing Royal European Circus, Big John Strong, and the Hunt Circus. In addition there are many circuses that don't use tents but play indoor dates or open-air parks. These range from the massive organization of the Ringling Barnum enterprises to the polar extreme of the Royal Lichtenstein Quarter-Ring-Sidewalk Circus, through which a Jesuit priest exercises his ministry to the people of God. In between come shows like Clyde Bros, Hubert Castle, Paul Kaye and Hamid Morton.

The Ringling Barnum programmes are lavishly printed and represent splendid value for the money.

172

In 1977 it was calculated that some 25 circuses in the United States were playing in tents and 34 in indoor halls or in shopping centres. Ten years earlier the number of tenting circuses had shrunk to about seven, so there has been a marked recovery in the last decade. In 1976, out of some 75 circuses that were recorded on the road, seven closed prematurely. Circus today is big business with union-approved contracts, but the days of the little under-capitalized show are not quite ended, and even if they sometimes fold in mid-season with their artistes stranded, one has a sneaking hope that they will never die.

A special feature of American circus activity is the interest in the history of the subject. There is a magnificent Circus World Museum at Baraboo, Wisconsin, with a fine archive collection, many old parade wagons beautifully restored, demonstrations of loading and unloading railroad cars, and performances of a high standard during the summer. You can easily spend a whole day there, and I can promise that it will be an enjoyable one. At Sarasota, Florida, the headquarters of Ringling Barnum, there is another Museum of the Circus housed in a building whose design is based on that of the Cirque d'Eté in Paris. There are excellent library collections at San Antonio, Texas, and at Illinois State University. Studies in circus history are beginning to appear as themes for university theses. The Circus Fans Association and the Circus Historical Society provide a link for enthusiasts from coast to coast.[9]

Several universities not only encourage the study of circus history but even teach circus skills. The New York School for Circus Arts is housed during the winter, thanks to a truly Christian act of hospitality, in the cathedral of St John the Divine; and during the past two summers it has presented a fresh and enthusiastic show as the Big Apple Circus in a tent pitched on a vacant lot in the heart of Manhattan. The Ringling Barnum organization runs a Clown College with an eight-week programme for training clowns, some of whom are accepted for work on the show.

Canada has always been much dependent upon the United States for its circuses, but there are at present a handful of smallish travelling circuses in the country which keep a native tradition alive. I have seen the Puck Circus, and have heard tell of Martin and Downs, and Gatini.

Central and South America

Mexico has always provided good support for the Circus, and it is the home of many brilliant performers. The oldest-established circus is Atayde, founded in 1888, which plays in three rings and has permanent winter quarters in Mexico City; there is also Circo Union, which is particularly strong in animal acts, and, among others, Gutierrez, which performs principally for Mexican audiences in the south-west of the United States. In Argentina one of the best-loved circuses was founded at the turn of the century by Frank Brown, an English clown and acrobat; today there are some forty circuses in the country, among which Tihany, founded by a Hungarian in 1955, is perhaps the best known. Every country of the continent, as well as Cuba, can boast its own native circuses with excellent acts, though, strangely in a continent with such a great equine tradition, there are almost no liberty acts in South American circuses today.

South Africa

The earliest circus brought to South Africa was by W. H. Bell in about 1870. In 1890 this show was taken over by Frank E. Fillis, of the far-flung English family of circus artistes, who built it up into a really big outfit. At the turn of the century Bostock and Wombwell sent out a menagerie and circus, and in 1904 William Pagel launched his own circus, which was particularly strong in animal acts.

In 1913 the Boswell brothers came out to Africa to work in the Fillis Circus, and later founded their own show. In 1954 W. H. Wilkie, an amusement caterer from the north of England, brought a circus to South Africa, and in 1963 this was amalgamated with Boswell's to form the Boswell Wilkie Circus. Meanwhile the Fillis, Bostock and Pagel shows have disappeared, so that the Boswell Wilkie is the only circus of any standing in South Africa today. It tours by rail – one of the few tenting circuses in the world still doing so – and presents excellent programmes.

South Africa can boast the most successful circus school in the English-speaking world. Keith Anderson runs a training school in Cape Town, mostly for poor boys, which has provided many excellent acrobats, especially on the flying trapeze, to professional circuses in Europe.

Australia

Circus was introduced here in the 1840s. Circus buildings were erected by Robert Radford in Launceston, Tasmania, in 1847, by Hayes in Melbourne in 1849, and by Jones in Sydney in 1850. These were followed by many tenting shows. The most famous of these was Wirth's, founded in 1878; it undertook a world tour in 1893, and engaged leading acts of world class for the benefit of Australian audiences. May Wirth, perhaps the finest woman rider in the history of the Circus, received her training with this family. The show closed down in 1963. Almost equal to Wirth's in quality was Bullen's, founded in the 1930s but folding in 1970, and Silver's, which ran for ten years from 1946. The oldest circus now performing in Australia is Ashton's, founded in 1852, which claims to have been the first tenting circus on the Australian continent, and has grown greatly in size since the disappearance of its larger rivals. There is also Sole Brothers, founded in about 1910, and the most recently formed is Royale.

The Far East

India, China and Japan have long enjoyed their own fine traditions of acrobatics and juggling; suspension from the hair was a speciality of Chinese girl acrobats; but Circus in the western form was not seen until

Juggling while suspended from the hair has been a speciality of Chinese circuses.

European and American companies arrived, of which the first appears to have been Soullier's in the 1860s. Other companies followed, and an Englishman, William Harmston, took a company that became resident in the Far East in the 1880s. The Clarkes were there during the period of the First World War. Indigenous circuses now exist in almost all Asian countries. The Gemini Circus presents a big tenting show in India, and I have seen a circus in Sri Lanka that compared well with the smaller European outfits. The Chinese People's Republic maintains a fine circus school, and several Chinese acrobatic troupes, both from the Mainland and Taiwan, have toured in the West in recent years with sensationally skilful acts.

The Middle East and North Africa

Indigenous circuses are not generally found in the Middle East, but European circuses have, from time to time, followed Rancy into this area. The Cirque Amar toured north Africa and Turkey in the early 1930s, and Gerry Cottle's Circus from England was invited to the Persian Gulf in 1976 and 1978. This was the first English circus to tour abroad for more than fifty years, and the first circus ever to be completely transported by air. Meanwhile, in Egypt a national circus has been set up with state support.

And so one could go on, but this incomplete list, which attempts to do no more than mention a few of the circus companies currently performing in the world, is surely a sufficient indication that, despite all the problems facing it, the Circus is far from dead. Moreover, let us not forget the little circuses that still wander across their chosen territories with a few simple acts and a family troupe. I recently came across a two-pole circus in Germany in which the performers consisted of two adults and seven children, aged, I should guess, between five and fifteen. Provided sensible regulations are observed there can be a wonderful atmosphere about these family shows, and they can provide an education in circus skills that not even the finest circus school can match. We probably need both: the family circus to plant the tradition, and the circus school to train the most promising students to higher standards.

36
Acts

BY THE BEGINNING of the twentieth century the mixture of drama and circus, that had dogged the development of the Circus ever since its origin, had almost disappeared. The last home of these spectacular semi-theatrical entertainments was the Circus Renz in Berlin.

In the early years of the century there was a craze for dare-devil acts, often with mechanical vehicles: bicycles were looping the loop by 1904, and the La Rague Sisters, driving primitive automobiles, were somersaulting in mid-air and passing each other in flight as they leaped gaps in a switchback runway as early as 1908. Similar acts appeared for several decades, but the attraction of such performances tends to lessen once the original sensation has worn off.

At one time big circuses like Sarrasani's and Ringling Barnum liked to carry round with them troupes of natives from remote areas of the globe, but nowadays the cinema and television have made exhibits of this kind less of a novelty.

A type of act that has appeared increasingly in circuses in this century is conjuring. Although some of these tricks are effective if you are sitting in the right place, very few magic acts are really suitable to be seen from all sides and, of course, many cannot be performed at all with the audience all round. From a purist point of view I feel that conjuring is out of place in a circus, as it inevitably involves trickery, which is the very antithesis of everything the Circus should stand for; I must admit, however, that I have found the trick in which a girl in a cage is transformed into a tiger absolutely stunning.

I am not such a purist as to object to the simulated falls and slips that some artistes introduce into their acts, so as to make the eventual achievement of their feats appear even more remarkable. It is, indeed, sad to observe the paltry applause with which circus audiences sometimes greet the performance of incredibly difficult feats, and one can hardly blame the performers for trying to "sell" their acts by occasionally "throwing" a trick in this way. But all the same, this kind of thing must be used with great discretion and circus proprietors must keep its use under strict control. The Bertram Mills Circus had a rule that no artiste could attempt a feat more than twice; it is embarrassing for everyone to watch an artiste on an off day make repeated attempts to bring off one of his feats.

By and large, the Circus today has reverted to the basic acts of skill, animal training and broad comedy upon which its appeal was originally built. Almost every act that is performed in the Circus today had been introduced, at least in principle, before the end of the nineteenth century; but enormous improvements have been made during the twentieth century. The frontiers of achievement are continually receding. The outstanding acts of the immediate pre- and post-war period have been well described in many books,[1] but here are some of the greatest acts that can be seen today.[2]

Horse Acts

The equestrienne balancing on horseback, weaving images of grace and beauty, striking attitudes from the ballet, down on one knee, on both knees, leaping the ribbons, adjusting herself to the rise and fall of the horse's back, an eye on her unstable mount, and a smile – a little too forced perhaps – at the ringside seats, is now almost a thing of the past. But twice in

The Richters are masters in the perilous feat of somersaulting on horseback.

recent years, and most notably by Martine Gruss in the Cirque à l'Ancienne, I have seen this act revived, and each time it met with warm appreciation from the audience. For me, this innocent and lovely spectacle contains all the magic of the Circus.

Between the wars group formations on horseback were featured by troupes like the Medrano Sisters and the Loyal Repenskys, and there were some fine voltige acts, notably the Hannefords, the Christianis, the Carolis, and the Baker Boys who put on a dashing display for Bertram Mills. But today the standard has unfortunately fallen. There are only two jockey acts of English origin performing today, and in America the situation is little better. One can, however, still see a superlative act of this kind performed by the Hungarian Richters. This family team of five not only puts on a sparkling demonstration of leaps on horseback, but achieves two feats of quite extraordinary brilliance: a head to head balance on a pad horse, which is technically very difficult but artistically a little ugly in execution; and two men somersaulting from different horses simultaneously, so that the rider on horse 1 arrives on horse 2 at the same moment as the rider on horse 2 arrives on horse 3. They didn't originate this feat, but only very few troupes have succeeded in mastering it; it demands the most precise coordination and judgment, and remains in my mind as one of the most exciting spectacles I have been fortunate enough to witness in a circus ring.

In high school the situation is better, as some riders who have competed at high level in horse shows have adapted their *dressage* for the requirements of the ring, and there are some very attractive acts to be seen. Mary Chipperfield and Katja Schumann, who fought out a closely contested final in the first Circus World Championship, are outstanding; as is Oreste Canestrelli in the United States.

In liberty horse acts, circuses like Bertram Mills were presenting troupes of as many as sixteen horses, perfectly matched in size and colour, in the 'fifties. Sadly, matched troupes of that size cannot be seen anywhere today. The circuses of England and America are not very strong in this area, but there are some fine troupes in Europe. I have particularly enjoyed the displays of the Jean Richard Circus, presented by Alexis Gruss, and of the Circus Krone. In the last decade a number of European circuses have introduced an act in which the unharnessed horses, usually greys, are allowed to wander, almost accidentally, around the ring, which is clothed, from the dry ice technique, in a light mist; when well lit, this almost gives the effect of horses grazing in the field at dawn. And then the trainer steps into the ring, and at one quiet word the horses range themselves immediately into the formation of their first exercise. I am not normally fond of theatrical lighting effects in the Circus, but this one seems to justify itself.

Ground Acts

We have seen the tendency for acrobatic feats with apparatus to replace the simpler leaps and somersaults by the end of the nineteenth century, and this tendency has continued to this day.

The trampoline, as we understand the term today, was illustrated in a primitive form in Hughes's poster of 1845, but at that time it seems to have consisted of no more than a small sheet of canvas lashed by cords to a metal frame. It does not seem to have been accepted as a common piece of circus equipment much before the early twentieth century, when either strips of rubber or springs of tempered steel were available to hold the canvas to the frame. In this form the trampoline was apparently introduced to Europe from America, and the first artistes to demonstrate its capabilities were Kelly and Gilette in the 1880s and the Max Franklin troupe at the turn of the century.[3] With its aid some enormous leaps can be made, and I have seen a man bounce to the roof of the Kelvin Hall in Glasgow and catch a small trapeze bar hanging there. Many of the effects of the flying trapeze act can be achieved with a trampoline and a hanging trapeze. Marco Canestrelli, in America, has created a record

Martine Gruss leaping the garters in a classical voltige act.

with a quadruple somersault from a trampoline to his brother's shoulders, Armando Cristiani throws a quadruple pirouette to his brother's shoulders, and Judy Wills has thrown a five-and-a-half twisting back somersault from it. Feats like these simply have to be seen to be believed. In recent decades, of course, trampolines have become commonly available on beaches and gymnasiums, and their use extends far beyond the circus ring.

Another effective device is the teeterboard, which had come into use by the end of the nineteenth century and was developed as an acrobatic turn by the Wotpert-Trio in the early decades of the twentieth century.[4] It is really a small see-saw. If one acrobat stands on the lower end, and another – or sometimes two others – jump on the higher end, the first one will be propelled into the air. With the aid of this simple device acrobats are now managing to throw single and double somersaults to land at the top of a column of colleagues standing on each other's shoulders, four or

even five high; one troupe, the Keharovi, have achieved a fantastic seven high, though they need the support of a perch to hold the column steady.

The Boitchanovi troupe from Bulgaria, who gained an award at Monte Carlo and performed before Queen Elizabeth II in her Jubilee celebrations, now round off a wonderful display with a unique and incredible *treble* somersault by a young boy to a three-high column. This is simply supreme daring, the utmost skill, and the beauty of the human body fused together in a flashing moment of time. Hazlitt would have given it immortality in his prose; so would Dickens, Hemingway or James Agate; but not a single theatre, ballet or athletics critic bothered to comment on this act when it appeared in London last year. The blindness of critics and the media to the art of the Circus fills me with despair.

A marvellous example of teeterboard work is provided when an elephant stamps on the board. This hurls the man on the other end to an enormous height, from which he can turn a lovely slow "backward layout" somersault to land on the head of a second elephant, or even on the shoulders of a second acrobat standing on the elephant's head. (A layout somersault is one with the body extended in a straight line, rather than tucked up in a ball; it is, I think, the more elegant of the two.) The Richters, Gebel-Williams, and Franco Knie perform this spectacular feat today. It is worth going a long way to see it.

A third type of equipment that has found its way into the Circus in recent decades is the Russian swing, introduced by the Soviet State Circuses. It is a swing on which two or more people can stand, and when it is swinging high one of the acrobats will "take off" and fly 30 ft or so into the air, somersaulting or pirouetting before he lands either on a mattress or on a colleague's shoulders. Teeterboard and Russian swing acts are much favoured by troupes from eastern Europe, who certainly achieve remarkable feats with their aid.

Another piece of apparatus, introduced apparently quite recently from Russia, is the *barre russe*. This is a thick rounded bar, possessing some elastic quality, held by two men, on which a third, usually a girl, stands. The supporters give the bar a good upward jerk which throws the girl high enough for her to execute a somersault before landing on the bar again.

Rudi Horn in his famous equilibristic act with tea cups and saucers.

The Metchkarovi troupe, among others, achieves a double somersault in this way. It can be a very attractive act, combining the teamwork of a group of ground acrobats with the precision of a somersault on the tight wire.

Extraordinary feats of balancing are now being achieved in perch acts, too. The Russian Kostiouk troupe has a top mounter who throws a backward somersault from the top of one perch to the top of another, six feet away, both perches being balanced, without hands, on the shoulders of the bearers. In the Risley act one of the Maroccan Rios brothers throws seven successive twisting somersaults and lands finally upon only one of the bearer's feet.

Among jugglers today, no-one quite takes the place of the phenomenal Rastelli, the charming young man who performed in simple sports kit and died prematurely in 1932. The best juggler I have seen is Kris Kremo, the latest in a line of famous circus performers, who does incredible things with cigar boxes; Bob Bramson performs a remarkable act with hoops, rolling them as well as throwing them in the air, and they really seem to obey his commands as they twist and turn; I understand that the Russian, Serge Ignatov, now equals Rastelli's achievement in keeping ten rings in the air simultaneously, getting a rhythm going with eight and then adding two more to complete the feat. Many jugglers now give variety to their act by juggling on the wire; on unicycles, like Rudi Horn who could throw up half a dozen tea cups and saucers, catch them on his head, and then add a lump of sugar and a tea spoon; or on a rola bola, a short plank balanced on a cylinder.

A type of ground act that does not attempt record feats but can be very good entertainment is comic acrobatics or the humptsi-dumptsi act. An English troupe called the Herculeans, dressed like Victorian acrobats and led by the over-sixty-years-old Johnny Hutch, is both funny and skilful, and any circus in which they appear is well worth a visit. I have also enjoyed the act put on by the Pauwels, who sometimes appear in the guise of wild French sailors sliding over and under tables and chairs in a mad carnival of eccentric tumbling.

Aerial Acts

Since the Wallendas performed a three-high pyramid on the high wire for Circus Gleich in 1924, artistes have vied with each other to create ever more sensational feats. The Wallendas achieved a seven-man, three-high pyramid in 1946; Karl Wallenda himself was killed in 1978 when a gust of wind blew him off the wire in Puerto Rico. A four-high column was

The Wallendas on the high wire in 1977.

achieved by the Solokhin Brothers in Moscow in 1962. I have seen two funambulists, Manfred Doval and Roger Regor, walk the high wire on stilts. One of the Colombian Castros leaps – without a balance pole – from his brother's shoulders to the wire on which he is balancing; the Carillos performed this a year previously, but the leaper fell in 1977 and was badly injured. The Russian Ahmed Abakarov troupe cross the wire three-high, with number two standing on one leg on number one's shoulder, and number three balancing on one hand on number two's head; and they round off an incredible display with a girl throwing a backward somersault from three-high to the shoulders of the man on the wire behind.

High wire acts are not usually performed with a net, but in several of these most daring feats – particularly with Russian troupes – the top mounter wears a safety lunge. Views about this are divided. Cyril Mills feels that its use should be restricted to practice, and that it is unfair and improper to use it at public performances. Some people feel that its use robs the feat of any risk, reduces it to a mere technical exercise, and spoils the breathless attention that should accompany its performance. Personally, I agree that it is wrong to use a taut safety lunge actually to help in

the execution of a feat; this reduces the performer to the level of a marionette. Some troupes today, among them the Abakarovs, are, I think, sometimes guilty in this respect. But I raise no objection to the use of a slightly slackened lunge as a safety device if the artiste falls, and I am relieved when I see one being fitted before a desperately dangerous feat. It is usually quite inconspicuous, and one can appreciate the artistry, the physical beauty, and the technical skill of the performance without fear of the appalling consequences of the tiniest miscalculation. Every year some circus artistes are killed and injured in the course of quite run-of-the-mill feats, often from faulty apparatus; last year some thirteen performers were badly injured and three killed in the United States alone; this is quite enough, without one wishing to add to their number by encouraging a dubious bravado.

High-wire acts appeal for the sensation of danger that they create, and I cannot deny that this is a compelling emotion, but, in my view, the height of the wire adds nothing to the skill of the exhibition, and for grace and artistry I find a low-wire act greatly preferable, especially as on the low wire the performer is not encumbered with the bulky balance pole.

On the low wire a forward somersault was not

Terry Cavaretta, the most graceful flyer on the flying trapeze today.

achieved until 1923 when Con Colleano succeeded in performing this difficult feat. A few performers are now including both forward and backward somersaults in their acts, but it remains a feat that only exceptional artistes can achieve. Even when they do so it is sometimes with so much wobbling and arm waving that all grace is lost, but when perfectly performed it is like a dream of unbelievable precision. Giuseppe Bricherasio, in his small Italian family circus, has recently achieved the incredible feat of a double somersault on the wire.

The corde lisse, or web, with a vertical rope, is often no more than a cover for erecting or dismantling the steel ring cage below, but this can be a fine act in its own right, especially when it culminates in spins from a mouth grip or one-arm planges, that is shoulder spins from a wrist hold. This act is usually performed by women, whose graceful figures are displayed to advantage. Lilian Leitzel was a renowned star in this type of performance before her tragic death from a broken swivel in 1931, sometimes achieving over two hundred planges in succession. Her feats are now being emulated by Fernanda Peris, who has turned 160 planges. The cloud swing, or swinging rope, has recently returned to popularity, and on this a hand-

some young Czech, named Dewart, is a superb performer.

The single trapeze, similarly, can be a very ordinary or a very exciting act. Isabella Nock, of the Swiss circus family, presents a singularly graceful performance, culminating in a breathtaking finale when she swings widely sitting on a chair that is balanced on two legs, and as it falls, crashing to the ring below, she is safely held by locking her insteps in the angle of ropes and bar. Gérard Edon is another fine performer, with a no-hands balance on a swinging and twisting bar. A few artistes can hang and swing, supporting themselves only by the heels or insteps; and Elvin Bale, a versatile performer with the Ringling Barnum Circus, has a truly sensational act in which he plunges forward from a swinging trapeze and catches himself by the heels. This is one of those feats that is performed so quickly that it is over almost before one realizes what is happening; only afterwards can one evaluate the fantastic speed of reaction that has made it possible. Elvin Bale also performs effectively on the giant Whirling Wheel, a massive piece of apparatus that is well-suited to three-ring circuses. Some performers try to jazz up the trapeze act by attaching their apparatus to some kind of imitation rocket or aeroplane circling round the roof; the Clarkes, in fact, introduced this as early as 1917. This kind of thing may impress audiences, but it does nothing to add to the grace or skill of the performance.

The flying trapeze remains one of the star acts in any circus programme. Not so long ago, when the Codonas and Concellos were supreme in this *genre*, a triple somersault to the catcher was regarded as the ultimate achievement. Now, within the last three years, two troupes, the Farfans and the Rock Smith Flyers, both from America, have achieved the three-and-a-half somersault at regular performances. The occasion when I first saw Don Martinez perform this with the Farfans at the second Monte Carlo Circus Festival is something I shall never forget. He is a small man, barely 5 ft high, and was some twenty-one years old when he was spotted jumping on a trampoline on a beach in California and invited to join the Farfan troupe; he practised for five years before he perfected his feat. He takes two enormous slow swings right up to the roof of the tent, then he lets go, transforming himself into a balled-up streak of human energy, whirling through the air, too fast for the eye to follow, and then – wham – there he is, caught by the legs in the catcher's safe hands. It had never been seen in Europe before.

The quadruple somersault has already been achieved in practice. It may not be long before it is seen in performance. At Monte Carlo Don Martinez missed it by centimetres. The strain upon the flyer is very great, as he usually blacks out during his rapid revolutions through the air. Nevertheless, others will certainly seek this elusive achievement. When someone performs this before an audience, that will be a day to remember! I hope I shall be there.

It is curious that while the first performer of the triple was a woman, most flyers have been men. An all-woman act that is outstanding for the grace of its execution is, however, the Flying Cavarettas (previously the Terrels), also from America, who were champions in the Circus World Championship in 1977. It is an eloquent indictment of our civilization that this beautiful display of choreographed skill has found it most profitable to appear as a kind of aerial sideshow at Las Vegas, coaxing a passing glance from the gamblers on the floor below.

There are two main training grounds for flying trapeze performers today: Mexico and South Africa. Novices need, of course, the proper equipment to practise on, and Keith Anderson's training school has produced many of the acts now performing in Europe. According to some judges, however, the Mexicans perform with greater style and artistry. In all these acts it must be remembered that the *style* is all import-

Elvin Bale on the giant Whirling Wheel which spins and revolves at the same time.

ant. The Circus is not, or should not be, concerned merely with sensation.

There is one aerial act that has appeared quite new in the twentieth century, and that is the swaypole. This is a flexible steel mast, as high as the tent or building will allow, on the top of which the performer sways perilously to and fro. Early exponents of acrobatics on what they called "a steel ship's mast" were the Winnepecs at about the turn of the century; in recent decades the master of this art has been a gentleman, now nearly seventy years old, called Fatini, who clambers up his vast "lamp post" – over 50 ft high – in the guise of a drunken reveller needing a light for his cigar, and then, lighting his cigar at the top, sets the thing in alarming motion. Some performers have devised a break in the middle of the pole, to be released at the right moment, to frighten audiences

Fatini on the swaypole at the Tower Circus, Blackpool.

into believing the pole has snapped. If you think this might be rather dangerous you are quite right. A man was killed doing this in America, a year or so ago, when his equipment failed.

Animal Acts

The gentling methods of wild animal training introduced by Hagenbeck found a disciple in Alfred Court, who, if not the first, is recognized as the greatest trainer of a mixed cat act in the history of the Circus. Court had his own Zoo Circus in France between the wars. He had a wonderful gift for persuading not only lions and tigers but leopards, pumas, jaguars, cougars, panthers, hyenas, and brown and polar bears to perform peacefully together. He brought eighteen different species of animals into the ring, and called his act "Peace in the Jungle".

Another outstanding animal trainer was Gilbert Houcke, a member of a famous family of circus proprietors and performers. Dressed like Tarzan in a leopard skin, he presented a group of tigers in a quiet but very effective performance, dispensing with the usual props and accessories. Despite all his experience, he was badly injured by one of his animals in 1961; when he came, as an honoured guest, to the Monte Carlo Circus Festival some fourteen years later he could barely stand upright unaided.

The best-known wild animal trainer today is Gunther Gebel-Williams, a German circus proprietor who has been lured to the Ringling Barnum Circus where he has become the idol of half America. Blond and handsome, with a fine ring presence, he presents his mixed groups with an enthusiastic vivacity and an infectious charm. Another trainer who has worked with Ringling Barnum but has now returned to Europe is Wolfgang Holzmair, whose superb figure is well displayed in the costume of a Roman gladiator; he shows up to twenty-one lions in the ring at once in an act that introduces plenty of excitement with roaring lions and simulated attacks, but which avoids the cruder forms of *en ferocité* exhibitions. He was injured in the cage in 1978 when trying to subdue a fight, but has now returned to work. A totally different approach is that of Gert Siemoneit-Barum, who shows up to twenty tigers at once in a playful, almost joky style. These trainers are all Germans, but England has produced a fine wild animal trainer in Mary Chipperfield, with a style of presentation that carries with it a cool authority that is, to my taste, much preferable to any amount of cheap showmanship.

The actual feats performed by the big cats have not materially changed, though some lions and tigers have been trained, like elephants, to walk the double tight

Gert Siemoneit-Barum gives the impression of playing with his tigers rather than commanding them.

rope. I personally find the performance of "tricks" by these noble animals somewhat belittling to their dignity, but I love to see them bounding round the ring with their muscles rippling beneath their gleaming coats. Circus animals are almost always in fine condition.

Elephants, on the other hand, can be trained to perform a great many feats, some of them very amusing. The Ringling Barnum troupe of elephants, presented by Axel Gautier, is the most impressive that I have seen; the Roberts and the Knie groups are the most agile. Most circus elephants are the Indian variety, but in recent years several trainers have shown that the African variety – the ones with the big ears – can be trained equally well.

The most entertaining animal performers are chimpanzees, bears and sea lions. Niccolini's chimpanzees, for instance, are amazingly acrobatic, even throwing somersaults to three high. The performances of the Russian-trained bears are fantastic: Berousek's bears balance on the rola bola; Kasseev's bears dance the pas de quatre from *Swan Lake*; Beljakow's bears turn themselves into highly efficient ring boys. As Californian sea lions are now a protected species whose export is banned by the Canadian government, Max Morris has trained Cape Fur seals to juggle and walk the tight rope.

Among dog acts, two that I have greatly admired have been performed by Dalmatians in a kind of liberty routine with Teddy Laurent; and by beautiful Borzoi hounds in conjunction with a Cossack riding act with the Golgojews.

Clowns

It is a common complaint that clowns are not funny any more. Grock, "Poodles" Hanneford and the Fratellini brothers are dead. Slivers Oakley, who used to hold the attention of the whole Barnum and Bailey tent as he mimed a baseball act alone in the centre ring, committed suicide when he was relegated to a walkaround. And where are the great clowns today?

Well, Charlie Rivel, now in his eighties, still occasionally performs, though it seems unlikely that the English-speaking world will see him again. When I was lucky enough to catch his act in Munich last year he was still wonderfully funny as the violinist who gets mixed up with the microphone, and in his long, tight, red dress as the burlesque prima donna; but his performance is now refined to a subtlety of gesture and interpretation that belongs rather to the cabaret than to the circus ring.

Russian clowns, in general, have entirely abandoned the traditional red-headed comic, the *r'izhii* of Tsarist times, and now appear in a naturalistic style with little make-up and no absurd costume. This style was pioneered by Karandash, who would drive a donkey cart round the ring, and was developed by his pupil, Oleg Popov, who aimed at creating the character of "a simple, happy chap, perhaps a bit soft-hearted and lyrical."[5] The young Russian clown, Anatoli Martchevski, has won the hearts of his audiences wherever he has appeared in the West with his gangling, charming manner; and another clown very popular in the Soviet Union is Yevgeny Maikhrovsky, who appears in a white shirt, black trousers speckled with white, and red braces, and whose distinctive voice carries to the back of the Leningrad Circus without a microphone. He creates a happy *rapport* with his audience and is greatly loved by children; like Martchevski, he often parodies the previous act, and one of his charming entrées is worth describing.

Mai (as he is popularly called) comes in after the strong man act but can't lift the weight. A pretty girl who gives him a bouquet, however, fills him with such delight that he finds he can throw the weight up into

Charlie Rivel, the greatest clown still performing today, has evolved a distinctive costume and style.

the air. A boxer coming along offers to fight him, but Mai performs very inefficiently with the boxing gloves on his feet and similar absurdities; his opponent, however, then kicks the bouquet away in disgust, and this so infuriates Mai that he throws himself into the fight with enthusiasm and in a hilarious display of comic fisticuffs emerges totally victorious. We are often told that clowns in the USSR are supposed to participate in the Marxist-Leninist education of the people, and they do sometimes poke fun at the bureaucratic absurdities of the regime, but what it amounts to when stripped of ideological verbiage is imaginative entrées with a moral like this.

But there is no need to go to Russia to see good clowning. In England there is Charlie Cairoli, who has been the resident clown at the Blackpool Tower since 1939. He strolls in as the incarnation of the "little man," originally conceived by Strube in his prewar cartoons, in an ill-fitting business man's suit, black jacket, striped trousers and bowler hat, and is immediately at one with his audience. He can time a slosh scene as well as anyone, drenching his stooge

Grock and partner. The classic circus double act of the auguste and the white-face clown.

(who is brilliantly played by Jimmy Buchanan) and himself with water, but he is also a subtle comedian who can make a raised eyebrow register to the back row; he is a marvellously inventive deviser of new entrées (he created over seventy in the ten years he spent at the Medrano in Paris before he came to England) and a fine musician who can play up to top G after top C on the trumpet.

In England, too, Jacko Fossett and Little Billy Merchant – one of several dwarfs who have enlivened circuses in their history – made themselves at home in the other resident circus, at the Great Yarmouth Hippodrome, with an honest-to-goodness bit of slapstick, not very subtle perhaps, but rich in the genuine circus spirit. And another member of that far-flung family, Tommy Fossett, with his attractive wife Vera, are not only expert jugglers but, as "Professor Grimble", present a tramp clown act that has something of the dramatic structure and contrast of a real clown entrée.

Then there is Lou Jacobs in the Ringling Barnum. It is not easy to put comedy over in a three-ring tent, and most American clowns have to rely on ingenious visual gags for a walkaround, but even in a vast arena Lou Jacobs' superb make-up – inspired by that of Albert Fratellini – carries, and he creates a very funny hunting scene with his little dog playing the part of

a rabbit. His face is familiar to millions and appeared on an American postage stamp.

Continental clowns talk too much for my taste, though I enjoy the visual contrast they offer when a brilliantly costumed white-face clown plays with an eccentric auguste. I suppose I have seen a dozen or so such acts in the past five years, but the only one that really sticks in my memory as outstanding is the Swiss, Pio Nock, who (despite anything Graham Greene may have written) is beautifully funny as the conjurer's assistant who is supposed to catch a bullet in his mouth and breaks innumerable plates in the process.

It isn't easy to be funny in the ring of a huge circus tent, especially if you are filling in as a run-in clown while the props are being changed. I know, because I've tried. Some clowns don't get beyond shouting "Hiya kids" as they run round; many of them rely on extravagant props, the chief of which is the comic motor car. This was first introduced as early as 1912 by Pimpo (Jimmy Freeman), the clown with John Sanger, and it can be a very funny act. But true clowning doesn't have to rely on props, and in a circus of intimate size a clown still has a chance. There is an English clown called Charlie Bale who, I suppose, will never make the headlines, but I have seen him play to a thin audience on a cold wet afternoon in a modest tenting circus and leave us gasping with laughter with no more elaborate props than a piece of music that keeps falling off a music stand and a bowler hat that falls off his head every time he stoops to pick it up.

It is, unfortunately, rare to see a really funny clown act in a circus today. But the tradition is there if you look for it.

Little Circuses

The acts I have described in this chapter are, mostly, to be found only in big circuses. But all the time acts that are close to them in skill and artistry are being performed in medium-sized and little circuses all over the world. Don't make the mistake of ignoring – or worse, despising – second- and third-ranking acts. The Circus can be enjoyed on many levels. Only last year, in a suburb of Munich, I saw a little circus, behind a flimsy canvas surround, present a learned pony that could have walked straight out of Astley's first Riding School, finding the hidden handkerchief and pointing out the prettiest girl in the town and the naughtiest boy in the school. While acrobats and trainers vie with each other to achieve the seeming impossible, the old traditional acts go on and on. And may they always do so.

The beauty and magic of the Circus on the corde lisse.

37
The Future

WHAT IS THE FUTURE for the Circus? There are many difficulties to be faced in the world today. Television familiarizes millions with the star acts in one transmission – the Bertram Mills Circus tried to prevent their artistes appearing on television. And the audience stays at home.

The enormous cost of travelling a big circus, of renting grounds, and feeding the animals has driven many circuses out of business. The difficulty of finding labour to erect and dismantle tents has forced others to close.

Animal cruelty cranks wage a continual war against circuses. They persuade local councils to refuse to let grounds to them, and in Scandinavia animal cage acts have been forbidden by law. Some of these fanatics have even plastered "Circus cancelled" stickers over the posters to keep people away. There is no evidence to support their belief that training performing animals is cruel, almost all countries have adequate laws to detect and punish this if it occurs, but this makes no difference to their virulent campaign. I am not going to mince words here. Some of these people are simply compensating for lack of love in their own lives by a sentimentalized over-indulgence of affection for animals whose nature they are incapable of understanding. Lovers of animals should rather be regular circus patrons, admiring the fascinating relationship between the performing animal and the human trainer but mindful, of course, of anything that might suggest harshness in that relationship. If they look with unbiased eyes they will find it hard to detect anything. In the past, it must be admitted, some trainers and proprietors have not been over-scrupulous in this matter. I believe that the standard of care today is very high, but the profession must safeguard its reputation with the utmost vigilance.

Another problem affecting animal acts is government regulations restricting the movement of animals. Because of the fear of rabies, many animals – including dogs, chimpanzees, lions, tigers and bears – that are brought into the United Kingdom from abroad have to spend six months in quarantine. This makes the importation of performing animal acts hopelessly uneconomic. In the United States regulations designed to preserve endangered species may result in preventing the movement of some animals even from one state to another.

A more general problem is the belief among the public that the Circus is something for children. It *is* a marvellous entertainment for children, but not only for children. Much of the art and skill of circus acts is quite beyond the appreciation of children. In the puppet theatre, in which I am also greatly interested, we encounter the same problem. The Circus is an art deserving and demanding an adult, a critical and an informed appreciation.

A further problem is that many of the feats that were once studied and applauded in circus rings are now studied and applauded elsewhere. Horse shows rather than circuses now attract connoisseurs of horsemanship; athletic competitions – and above all the Olympic Games – have replaced competitive leaping and somersaulting in the Circus; gymnastic events, with wonderful girl stars, have gained an enormous public that once might have admired not dissimilar feats in the ring. The answer to this may be to introduce a competitive element into the Circus, and recent years have seen the first signs of this. The Monte Carlo Circus Festivals, first held in 1974, attract leading artistes from all over the world, and the gold and silver trophies awarded there are a recognition of outstanding performances. There is no more pleasant way of spending a week in December than in strolling in the delightful gardens of Monaco during the day and attending the circus at night.

The Circus World Championship, introduced in London in 1976, is more directly competitive and limited to certain classes of acts for the awards, with the score for each act flashed on a screen after the jury's marking in the manner made familiar at skating and gymnastic competitions. This, too, has attracted some really outstanding acts to a city that has been starved of top quality Circus for too long.

In an age when art and entertainment of many forms can only survive with the help of state or private subsidy, the Circus in western Europe feels ignored. Only in Italy does the state offer any kind of aid, though in France President Giscard d'Estaing is said to be sympathetic to preserving the future of the Circus and a study has been put in hand to ensure this. The performing arts are tending to grow closer together, with opera and music hall, mime and puppetry, enter-ing more and more into the world of the theatre. Should not Circus, too, receive a helping hand? The Circus is recognized as an art and entertainment form that receives state support in the countries of eastern Europe. Without accepting all the qualifications that go with that, should not our circuses be assisted too?

In the last resort, however, Circus will survive as long as people want to see it. The Circus is skill and daring, with no trickery, transmuted into beauty and art. The Circus is the place where animals and men almost become one in a joint physical action. The Circus is the primeval theatre in the round. Whether it is in vast arenas, or in intimate amphitheatres redolent of the Belle Epoque, in huge tents on dusty downtown lots, in little tents in wet English meadows, or in the open air on the sunbaked *place* of a Mediterranean village, wherever courageous and sometimes hungry men display the skills and traditions of this ancient art, there is the Circus. And as long as men and women and children are drawn to wonder and delight as they gather round the ring, the Circus will not die.

Appendix

IT MAY BE USEFUL to list here the buildings that have been used for circuses in three major cities. In principle, subject to certain exceptions to make the information more complete, the list is limited to permanent, or at least semi-permanent, buildings that were either erected specifically to serve as circuses, or were converted for that purpose. As far as possible the names and dates of the managers or proprietors have been added.

Circus Buildings in London

ASTLEY'S AMPHITHEATRE, Westminster Bridge Road

1769-1779	an open-air arena
1779-c1784	a partially covered arena
c1784-1794	first circus-theatre
1795-1803	second circus-theatre
1804-1841	third circus-theatre
1842-1893	fourth circus-theatre

Managers: Philip Astley   1769-1814
John Astley   1814-1821
William Davis   1822-1823
Andrew Ducrow   1824-1842
William Batty   1843-1853
William Cooke   1853-1861
not used for circus acts   1862-1870
George Sanger   1871-1893

THE ROYAL CIRCUS, Blackfriars Road

1782-1805	first circus-theatre
1806-1809	second circus-theatre
1810	converted to the Surrey Theatre

Managers: Charles Dibdin   1782
Giuseppe Grimaldi   1783
Charles Hughes   c1784-c1790
Carlo Delpini   c1790-1794
James and George Jones   1794-1809

reverted to circus under
James West   1814-1816
Andrew Ducrow   1841-1842

THE CIRCUS, Marlborough Street
1785
Manager: Jones

JONES'S EQUESTRIAN AMPHITHEATRE, Union Street, Whitechapel
c1786–1794
Managers: James and George Jones

THE OLYMPIC PAVILION, Wych Street
1806   opened as a circus
1813   converted to a theatre
Manager: Philip Astley

THE EQUESTRIAN THEATRE, Edgware Road
1811
Manager: William Davis

THE ROTUNDA CIRCUS, Blackfriars Bridge Road
1827
Managers: the Cooke family

COOKE'S CIRCUS, The Old Tennis Court, Great Windmill Street
1831–1832
Managers: the Cooke family

THE NEW ROYAL NATIONAL AND OLYMPIC ARENA, Whitechapel
1833
Manager: Andrew Ducrow

THE ROTUNDA, Vauxhall Gardens
1839   converted to a circus
1859   demolished
Manager: Alfred Bunn

THE OLYMPIC CIRCUS, National Baths, Westminster Road
1841–1842   in use during the rebuilding of Astley's
Manager: William Batty

THE YORKSHIRE STINGO, New Road, Marylebone
1843
Manager: William Allen

THE CREMORNE CIRCUS, Cremorne Gardens
c1849–c1876
Managers: T. B. Simpson 1846–1861
                E. T. Smith 1861–1869
                John Baum 1870–1877

BATTY'S HIPPODROME, opposite the Broad Walk, Kensington
1851–1853
Manager: William Batty

THE ALHAMBRA, Leicester Square
1854   building opened as Panopticon of Science and Art
1858   converted to a circus
1860   converted to a music hall
Manager: E. T. Smith

THE HOLBORN AMPHITHEATRE, High Holborn
1867   opened as a circus
1873   converted to a theatre

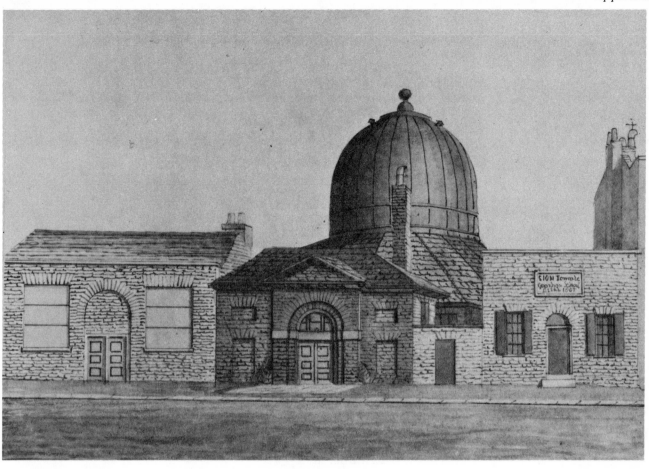

Jones's Riding School at Union Street, Whitechapel, 1786.

1874–5	used as a circus again
1876	converted to a roller skating rink
Managers:	Thomas McCollum 1867–1870
	William Charman 1870–1872
	James Newsome 1874–5

HENGLER'S CIRQUE, Argyll Street

1870	building opened as the Corinthian Bazaar
1871	converted to a circus
1885	reconstructed in brick
1910	rebuilt as the Palladium Theatre
Managers:	the Hengler family 1871–1895
	various short tenancies 1895–1910

THE DALSTON CIRCUS, Dalston Lane, Hackney

1886	opened as circus
1890	licence withdrawn
1897	reconstructed as a music hall

THE LONDON HIPPODROME, Cranbourne Street

1900	opened as a circus-theatre with aquatic facilities
1909	converted to a music hall
Manager:	H. E. Moss

In addition to these, circuses have been presented in several theatres, usually on the stage but sometimes with an attempt at a performance in the round. The most important seasons were as follows:

THE ENGLISH OPERA HOUSE, or THE LYCEUM

c1793–5	Benjamin Handy
1794	Philip Astley
1843	Van Amburgh and Sands

THE THEATRE ROYAL, DRURY LANE

1848	Cirque National de Paris
1848/9	Cirque National de Paris
1851	Thomas McCollum
1853	Hernandez and Eaton Stone
1857	Miss Ella

THE THEATRE ROYAL, COVENT GARDEN

1884/5	International Cirque
1885/6	International Cirque
1886/7	International Cirque
1888/9	Hengler's Cirque
1889/90	Covent Garden Circus
1893/4	William Holland's Noah's Ark

THE ROUND HOUSE, Primrose Hill

| 1969/70 | Robert Brothers |

Several exhibition halls have been used for seasonal circuses. The most important are the following:

THE CRYSTAL PALACE, Sydenham

| 1854–1936 | Many circuses and circus-type acts, notably those provided by Eduard Wulff in the 1890s. |

THE AGRICULTURAL HALL, Islington

| 1863–1939 | Christmas circuses almost every year, provided by the Sangers, Myers, Robert Fossett, John Swallow, and others. |

THE ALEXANDRA PALACE, Muswell Hill

| 1877–1913 | Some circuses and circus-type acts. |

THE ROYAL AQUARIUM, Westminster

| 1876–1907 | Many circus-type acts, notably those provided by G. A. Farini during the 1870s and 1880s. |

OLYMPIA, Kensington

1886/7	Paris Hippodrome
1887/8	Paris Hippodrome
1889	Barnum and Bailey
1896	Royal Netherlands Circus
1897/8	Barnum and Bailey
1898/9	Barnum and Bailey
1906/7	Cirque Metropole in Mammoth Fun City
1907/8	Berketow's Russian Circus in Mammoth Fun City
1913/14	Carl Hagenbeck, presented by C. B. Cochran
1919/20	Wilkins and Young
1920/1–1966/7	Bertram Mills (less war years)

EARLS COURT, EMPRESS HALL

| 1912 | C. B. Cochran |

1928/9	Bostock
1939/40	S. V. Parkin
1952/3–1953/4	Jack Hylton

HARRINGAY ARENA
1947/8–1957/8 Tom Arnold

WEMBLEY ARENA

1959	Moscow State Circus
1960	Moscow State Circus
1961	Moscow State Circus
1971	Moscow State Circus

Information partly based on Raymond Mander and Joe Mitchenson, *The Lost Theatres of London*, 1968, and Diana Howard, *London Theatres and Music Halls*, 1970.

Circus Buildings in New York

THE CIRCUS, Greenwich Street, near the Battery
1793	John Ricketts
1794	Thomas Swann

THE AMPHITHEATRE, Broadway, corner of Exchange Alley
1794–6	John Ricketts

RICKETTS' AMPHITHEATRE, Greenwich Street, by Rector Street
1797	John Ricketts
	Philip Lailson
1798	John Ricketts

LAILSON'S AMPHITHEATRE, Greenwich Street, south of Rector Street
1797–8	Philip Lailson
1799	Thomas Franklin

THE BROADWAY ARENA, corner of Magazine (now Pearl) Street
1808	Pepin and Breschard

THE CIRCUS, Broadway, by Wirth Street
1809–10	Pepin and Breschard

THE OLYMPIC CIRCUS, Broadway, by Anthony Street
1810–12	Pepin and Breschard
1820–22	James West
1823–28	Price and Simpson (as the Broadway Circus)

THE CIRCUS, Broadway, by White Street
1812	Cayetano
1813	Pepin and Breschard

THE NEW CIRCUS, Broadway, by Canal Street
1817	James West
1823–4	Rogers

THE CIRCUS, Broadway, between Hester and Broome
1818–19	Pepin and Breschard

LAFAYETTE'S AMPHITHEATRE, Laurens Street
1825–6	C. W. Sandford

THE MOUNT PITT CIRCUS, Grand Street
1826–8	C. W. Sandford

THE BOWERY AMPHITHEATRE (formerly The Zoological Institute; later The

Franconi's Hippodrome on Broadway, New York, 1853.

Amphitheatre of the Republic, The New York Amphitheatre, The Zoological Hall, The Varieties), 37 Bowery
    1838–65   June, Angevine and Titus

THE BROADWAY CIRCUS, 509 Broadway, between Spring and Broome Street
    1839

THE NEW BROADWAY CIRCUS, 559 Broadway
    1848   Tryon and Thompson
                  Welch, Delavan and Nathan
    1849   Sands, Lent and Co.

THE HIPPODROME, Broadway and 23rd Street
    1853–5   Henri Franconi

THE BROADWAY AMPHITHEATRE (formerly Wallack's Theatre), Broome Street
    1863   Lewis B. Lent

THE HIPPOTHEATRON, or The New York Circus, 14th Street
    1864–72   Lewis B. Lent
    1872   Phineas T. Barnum

BARNUM'S ROMAN HIPPODROME (later Madison Square Garden), Madison Square
    1874–89   Phineas T. Barnum

DORIS WINTER CIRCUS, 42nd Street between Seventh and Eighth Avenue
    1897

Theatres in which Circuses were presented

THE BOWERY THEATRE (later The American Theatre), Bowery, south of Canal Street

1837–78	various circus seasons

THE PARK THEATRE, Park Row

1843	Welch
1845	Welch
1848	Sands, Lent and Co.

THE CHATHAM THEATRE

1844	Rockwell and Stone
1846–7	Sands, Lent and Co.

PALMO'S OPERA HOUSE, Chambers Street

1846	Howes

THE NATIONAL THEATRE (later The Chatham Amphitheatre), Leonard and Church Street

1854	Tourniaire
1859	Nixon and Aymar

THE METROPOLITAN THEATRE, Broadway and Bond Street

1855	Nathan and Sands

THE BROADWAY THEATRE, between Pearl and Anthony Street

1857	Van Amburgh
1858	Sands, Nathan and Co.

Pleasure Gardens in which Circuses were presented

NIBLO'S GARDEN, Broadway and Prince Street

1822–61	Sands, Lent and Co.; James M. Nixon; and others

VAUXHALL GARDEN, Bowery

1830–43	Blanchard; Cooke; Bancker, Sweet and Gardner; and others

RICHMOND HILL AMPHITHEATRE, Charlton and Varick Street

1833–45	Bancker and Sweet; J. Whitaker; and others

ARCADIAN GARDEN, 255 Bleecker Street

1841–2	H. Rockwell

PALACE GARDEN (later Cremorne Gardens), Sixth Avenue and 14th Street

1858–62	Nixon

GILMORE'S GARDEN, Third Avenue and 63rd Street

1876–8	Barnum's Greatest Show on Earth

Exhibition Halls in which Circuses were presented

THE EMPIRE SKATING RINK (later The American Institute Building), Third Avenue between 63rd and 64th Street

1870	Quagliani
1871	Howes
	Phineas T. Barnum
1873	Phineas T. Barnum
1879	Phineas T. Barnum

1880	Phineas T. Barnum
1888	Frank A. Robbins

THE AQUARIUM, Broadway and 35th Street

1879	Lewis B. Lent
1880	John H. Murray
1883	The Australian Circus

MADISON SQUARE GARDEN

1874–89	a converted railroad station at Madison Square, originally titled Barnum's Roman Hippodrome
1890–1924	rebuilt on Madison and Fourth Avenues, 26th to 27th Street
1925–67	new building at Eighth Avenue and 50th Street
1968–	new building at Eighth Avenue and 32nd Street P. H. Barnum; Barnum and Bailey; Ringling Brothers, Barnum and Bailey

The sites listed are limited to Manhattan. The early circus sites are based on information in Stuart Thayer, *Annals of the American Circus 1793–1829*, 1976; the later sites are from T. Allston Brown, *A History of the New York Stage*, 1903, and George C. D. Odell, *Annals of the New York Stage*, 1927. It is not certain whether all of these sites were, in fact, covered buildings. Many theatres and variety houses included occasional circus acts, and no attempt has been made to list all of these.

Circus Buildings in Paris

AMPHITHEATRE ASTLEY, faubourg du Temple

1783–91	Philip Astley
1791–1802	Antonio Franconi (as Amphithéâtre Franconi)
1817–26	Antonio Franconi (as Cirque Olympique)

CIRQUE DU PALAIS ROYAL

1787

THEATRE DE L'EQUITATION, l'enclos des Capucines

1802–6	Antonio Franconi

CIRQUE OLYMPIQUE, rue du Mont Thabor

1807–16	Antonio Franconi

CIRQUE OLYMPIQUE, boulevard du Temple

1827–36	Adolphe Franconi
1836–47	Louis Dejean and Adolphe Franconi

CIRQUE D'ETE or NATIONAL or DE L'IMPERATRICE, Carré Marigny, Champs Elysée

1838–41	wooden building
1841–70	stone building on a different site. Dejean and Adolphe Franconi
1870–97	Victor Franconi

CIRQUE D'HIVER or NAPOLEON, boulevard des Filles du Calvaire

1852–70	Louis Dejean and Adolphe Franconi
1870–1907	Victor Franconi
1907–23	used as cinema
1923–33	Desprez
1934–	Bouglione

CIRQUE DU PRINCE IMPERIAL, rue de Malte

1866–7	Bastien Gillet-Franconi

The Cirque d'Hiver on the boulevard des Filles du Calvaire, 1893. It remains almost unaltered today.

CIRQUE FERNANDO or MEDRANO, boulevard Rochechouart, Montmartre
    1874–97   Fernando Beert
    1898–1963   Medrano
    1963–71   Bouglione

NOUVEAU CIRQUE, rue St Honoré (formerly rue du Mont Thabor)
    1886–1926   Raoul Donval

CIRQUE METROPOLE or DE PARIS, avenue de la Motte-Piquet
    1906–30

Hippodromes

HIPPODROME, barrière de l'Etoile
    1845–54   Franconi

NOUVEL HIPPODROME, la porte Dauphine
    1856–69   Arnault

HIPPODROME DE L'ALMA, pont de l'Alma
    1877–92   Zidler

HIPPODROME, place de l'Exposition
  1894–1900   Medrano. Raoul Donval

HIPPODROME DE LA PLACE CLICHY
  1900–07   Frank Bostock and Hyppolite Houcke

The dates for the earlier circuses are as given in A. H. Saxon, *Enter Foot and Horse*, 1968; for the Hippodromes as given in Adrian, *Cirque Parade*, 1974.

Notes

I AM WELL AWARE of the importance of providing authority for my statements, especially in a subject like Circus where rumour, gossip and lies have taken the place of facts for too long. However, if the authority for every statement in this book were given in a footnote, there are pages in which a note would have to be provided for almost every line of text. This is just not that sort of book. The compromise that I have adopted is to give a footnote *once only in each chapter*, usually at the first reference, to the principal printed sources that I have used in that chapter. As each title quoted may refer to more than one reference, page numbers are not given, but I hope that intelligent use of indexes and contents will usually lead an enquirer to the passage he is seeking without much difficulty; if a pertinacious student is sometimes obliged to read a book instead of just glancing at a page, I may perhaps venture the hope that the experience will give him as much pleasure as it has me. Where a source has been referred to in more than one chapter it is given in an abbreviated form in each note; a key to the abbreviations is provided below.

Broadly speaking, I have relied upon books and journals for my information in parts I, IV, V and VI.

For parts II and III, however, I have, wherever possible, used original sources, such as manuscript accounts, newspaper reviews, playbills, posters and other advertisements. It has not been feasible to give individual references to the playbills and programmes, but I have used the collections in the British Library, the Enthoven Collection at the Theatre Museum, the John Johnson Collection at the Bodleian Library, the Robert Wood Collection at the National Museum of the Music Hall, Sunderland, and the Fenwick Collection at the Tyne and Wear Archives Department, Newcastle on Tyne, as well as my own private collection. In any cases of doubt, I should be happy to provide students with more detailed references; it is my intention that my indexed notebooks shall, in due time, be lodged in the Theatre Museum.

There is one book not listed in the Notes that has, nevertheless, been invaluable to me. This is *Circus and Allied Arts. A World Bibliography* by R. Toole Stott, 4 vols, 1958–71. It is no exaggeration to say that this massive work has, for the first time, made the writing of circus history possible, and I cannot adequately express my indebtedness to it.

Abbreviations

Astley	Philip Astley, *The Modern Riding Master*, 1775.
Auguet	Roland Auguet, *Histoire et Légende du Cirque*, 1974.
Barker	Kathleen Barker, *Bristol at Play*, 1976.
Bentley	G. E. Bentley, *The Jacobean and Caroline Stage*, 1941–68.
Boase	Frederick Boase, *Modern English Biography*, 1892.

Boulton   W. B. Boulton, *The Amusements of Old London*, 1901.

Boz   Charles Dickens, "Astley's" in *Sketches by Boz*, 1836.

Broadbent   R. J. Broadbent, *Annals of the Liverpool Stage*, 1908.

Buckland   Francis T. Buckland, *Curiosities of Natural History*, Fourth Series, 1873.

Buckskin Joe   *Buckskin Joe, being the unique and vivid memoirs of Jonathan Hoyt, 1840–1918*, edited by Glen Shirley, 1966.

Campardon   Emile Campardon, *Les Spectacles de la Foire, 1595–1791*, 1877.

Chapin May   Earl Chapin May, *The Circus from Rome to Ringling*, 1932, revised edition 1963.

Chindahl   George L. Chindahl, *A History of the Circus in America*, 1959.

Chipperfield   Jimmy Chipperfield, *My Wild Life*, 1975.
Clarke   John Clarke, *Circus Parade*, 1936.
Decastro   Jacob Decastro, *Memoirs*, 1824.
Delzant   Alidor Delzant, *Les Goncourts*, 1889.
Dibdin   Charles Dibdin the Younger, *Professional and Literary Memoirs*, edited by George Speaight, 1956.

Disher   W. Willson Disher, *Greatest Show on Earth*, 1937.

Ducrow   A. H. Saxon, *The Life and Art of Andrew Ducrow, and the Romantic Age of the English Circus*, 1978.

Durang   *The Memoir of John Durang, American Actor, 1785–1816*, edited by Alan S. Downer, 1966.

Eberstaller   Gerhard Eberstaller, *Circus* (text in German), 1976.

Findlater   Richard Findlater, *Grimaldi: King of Clowns*, 1955.

Fox and Parkinson Charles P. Fox and Tom Parkinson, *The Circus in America*, 1959.

Frost   Thomas Frost, *Circus Life and Circus Celebrities*, 1875.

Glynne Wickham   Glynne Wickham, *Early English Stages*, vol. ii, part 2, 1972.

Le Grand Livre   *Le Grand Livre du Cirque*, edited by Monica J. Renevey, 1977.

Halperson   Joseph Halperson, *Das Buch vom Zirkus*, 1926.
Hippisley Coxe   Antony Hippisley Coxe, *A Seat at the Circus*, 1951.

Hodgkinson   J. L. Hodgkinson and Rex Pogson, *The Early Manchester Theatre*, 1960.

Hone   William Hone, *The Everyday Book* (for September 5), 1838.

Jando   Dominique Jando, *Histoire Mondiale du Cirque*, 1977.

Jensen   Dean Jensen, *The Biggest, the Smallest, the Largest, the Shortest*, 1975.

Lano   David Lano, *A Wandering Showman, I*, 1957.
Le Roux   Hughes Le Roux and Jules Garnier, *Acrobats and Mountebanks*, 1890.

Lloyd   James Lloyd, *My Circus Life*, 1925.
Lukens   John Lukens, *The Sanger Story*, 1956.

Lumsden	Harry S. Lumsden, "History of Cooke's Royal Circus", reprinted in *The Sawdust Ring*, iii, 1936.
Markschiess-van Trix	J. Markschiess-van Trix and Bernhard Nowak, *Artisten- und Zirkus Plakate*, 1975.
Mayhew	Henry Mayhew, *London Labour and the London Poor*, vol. iii, 1861.
McKennon	Joe McKennon, *Horse Dung Trail*, 1975.
Montague	Charles W. Montague, *Recollections of an Equestrian Manager*, 1881.
Mudshows	Stuart Thayer, *Mudshows and Railers: the American Circus in 1879*, 1971.
Munby	The Munby Papers. MS diaries of Arthur J. Munby at Trinity College, Cambridge, extracts from 'which are published in Derek Hudson, *Munby: Man of Two Worlds*, 1972.
Odell	George C. D. Odell, *Annals of the New York Stage*, 1927–49.
Paterson	[James Bertram], *Glimpses of Real Life . . . the Confessions of Peter Paterson, a strolling Comedian*, 1864.
Pinder	Jacques Garnier, *Les Histoires de Cirque de Lewis-James Pinder dit Arthur*, 1978.
Polacsek	John F. Polacsek, "The Development of the Circus and Menagerie 1825–1860". Thesis submitted to the Graduate School of Bowling Green University, 1974.
Price	Marian Hannah Winter, "The Prices – an Anglo-Continental Theatrical Dynasty", *Theatre Notebook*, xxviii, 1974.
Rennert	Jack Rennert, *100 Years of Circus Posters*, 1974.
Sanger	"Lord" George Sanger, *Seventy Years a Showman*, [1908].
Saxon	A. H. Saxon, *Enter Foot and Horse: a History of Hippodrama*, 1968.
Speaight	George Speaight, *The History of the English Puppet Theatre*, 1955.
Strehly	Georges Strehly, *L'Acrobatie et les Acrobates*, [1903].
Strutt	Joseph Strutt, *The Sports and Pastimes of the People of England*, 1801.
Thayer	Stuart Thayer, *Annals of the American Circus 1793–1829*, 1976.
Thétard	Henry Thétard, *La Merveilleuse Histoire du Cirque*, 1947; new edition 1978.
Towsen	John H. Towsen, *Clowns*, 1976.
Vail	R. W. G. Vail, *Random Notes on the History of the Early American Circus*, 1934.
Van Hare	Van Hare, *Fifty Years of a Showman's Life*, 1888.
Varey	J. E. Varey, "Notes on English Theatrical Performers in Spain", *Theatre Notebook*, viii, 1953.
Vaux	Baron de Vaux, *Ecuyers et Ecuyères*, 1893.
Wallett	W. F. Wallett, *The Public Life*, 1870.
Wild's	*"Old Wild's" . . . The Reminiscences of "Sam" Wild*, [1888].
Winter	Marian Hannah Winter, *The Theatre of Marvels*, 1964.

Specialist Journals referred to

Theatre Notebook, published by The Society for Theatre Research, 77 Kinnerton Street, London, SW1.

Theatre Survey, published by The American Society for Theatre Research, 1117 CL, University of Pittsburgh, Pittsburgh, Pa. 15260.

Nineteenth Century Theatre Research, Department of English, University of Arizona, Tucson, Arizona 85721.

The Sawdust Ring (1934–39), published by The Circus Fans Association of Great Britain.

King Pole (1948–   ), published by The Circus Fans Association of Great Britain, 8 Casslee Road, Catford, London, SE6.

The White Tops, published by The Circus Fans Association of America, P.O. Box 69, Camp Hill, Pa. 17011.

Bandwagon, published by The Circus Historical Society, 2515 Dorset Road, Columbus, Ohio 43221.

Le Cirque dans l'Univers, published by Le Club du Cirque, 40 rue Chateaubriand, 45100 Orleans, France.

Die Circus Zeitung, published by Die Gesellschaft der Circusfreunde in Deutschland, 31 Celle, Harburger Strasse 53, German Federal Republic.

Circus-Parade, published by Circus Club International, D2308 Preetz, Klosterhof 10, German Federal Republic.

Chapter 1

1   Xenophon, *Symposium,* 4, 55.
2   Petronius, *Satyricon,* liii.
3   Vopiscus, *Scriptores Historiae Augustae:* Carus, Carinus, Numerian xix.
4   Allardyce Nicoll, *Masks, Mimes and Miracles,* 1931; Margarete Bieber, *The History of the Greek and Roman Theater,* 2nd ed., 1961.
5   Suetonius, *Lives of the Caesars:* Galba vi; Pliny, *Natural History,* viii, 2; Seneca, *Epist. 86.*
6   Speaight.
7   *The Romance of Alexander,* with introduction by M. R. James, 1933. See also Strutt.
8   Muhammad Ibu Dànial, *Baba Ajib wa Gharib,* translated in a thesis by Saffana al-Khayer submitted to the University of Exeter, 1977.

Chapter 2

1   J. T. Murray, *English Dramatic Companies 1558–1642,* 1910; Joseph Quincey Adams, *The Dramatic Records of Sir Henry Herbert,* 1917.
2   Speaight.
3   Strutt.
4   Note by H. Furness in New Variorum Edition of Shakespeare, *Love's Labour's Lost,* 1904; "Moraco, le Cheval de l'Ecossais", *Le Cirque dans l'Univers,* 110, 1978; Chipperfield.
5   William Stokes, *The Vaulting Master,* 1641. This book is incorrectly stated by Frost to depict vaulting over a live horse. See also Bamber Gascoigne, *World Theatre,* 1968, fig. 164.
6   Bentley.
7   Glynne Wickham.
8   Bamber Gascoigne, *World Theatre,* 1968, figs. 99, 100, 101.

Chapter 3

1 The information on French fairs is from Campardon, supplemented by Maurice Albert, *Les Théâtres de la Foire, 1660–1789*, 1900. On English fairs from Henry Morley, *Memoirs of Bartholomew Fair*, 1859; John Ashton, *Social Life in the Reign of Queen Anne*, 1882; Thomas Frost, *The Old Showmen and the London Fairs*, 1874; and Sybil Rosenfeld, *The Theatre of the London Fairs in the Eighteenth Century*, 1960.
2 Findlater.
3 Hodgkinson.
4 *Humphry Clinker*, 1771, letter from Winifred Jenkins dated June 3; Winter.
5 *The London Spy*, 1700.

Chapter 4

1 Warwick Wroth, *The London Pleasure Gardens of the Eighteenth Century*, 1896.
2 Disher.
3 Barker.
4 Decastro.
5 *The Gazetteer*, 10 April 1773.
6 Halperson.
7 Vail.
8 Varey.
9 Compardon.
10 Boulton.
11 Eugeny Kuznetzov, *Tsirk* (text in Russian), 1931.
12 Jacob Bicker, "Notietie van het merkwaardigste meyn bekent" (Account of remarkable things I have known) 1732–1772, MS in the Gemeentelijke Archiefdienst van Amsterdam.

Chapter 5

1 The particulars in this chapter are drawn from advertisements in *The Gazetteer, The Public Advertiser* and *The Morning Chronicle*, 1768–1773.
2 George Speaight, "Some Comic Circus Entrées", *Theatre Notebook*, xxxii, 1978.

Chapter 6

1 Disher; Saxon; E. W. Brayley, *Accounts of the Theatres of London*, 1826.
2 An advertisement for Astley's Riding School to Let in the *Morning Chronicle* for March 20, 1779 gives the diameter of the circle as 95 ft; I think this must be the overall dimensions including the seating, as a manuscript note by William Capon on his watercolour drawing of Astley's as in 1777, in the Greater London Council print collection, gives the diameter of the ring as 60 ft.
3 Dibdin.

Chapter 7

1 Boulton.

2 Charles Dibdin, *Royal Circus Epitomized*, 1784; Charles Dibdin, *The Professional Life*, ii, 1803.

3 *The Circus: or British Olympicks, A Satire on the Ring in Hide-Park*, 1709; Jacob Larwood, *The Story of the London Parks*, n.d.

Chapter 8

1 Decastro; Robert Fahrner, "The Turbulent First Year of the Royal Circus", *Theatre Survey*, xix, 2, 1978.

2 A. H. Saxon, "Capon, the Royal Circus and The Destruction of the Bastille", *Theatre Notebook*, xxviii, 1974.

3 Saxon.

4 Hippisley Coxe.

Chapter 9

1 La T. Stockwell, *Dublin Theatres and Theatre Customs*, 1938; Lou Warwick, *Drama that Smelled, or Early Drama in Northampton*, 1975.

2 Dibdin.

3 Barker; Hodgkinson; Broadbent; James C. Dibdin, *Annals of the Edinburgh Stage*, 1888. See also lists in *The World's Fair*, June 22, 29, July 6, 1957.

4 Paterson.

5 Charles Mackie, *Norfolk Annals*, 1901.

6 Wallett.

7 J. P. Robson, *The Life and Adventures of the far-famed Billy Purvis*, 1849; Frost; Mayhew, "The Street Juggler"; David Prince Miller, *The Life of a Showman*, 1849.

8 Wild's.

9 Lukens; W. S. Meadmore, "Sangers' Circuses", *The Sawdust Ring*, Summer 1938.

10 Astley.

11 Montague.

12 Hone; Terence Rees, *Theatre Lighting in the Age of Gas*, 1978.

13 Clifford Musgrove, *Life in Brighton*, 1970; Le Grand Livre; Mudshows.

Chapter 10

1 Dibdin.

2 James Meikle, "Old Scottish Show Life", *The Scottish Field*, October 1921; "Royal Circus Shows", *King Pole*, 36, 1977; Pinder.

3 Decastro.

4 *Life at Fonthill 1807–1822 . . . from the Correspondence of William Beckford*, edited by Boyd Alexander, 1957; Joseph Cave, *A Jubilee of Dramatic Life*, [1892].

5 Charles Keith, *Circus Life and Amusements*, 1879; Le Grand Livre; Hone.

6 Ducrow. This work is outstanding in the field of circus history.

7 Lumsden; family tree in *Who's Who in the Theatre*, 5th edition, 1926; Frost.

8 Boase; Wild's.

9 "The Romance of the Ginnetts", *The Sawdust Ring*, iii, 1936.

10 Rupert Croft-Cooke and W. S. Meadmore, *The Sawdust Ring*, [1951].

11 Sanger.

12 Lukens.

13 Charles Dickens, *Hard Times*, 1854; Wallett.

Chapter 11

1 Munby.

2 John H. Glenroy, *Ins and Outs of Circus Life*, 1885.

3 Frost; Strehly; Thétard; *Le Cirque dans l'Univers*, 2e, 1977.

4 Henry D. Stone, quoted by Vail.

5 Ducrow.

6 Erroll Sherson, *London's Lost Theatres of the Nineteenth Century*, 1925.

7 Hone.

8 Lukens.

9 Mudshows.

Chapter 12

1 Eberstaller; Winter.

2 Le Roux.

3 Van Hare.

4 Le Grand Livre; Frost says the result was a draw.

5 Thétard; Paterson; Chapin May.

6 Ducrow.

7 W. Hazlitt, "The Indian Jugglers", *Table Talk*, 1821.

8 Strehly.

9 "Signor Saltarino" [H. W. Otto], *Fahrend Volk*, 1895.

10 Mayhew, "The Street Risley".

11 Roy Busby, *British Music Hall: an Illustrated Who's Who*, 1976.

Chapter 13

1 Broadbent.

2 Ducrow.

3 Frost; Lloyd.

4 Findlater; Thétard.

5 Van Hare.

6 Strehly.

7 Munby.

8 Le Roux.

9 Pierre Couderc, "Fiction or Fact – Truth or Legend. Installment no. 9. Important Trivia", *Bandwagon*, July–August 1965. This is part of an important series of articles on achievements of "the triple" in various types of circus acts. It appeared in *Bandwagon* through 1965, and was translated in *Le Cirque dans l'Univers*, the articles on the flying trapeze appearing in nos. 54, 55, 56 and 62, 1964–6.

10 Dibdin.

11 Buckland.

12 Boase.

13 Mayhew, "The Strong Man".

Chapter 14

1 James and Horace Smith, "Playhouse Musings" in *Rejected Addresses*, 1812; Lloyd; Wild's.

2 E. A. Brayley Hodgetts, "The Training of Performing Animals", *The Strand Magazine*, September 1894; Le Roux; Hippisley Coxe.
3 Mayhew, "The Happy Family Exhibitor".
4 Buckland.
5 Van Hare.
6 Hone.
7 Alfred Bunn, *The Stage, both Before and Behind the Curtain*, 1840; George Rowell, *Queen Victoria Goes to the Theatre*, 1978.
8 A. H. Saxon, "Edwin Landseer's Joke on Macready", *Nineteenth Century Theatre Research*, 6, 2, 1978.
9 Edward Campbell, "The Bounce", *King Pole*, 33, 1976.
10 "Wild Animal Training", *The Strand Magazine*, September 1891.
11 Lukens.
12 Winter.
13 *Cirque Knie: une Dynastie du Cirque*, 1975.
14 Frederick Dolman, "Four-Footed Actors", *The English Illustrated Magazine*, September 1899; Pinder.
15 W. Smith, "Animal Training Extraordinary", *Chums*, July 1898.
16 Astley.
17 *Report from the Select Committee on Performing Animals*, 1922.

Chapter 15

1 M. Willson Disher, *Clowns and Pantomimes*, 1925.
2 Dibdin; Findlater.
3 Van Hare.
4 William Tinsley, *Random Recollections of an Old Publisher*, 1900; Grock, *Life's a Lark*, 1931.
5 Frost.
6 Boz.
7 Paterson.
8 Boase; Mayhew, "Silly Billy".
9 The *Bristol Mirror*, July 18, 1857.
10 Delzant.
11 Chipperfield.
12 Strehly.
13 *Journal*, December 27, 1876; *The Brothers Zemganno*, 1879.
14 Tristan Rémy, *Entrées clownesques*, 1962.
15 Price.
16 Tristan Rémy, *Les Clowns*, 1945.
17 "Signor Domino" [Emil Cohnfeld], *Der Cirkus und die Cirkuswelt*, 1888.
18 [H. Meyer], *Der richtige Berliner in Wörtern und Redensarten*, 4th edition, 1882.
19 Edouard de Perrodil, *Monsieur Clown*, 1889.
20 Albert Fratellini, *Nous, les Fratellini*, 1955.
21 Towsen.
22 Mayhew, "Street Clown".
23 Ifan Kyrle Fletcher, "A Portrait of Thomas Barry", *Theatre Notebook*, xvii, 1963.

Chapter 16

1 Boz; Henry Valentine, *Behind the Curtain*, 1848.
2 Strehly.
3 Sanger.
4 "Town and Country Circus Life", *All the Year Round*, November

16, 1861; Olyslager Auto Library, *Fairground and Circus Transport*, 1973.

5   Paterson; Clarke.
6   Ducrow.
7   Wallett; Speaight.
8   Lukens.
9   Montague; Frost.
10 Paterson; Antony Hippisley Coxe, "Great Days of the Circus", *The Times*, December 15, 1962.
11 Mayhew, "The Penny Circus Jester", "The Strong Man".

Chapter 17

1   Varey.
2   Thayer.
3   Jensen.
4   Frost.
5   Montague; Sanger.
6   Boase.
7   McKennon.

Chapter 18

1   Vail.
2   *Theatre Notebook*, x, 1956.

Chapter 19

1   Vail; Thayer; James S. May, "A Checklist of Circus Buildings constructed by John B. Ricketts", *Bandwagon*, xxii, 5, 1978.
2   Decastro.
3   Odell.
4   Thomas Clark Pollock, *The Philadelphia Theatre in the Eighteenth Century*, 1933.
5   Durang.
6   C. H. Amidon, "Inside Ricketts' Circus", *Bandwagon*, xix, 3, 1975.

Chapter 20

1   Chindahl.
2   Odell.
3   Durang.
4   R. W. G. Vail, "This Way to the Big Top", *New York Historical Society Quarterly Bulletin*, July 1945.
5   Decastro.
6   Thayer is outstanding for its detailed coverage of the early period. See also Chapin May; Jensen; Chindahl; Fox and Parkinson.

Chapter 21

1   Bill reproduced in Chapin May.
2   Thétard.
3   Thayer.

Chapter 22

1 Odell.
2 Thayer.
3 William Lawrence Slant, *Theatre in a Tent*, 1972.
4 Polacsek.
5 C. H. Amidon, "Circus Wheels", *The White Tops*, xlviii, 4, 1975; McKennon.
6 Frost.
7 Philip Graham, *Showboats*, 1951, which, however, gives the dimensions as 200 ft by 35 ft. If this is correct it could not have housed a standard size ring.
8 Articles by Charles Amidon and Stuart Thayer, and George Speaight in *Bandwagon*, xxi, 6, 1977.
9 Richard E. Conover, *The Telescoping Tableaus*, 1956; C. H. Amidon, "A History of Circus Parades in America", *The White Tops*, xlix, 3, 1976; Charles Philip Fox and F. Beverly Kelley, *The Great Circus Street Parade in Pictures*, 1978.
10 C. H. Amidon, "Stalking the Apollonicon", *Bandwagon*, xx, 2, 1976.
11 Rennert.
12 Buckskin Joe.

Chapter 23

1 Vail.
2 Stuart Thayer, "One Sheet", *Bandwagon*, xix, 3, 1975.
3 Jensen.
4 Fox and Parkinson.

Chapter 24

1 Chindahl; Fox and Parkinson.
2 Jensen.
3 Lano.

Chapter 25

1 Thayer; T. Allston Brown, *A History of the New York Stage*, 1903.
2 Robert Montilla, "The Building of the Lafayette Theatre", *Theatre Survey*, xv, 2, 1974.
3 Odell; P. T. Barnum, *Struggles and Triumphs*, 1889 edition.
4 J. Thomas Scharf, *History of Baltimore City and County*, 1881; Polacsek.
5 Lumsden.
6 A. H. Saxon, "A Franconi in America: the New York Hippodrome of 1853", *Bandwagon*, xix, 5, 1975.
7 Lano.

Chapter 26

1 Polacsek.
2 Copeland MacAllister, "The First Successful Railroad Circus was in 1866", *Bandwagon*, xix, 4, 1975.
3 McKennon. Despite its semi-fictional form I have found this book of great value for detail and atmosphere in the circuses of this period.

4 J. Y. Henderson, *Circus Doctor*, 1952.
5 Fred D. Pfening Jr, "Circus Train Wrecks", *Bandwagon*, xix, 5, 1975.

Chapter 27

1 Carl Landrum, "W. W. Cole's Five-Continent Circus", *Bandwagon*, xix, 2, 1975.
2 Buckskin Joe.
3 Chapin May; Thétard.

Chapter 28

1 Jensen.
2 McKennon.
3 Fox and Parkinson.
4 Rennert.
5 Eberstaller; Hans Rettig, "Circus Krone damals ...", *Die Circus Zeitung*, xxii, 3, 1976.

Chapter 29

1 Chapin May; Fox and Parkinson; Chindahl; McKennon; Jensen.

Chapter 30

1 Jensen.
2 Joseph T. Bradbury, "Downie Bros Wild Animal Circus", *Bandwagon*, xix, 6, 1975.

Chapter 31

1 Most of this chapter is based on McKennon.
2 Lano.
3 Bert J. Chapman, *Hey Rube*, 1933.
4 Lukens.
5 C. Sturtevant, "Check List of American Circus Route Books", *The Rare Book Speculator*, i, 8, 1937.
6 But *The Era*, particularly from the 1860s, could yield some valuable information to any student with the time and pertinacity to work through its files.

Chapter 32

1 Disher.
2 Manfred Roitzsch, "Kunstreiter mit Priveleg", *Circus-Parade*, 7, 1978.
3 Price.
4 Thétard.
5 Compardon.
6 Decastro.
7 The most recent histories of the Circus on an international scale are Le Grande Livre and Jando, both well illustrated – the former quite

magnificently. Thétard and Halperson are excellent. A brief survey is provided by Auguet. There is a useful chapter in Vaux and a convenient summary of names in Markschiess-van Trix. Rupert Croft Cooke and Peter Cotes, *Circus: A World History*, 1976, does not really live up to its title.

8 Rennert; Markschiess-van Trix; *Menschen – Tiere – Sensationen. Zirkusplakate 1880–1930*, Münchner Stadtmuseum, 1978.

Chapter 33

1 Vaux.
2 Auguet; *The Tatler*, November 22, 1901.

Chapter 34

1 Strehly.
2 Ernest Molier, *Cirque Molier 1880–1904*, 1905.
3 Quoted by Delzant.
4 Marc Chagall, *Cirque*, 1967.

Chapter 35

1 E. H. Bostock, *Menageries, Circuses and Theatres*, 1927; David Jamieson, "The Wombwells and Bostocks", *King Pole*, 35–37, 1977.
2 Malcolm Airey, "The Chapman Story", *King Pole*, 31–34, 1975–6.
3 Cyril Bertram Mills, *Bertram Mills Circus*, 1967.
4 Chipperfield.
5 On contemporary British circuses the best sources are *King Pole* and the Motley page of *The World's Fair*.
6 On contemporary European circuses the best sources are Le Grand Livre and Jando, and more particularly *Le Cirque dans l'Univers*, the admirable journal of the French circus society.
7 Gerhard Eberstaller, *Zirkus und Varieté in Wien*, 1974.
8 André Heller, *Es werde Zirkus: ein poetisches Spektakel*, 1976.
9 On the contemporary and recent American Circus the best sources are *The White Tops* and *Bandwagon*.

Chapter 36

1 Notably Clarke, Hippisley Coxe, and Eberstaller.
2 Some current acts are described and illustrated in Le Grand Livre and Jando. There is a woeful lack of critical reviews of circus performances, but the best informed accounts of contemporary circus acts are to be found in *Le Cirque dans l'Univers* and *King Pole*.
3 George Foster, *The Spice of Life*, [1933]; Markschiess-van Trix.
4 Eberstaller.
5 Towsen.

Colour

Illustrations A, E, G and H are from [J. L. Blamire], *The Children's Circus and Menagerie Picture Book*, 1882. Toronto Public Libraries, Osborne Collection of Early Children's Books.

Illustration J is from the collection of Mr Terence Benton

Illustrations B, C, F and I are from the Marian Hannah Winter Collection.

Illustration D is from *Aunt Louisa's National Album*, printed by Kronheim, c. 1875.

Black and White

Illustrations not otherwise acknowledged are from the author's collection.

Index

PERFORMERS AND PROPRIETORS